DEDICATION

To Sister Nancy Vendura, C.S.J.

Best friend,
Inspiration for sanctity,
Inspiration for service.

CONTENTS

ACKNOWLEDGMENTS

For her assistance in the preparation of this book, I thank my secretary, Mrs. Mary Ann Osborne, who corresponded with more than a hundred promoters of causes for Asian candidates. Mrs. Helen Kelley proof read the entire text and provided much needed and appreciated editing. Mrs. Rina Roca and Rev. Francis Nguyen translated works from Italian and Vietnamese texts respectively. For providing statistical data relevant to Asian Catholics, I thank Cecile Motus, interim director for the USCCB Office for the Pastoral Care of Migrants and Refugees, and Professor Ruth Narita Doyle, visiting senior research scholar in sociology and anthropology at Fordham University and former director for over twenty years for Cardinal O'Connor's Office of Pastoral Research and Planning for the Archdiocese of New York.

For providing me the opportunity to travel to Asia to preach retreats to Vincentian Fathers and Daughters of Charity and to do necessary on-site research, I thank my provincial, Rev. Thomas F. McKenna, C.M. I also must thank many people for having provided hospitality to me in Asia. In Beijing, China, the confreres of the Vincentian China Province. In India, at Mysore, Father Jose Aikara, C.M., provincial of the Vincentian Southern India Province; Rev. Johnson Nedungadan, C.M., rector of the major seminary at Adway; Rev. Joy Thuruthel, C.M., director of the Retreat and Seminar Center at Belwady; and the Daughters of Charity at Mysore and Bangalore. In Japan, I thank the Jesuit Fathers at Nagasaki, namely, Rev. Renzo de Luca, S.J., assistant director of the Twenty-six Martyrs Shrine; Rev. Patrick Dermott Brangan, S.J., minister of the local Jesuit community; and Rev. Yuki, S.J., director of the Twenty-six Martyrs' Shrine. At Kobe City, Japan, I received wonderful hospitality from Rev. Victoriano Torres, C.M.; Sr. Mary Moran, D.C., fifty year veteran of ministering in Japan and former Visitatrix of the Japanese Province of the Daughters of Charity; and Sr. Gratia, D.C. At Seoul, South Korea, Rev. Kim Yong Ki, C.M., Vincentian parish priest, and his parishioners graciously hosted me. At Manila, in the Philippines, I enjoyed the company of Rev. Maximilian Rendon, C.M., religious superior of Vincentians ministering at Adamson University. In Saigon, Vietnam, Miss Tuoi Nguyen, sister of my U.S. Vincentian confrere, Rev. Michael Nguyen, C.M., introduced me to native Vietnamese who provided valuable information and insights.

Every researcher appreciates people who respond to requests for information. This book, like my previous books, is produced only with the cooperation of countless postulators, vice-postulators, historians, archivists, shrine directors, museum curators, guild presidents, librarians, promoters, and secretaries. In each biography, where applicable, I name the person(s) who provided information for and read the draft of the biography for the particular saint or candidate for sainthood.

Writing about the saints is my avocation. My primary responsibility is serving as pastor for the people of St. Joseph Church in Emmitsburg, Maryland. Rev. Stephen Trzecieski, C.M., the assistant pastor, freed me from many pastoral activities so that I could complete this book. I thank him for the wonderful contribution he makes to the parish and for his encouragement in my writing this book.

INTRODUCTION

Saints of Asia[1]: 1500 to the Present

Purpose of This Book

Christianity originated in Asia. Catholics will benefit from knowing and appreciating the two-thousand-year witness of Church history, plus Church heroes and heroines in Asia. Jesus founded the Church in Palestine, whence the apostles and disciples quickly spread the faith throughout Asia: north to Syria, east to India, and west to Asia Minor, as well as beyond Asia to Africa and Europe. In the third century, Armenia became the first nation to embrace Christianity. In the same century, Edessa became a center of Christian spirituality. By the fifth century, the Church had reached Arab lands. Persian merchants introduced Christianity to China in the fifth century. Two centuries later, missionaries built the first church in China, where the Church flourished for the next two hundred years. Pope John Paul II writes, "the decline of this vibrant Church in China by the end of the First Millennium, [however], is one of the sadder chapters in the history of God's People on the continent."[2]

In the thirteenth century, missionaries brought the gospel to the Mongols, Turks, and again the Chinese. Many factors, however, contributed to the next century's "drastic diminution of the Church in Asia": the expansion of Islam, the "absence of an appropriate adaptation to local cultures," and the Black Death, which claimed the lives of almost fifty million people in Europe and Asia, including one-third of the European clergy, thereby reducing personnel available for missionary ministry in Asian countries.[3] The sixteenth, seventeenth, and nineteenth centuries experienced growth of missionary movements, not only in evangelization but also in education, health care, and social services. Nonetheless, the Church's ministry in Asia resulted in only a minimal number of conversions.

"Despite her centuries-long presence and her many apostolic endeavors, the church in many places was still considered as foreign to Asia, and indeed was often associated in people's minds with the colonial powers."[4]

Only in 1514 did Asia receive its first diocese, namely Funchai (now Madeira, India). During the remainder of the century, Goa, Malacca, Macao, Manila, Funay, and Malabar also became dioceses. In the next century were added Cranganore, Meliapore, Peking (now Beijing), Nanking, Mylapore, and the vicar apostolic of Siam (now Thailand). Today, the Asian countries with the most archdioceses and dioceses are India with 146; China, 105; Philippines, 70; Indonesia, 35; Vietnam, 25; Japan, 16; South Korea, 14; Lebanon, 14; Sri Lanka, 11; Myanmar, 11; and Syria, 10.

The number of Catholics has burgeoned across Asia in recent centuries.[5] The increase is due generally to natural increase rather than conversions. The Asian countries with the most Catholics include the Philippines with 63 million; India, 16 million; Vietnam, 5 million; and South Korea, 4 million. The Philippines ranks right behind Brazil and Mexico in its number of total Catholic population. The countries with a majority portion of Catholic population are East Timor at 94%; the Philippines, 83%; and Lebanon, 52% (prior to the month-long July War of 2006).

Asian and Pacific Island Catholics in the world and in the USA represent ever-increasing proportions. In the last quarter century, the Asian Catholic population in the world has increased from 7% to 10%.[6] In the USA, Asian Catholic population is estimated at 2.6% of the total Catholic population.[7] This figure includes approximately a half-million Catholics from the Armenian, Chaldean, Maronite, Melkite, and Syriac churches, which include the Syro-Malabar and Syro-Malankara churches.[8] Asian clergy serve now in over a thousand Catholic parishes in the USA.

Who Is Included in This Book

Modern-era saints and candidates for sainthood, who either were born in Asia or ministered extensively in Asia are included. Only people whom the Vatican has either canonized as saints or officially introduced into the process as Servants of God are included.

Not included are saints or candidates prior to the Modern Era, which historians identify as A.D. 1500. Sadly, this criterion eliminates the hundreds of saints from the first century apostolic era and second to eighth centuries patristic era. Numerous encyclopedia articles and dictionaries of saints, however, include ample description of these saints from the earliest centuries of the Church. Also not included are those saints and candidates who spent little time in Asia. Blessed Emilie Van der Linden D'Hoogvorst (1818-1878), known in religious life as Sister Mary of Jesus, founded the Sisters of Mary Reparatrix and began many houses throughout India, but she never ministered there. The Servant of God, Father Joseph McKniff, O.S.A. (1905-1994) served in the Philippines for only three years before ministering in Cuba from 1939-1968, and in Peru from 1972-1994. These are just a few examples.

Names of the Saints

In the "Index of Names," individuals are listed alphabetically according to first names. Because Westerners are accustomed to using in liturgical texts the Anglicized order of the Christian name appearing before one's surname, the author applies that same word order even though among Far Eastern Christians, the word order would be surname, the non-Christian birth name, and lastly one's Christian name.

Calendar of Saints

Entries are arranged according to the Church's liturgical calendar. Because saints and blesseds have official feast days, their biographies appear on those dates. Because Venerables and Servants of God do not have official feast days, the biography appears on either the date when the individual died, or the date when the promoters celebrate the memory of their particular candidate. On feast days when approximately a hundred or more martyrs are celebrated, namely, the Martyrs of China, Japan, Korea, and Vietnam, I have presented the group's prototypical saint on that day, and have included other representatives on their particular dates of martyrdom.

Marian Shrines

Church-approved Marian apparitions at Vailakanni, India, and Our Lady of La Vang, Vietnam, are included. Alleged apparitions which are not yet Vatican-approved are not included.

Representation

All of the Modern-era, Asian-born saints and Church-approved candidates for sainthood have been included. Also included are a few representative European missionaries who ministered and died for the spread of the faith in Asia.

Some saints or candidates may be associated with more than one country. The renowned Jesuit missionary Francis Xavier worked for a few months in the Malaysian Peninsula, and died off the coast of China, but is remembered especially for his three years of ministry in India and almost three years at Japan. The Frenchman Bishop Melchior Marion de Brésillac, who near the end of his life founded the Society of African Missions, spent a dozen years in India before beginning his short-lived ministry in Sierra Leone.

An attempt has been made to provide an as wide as possible representation from Asia's six geographical regions, four dozen countries, both sexes, various vocations, and paths to sanctity.[9] The saints and candidates from the last half-millennium come mostly from China, Japan, Korea, and Vietnam, each of which is blessed with nearly a hundred or more martyrs. India has suffered few martyrdoms, but still lays claim to about two dozen saints and candidates. Ironically, the centuries-long Catholic country of the Philippines has very few canonized saints because it wholeheartedly embraced the faith and has not suffered significant anti-Catholic persecution and martyrdoms.

The Mission Continues

About three percent of the Asian population is Catholic. Approximately three times that number is Christian. Persecution against the property and lives of Catholics and Christians continues to this day. The U.S. Commission on International Religious Freedom (USCIRF) annually recommends to the U.S. Secretary of State, in fulfillment of the 1998 International Religious Freedom Act, those countries whose governments "engage in or tolerated systematic and egregious violations of the universal right to freedom of religion or belief." USCIRF reported in 2006 the following three categories and its representatives from Asia: (1) regarding countries of particular concern, nine of the eleven are Asian: Burma (now Myanmar), North Korea, Iran, Pakistan, People's Republic of China, Saudi Arabia, Turkmenistan, Uzbekistan, and Vietnam; (2) regarding countries which require very close monitoring, three of the seven are Asian: Afghanistan, Bangladesh and Indonesia; and (3) of the countries which require close monitoring, all four are Asian: India, the Russian Federation, Sri Lanka, and Iraq.

In Pope John Paul II's apostolic exhortation *Ecclesia In Asia*, he concludes:

> The peoples of Asia need Jesus Christ and his Gospel. Asia is thirsting for the living water that Jesus alone can give (cf. Jn. 4:10-15). The disciples of Christ in Asia must therefore be unstinting in their efforts to fulfill the mission they have received from the Lord, who has promised to be with them to the end of the age (cf. Mt. 28.20). Trusting in the Lord who will not fail those whom he has called, the Church in Asia joyfully makes her pilgrim way into the Third Millennium. Her only joy is that which comes from sharing with the multitude of Asia's peoples the immense gift which she herself has received: the love of Jesus the Savior. Her one ambition is to continue his mission of service and love, so that all Asians "may have life and have it abundantly"(cf. Jn. 10:10).[10]

JANUARY

3. ✠ Blessed Kuriakose Elias Chavara, C.M.I.

Place: Mannanam, Kerala State, India
Fame: Founder of Carmelites of Mary Immaculate (C.M.I.) and the Congregation of the Mother of Carmel (C.M.C.); Reconciler of Church factions

KURIAKOSE ELIAS CHAVARA

Kuriakose Elias Chavara (1805-1871) was born on the Arabian Coast at Kainakary, Kerala.[11] The Chavara family descended from the Pakalomattam family, one of the four that claim descent from the Brahmin converts of Saint Thomas the Apostle.

Kuriakose, at ten, having completed his elementary education, moved to the local rectory, where he spent two years under the tutelage of the parish priest. In 1818, the youth entered Pallipuram Seminary, whose rector was Malpan Thomas Palackal. Not long afterwards, an epidemic struck Kainakary, and Kuriakose's father, mother, and only brother succumbed to the disease.

After mourning his great loss, Kuriakose arranged the family's affairs, continued his priestly studies, and on November 29, 1829, was ordained a priest.

Fathers Thomas Palackal, Thomas Porukara, and Kuriakose shared a desire to live a communal life. The trio approached the Vicar Apostolic, who granted the three priests the permission to establish a religious house. On May 11, 1831, the priests laid the house's foundation at Mannanam. This institute, now known as the Carmelites of Mary Immaculate, was the first indigenous religious institute for men in the modern Indian Church.

In 1841, Malpan Palackal, and in 1846, Malpan Porukara died, leaving to Father Kuriakose the responsibility for developing the nascent religious community. On December 8, 1855, Father Chavara and eleven companions professed their religious vows with Father Kuriakose serving as superior of the religious community.

During Father Chavara's fifteen years as provincial superior, the congregation made huge impact on the religious renovation of Kerala. Besides the first house at Mannanam, Father Chavara founded seven additional houses throughout Kerala. To develop vocations to priesthood, Father Chavara established numerous seminaries. For priests and laity, he introduced the practice of annual retreats. One of the first printing presses in India, came about through his initiative; he started the country's first Catholic Publishing House to disseminate Catholic teachings. To educate the Catholic populace, he built many schools wherein children studied during the day, and catechumens studied in the evening. For the destitute and dying, he built hostels. Many valuable innovations in the Syro-Malabar liturgy are attributed to him. On February 13, 1866, Father Kuriakose co-founded the first indigenous women's religious community in India, the Third Order of Discalced Carmelite Nuns, now known as the Congregation of the Mother of Carmel.

In 1861, a schism threatened the Syro-Malabar Church in southern India. The Saint Thomas Christians, who trace their origins to the apostle, had enjoyed a native Indian bishop for their first three hundred years, and a Syrian bishop for the next 1200 years. In the sixteenth century, however, the Synod of Diamper transferred the jurisdiction of India to Latin bishops, who neither understood nor appreciated the Syriac Rite and culture. After decades of requests, representatives of the Syro-Malabar Rite succeeded in having the Patriarch of Babylon make an investigation. The patriarch commissioned Bishop Thomas Rocos of Bagdad to study the situation, and report his findings to the patriarch.

Rocos arrived at Cochin, India, on May 9, 1861. Many Indians welcomed Rocos as the new bishop of Malabar. Rocos acceded to the people's yearnings, and pretended to have been missioned to the see by the pope and patriarch. Chavara was shocked; Rocos was "playing bishop." In June, the Latin Archbishop of Verapoly, alarmed that more than two-thirds of the Syriac churches had gone over to Rocos, appointed Chavara the Vicar General of the Syro-Malabar Church in order to avert a schism. Chavara visited the churches, reasoned with the clergy and congregations, and publicly pointed out that Rocos lacked ecclesiastical credentials.

Chavara urged the Catholics to remain faithful, and not to become schismatics. In March 1862, Rocos renounced any claims attributed by or to him, and returned in good standing to the Church in Bagdad. Pope Pius IX sent a personal note to Kuriakose, thanking him for having saved the people from schism.

Amidst his diverse activities, Father Chavara wrote prose and poetry: *Atmanuthapam* (The Lamentations of a Repentant Soul), *Maranaveettil Paduvanulla Pana* (A song of bereavement), *Anasthaciayude Rakthasakshyam* (The Martyrdom of Anasthacia), *Dhyana Sallapangal* (Colloquies in Meditations), and "*Testament of a Loving Father*" as counsels for Christian families.

During his multiple activities, Father Kuriakose remained a man of prayer. He introduced to India the Forty Hours Adoration, Marian devotions during May and October, prayed the rosary daily, and founded for the sick and dying a Confraternity of Saint Joseph for a Happy Death.

Father Chavara became very ill in October 1870. Sensing death approaching, he placed a note on his door requesting that visitors restrict themselves either to speaking with him about spiritual matters or reading spiritual books to him. After taking a turn for the worse, he spoke to those surrounding his bed, "Why are you sorry, and why are you crying? Everyman whoever he is, has to die someday. Now it is my time."[12] After these words he received the sacrament of the anointing. On January 3, 1871, he calmly fell asleep in the Lord.

After his death, the founder's last will and testament was copied and distributed to members of the C.M.I. In this document, the founder urges the members of the community to grow in communal love, obedience to superiors, cooperation with local bishops, prudence in accepting candidates for the community, and to assist the family who once had sued him unsuccessfully. The introductory paragraph reveals the founder's desire to serve God completely:

> Dear children, by the special grace of God we have been called to be members of the Carmelite Congregation which is very dear to our Blessed Mother. I'm sure that this has been so because God willed it so, not because man planned it. . . . But neither you nor I have become truly religious. The only sign of a true religious is an unconditional obedience as a complete surrender of oneself to

God. If one has this virtue, he is a true and full religious. Even though this seems not difficult to achieve, you have to struggle to do it. In the beginning you may be unwilling to do it because you find it difficult. But as the days go by, you will find it good and necessary. Then you will be happy over it and enjoy peace of mind.[13]

9. ✠ Saint Agatha Yi

***Place:** Seoul, South Korea*
***Fame:** Teenage martyr*

Agatha Yi (1823-1840) was arrested on April 8, 1839, along with her parents and brother.[14] A few hours earlier, Bishop Lawrence Imbert had finished celebrating Mass in their home, and had urged the family to hide the Mass vestments and vessels. The exhausted family, however, went to sleep, intending to conceal the materials the next morning. In the middle of the night, however, soldiers burst into the home and found the evidence about which an apostate had informed them. The family of four was arrested. Nine months later, Agatha Yi was strangled to death because of her refusals to renounce the Catholic faith.

In prison, the soldiers repeatedly tortured young Agatha. Her military guards whipped her three hundred times, and beat her ninety times. She was deprived of food and drink. That she remained a virgin while in the hands of the malevolent guards is astounding. Having separated the parents and children, the prison officials misinformed Agatha that her mother and father had recanted their profession of faith, and that the couple subsequently was released from prison. Agatha rejected her captors' lie, and replied courageously for her twelve-year-old brother Damian and herself, "Whether or not our parents denied their religion is not our business. We cannot deny God."[15] Actually, Agatha's father, Augustine Yi Kwang-hŏn, already had suffered decapitation on May 24, 1839 at the age of 53; and her mother Barbara Kwŏn Hŭi had suffered the same fate three months later, on September 3, at 46 years of age. When Agatha's father had been offered release for himself, and his family, and the return of his property, if he would apostatize, he replied, "Whatever happens, I cannot betray God."[16]

Because minors could not be beheaded, Agatha Yi was strangled to death at Seoul on January 9, 1840. The father, mother, and daughter were canonized together.

10. ✠ Blessed Diego Luis de San Vitores, S.J.

Place: Agana, Guam
Fame: Apostle of Guam

Having been born into nobility at Burgos, Spain, and educated in the Jesuits' Colegio-Imperial at Madrid, Diego Luis de San Vitores (1627-1672) entered the Society of Jesus in 1640, with the expressed desire of ministering as a missionary.[17]

After ordination in 1651, and the three-year internship for newly ordained priests, Diego served in various priestly duties until 1660. He was missioned to the Philippines for five years, and to Mexico for two years. From Acapulco he traveled to Manila, where Diego volunteered to start a mission at *Las Islas de los Ladrones*, an archipelago of fourteen main islands located 1,350 miles southeast of Manila.[18] Because no direct route existed between the Philippines and *Las Islas*, Diego had to sail from Manila to Acapulco, and during the ship's return to the Philippines, he disembarked at Guam. This circuitous route took ten months. Diego and companions arrived at Hagatna (now Agana, Guam) on June 15, 1668.

At Guam, Chief Kepuha welcomed Father Diego and the other Spanish priests, catechists, and soldiers. The chief accepted baptism, and granted to the missionaries the land upon which to build a church. Chief Kepuha died in 1669.

Father Diego acculturated himself to the native Chamorros. He learned their language, and composed in Chamorro and Latin a grammar book, a catechism, and liturgical texts. He taught doctrine through songs. He served the people in the usual pastoral ways: catechizing, baptizing, performing marriages, visiting the sick, and burying the dead. Traveling to neighboring islands, he served the inhabitants with apostolic zeal. He led the islanders in constructing a church, which was completed in 1669. The name of the islands he changed from *Las Islas de los Ladrones* to *Las Islas Marianas*, named after Queen Maria Anna of Austria. He gave each island a saint's name — Guam's name derives from Saint John. To develop a native clergy, he founded a school, which grew into today's Royal College. Opposed to mass conversions, he insisted on individual acceptance of the faith, "even though all begged for baptism."[19] He asked people to bury the skulls of their ancestors which had adorned the families' living quarters as objects of worship, and to replace that belief with faith in Jesus' death and resurrection.

Not everyone appreciated Father Diego's efforts. The new Chief Matapang (r. 1669-1680), received baptism, but later felt threatened by the moral influence of the priests, and the political-military power of the Spaniards over the Chamorros. A Chinaman named Choco, who had claimed magical powers, feared the power of the priests. Native self-appointed sorcerers who claimed control over health, weather, and crops, felt threatened by the Catholic priests. Young men who lived with unmarried women whose services they purchased with tortoise shells, opposed the priests, who opposed the young men's live-in arrangements.

Matapang went to war against the foreigners. The initial battle lasted six weeks in fall 1671. Peace was restored, and perdured for five months. Old wounds were reopened, however, when nonbelievers murdered a boy-catechist. Father Diego ordered all the catechists to return to the safety of the central mission house at Agana. Pedro Calungsod, who served as aide to the severely near-sighted Father Diego, remained with the priest.

On April 2, 1672, Father Diego and Pedro Calungsod entered Chief Matapang's village. The priest inquired of the chief if any women had given birth recently so that the priest might baptize the infants. The chief angrily told the priest not to baptize any child. The priest's enemies had advised the chief that baptism oftentimes resulted in the death of infants. The priest left the chief alone to calm down, and gathered around himself many children who began chanting their catechism lessons. Matapang left the village to enlist other enemies of the religion. During the chief's absence, the priest baptized the chief's newly born daughter.

When Chief Matapang returned to the village, he became infuriated upon learning that Father Diego had baptized the chief's daughter. Some evidence suggests that the missionary had received permission from the mother of the child. The chief began searching furiously for the priest.

When Matapang discovered Father Diego and Pedro Calungsod, the chief and his assistant hurled spears at Pedro. Initially, he deftly averted the weapons, but one spear soon struck him in the chest. Wounded, he fell. Matapang approached and with a machete crushed the youth's skull. Father Diego knelt down, absolved the catechist of any sins, and stood up, preaching Jesus to the attackers. They flung a spear into the priest's chest, and crushed his skull with a machete. Allegedly, just before being killed, the priest uttered to the chief, "May God have mercy on you."[20]

12. ✝ Blessed Nicholas Bunkerd Kitbamrung

Place: Bangkok, Thailand
Fame: Thailand's first priest martyr

As World War II erupted in 1939, a period of nationalism swept across Asia with the soul-felt cry, "Asia for the Asians."[21] In Siam (now Thailand) the Portuguese had sent the first missionaries in 1567, and the Vatican had assigned the French there in 1669. Over the centuries, animosity percolated between the Siamese and the French. The hatred heightened after France annexed in 1893, 1904, and 1907, almost a half-million square meters of Siamese territory.

A vigilante group of Siamese nationalists called the Thai Bloods began an armed resistance against the colonial government in 1939. The Thai Bloods preached that Buddhism was the national religion, and that "Catholicism is an alien religion."[22] Thai Bloods urged their countrymen not to buy from or sell to Catholics, not to allow Catholics to use public transportation, and to "refuse to see Catholics as true Thais."[23] Many Catholic schools, hospitals and churches were closed, and many staff members were imprisoned and tortured.

On January 12, 1941, the native Thai priest Nicholas Bunkerd Kitbamrung (1895-1944) was arrested by fellow Thais. They charged him with spying for France.

After nine months at Klong Prem Prison, Nicholas was sentenced to ten years at Bangkok Prison. In prison, the priest served the sick, consoled the sorrowing, and evangelized fellow inmates. He is credited with having baptized sixty-eight prisoners. After two years in prison, he contracted tuberculosis. He continued his ministry until poor health prohibited him. On the third anniversary of his arrest, he died from the privations of prison and sickness. Nicholas Bunkerd Kitbamrung is regarded as Thailand's first priest martyr.

In a letter to the archbishop, the priest attests to the love of his country and countrymen, the acceptance of God's will, and forgiveness towards his opponents.

> Your Excellency knows very well that I love my country so much that I have sacrificed myself and my secular happiness. I then endeavoured to preach a life of morality to my Thai brothers for fifteen years. So I have helped the Thai nation both directly and indirectly. I have also instructed others to be patriots. . . . I am willing to accept this punishment according to God's will in order to atone for my mistakes and sins, and for world peace and the civilization of my country. . . . I have always prayed God to forgive the guilt of those three false witnesses who filed false accusations against me, thus following the example of Jesus the Universal Master.[24]

The parents of Nicholas had converted to Catholicism, and raised all six of their children in the faith. At thirteen, Nicholas left his hometown of Nakhon Chaisri and entered the seminary, and at twenty-five began studies at Penang International Major Seminary at Malaysia. On January 24, 1926, he was ordained a priest for the archdiocese of Bangkok.

After serving as pastor at Bang Nok Khneuk and Phitsanulok, Father Nicholas ministered in territory that is now North Vietnam. In 1937, he was assigned to Khorat, where he served well until his arrest in 1941.

16. ✠ Blessed Joseph Vaz, C.Or.

Place: Goa, Gujarat State, India; and Colombo, Ceylon (now Sri Lanka)
Fame: Apostle of Sri Lanka

Portuguese Catholics between 1505-1658, and Dutch Calvinists between 1658-1796 colonized Ceylon (now Sri Lanka).[25] The Dutch Calvinists attempted to eradicate every vestige of Catholicism by prohibiting the practice of the religion.

Joseph Vaz (1651-1711) was born on the island of Salsette off the coast of Goa. His native Indian Catholic parents had descended from high-caste Brahmins. After Joseph's ordination to priesthood in 1676, his superiors assigned him first to Goa in 1681, and three years later, to Ceylon.

For years, Joseph had dreamed of going to Ceylon to bring back to the faith those Catholics whom the Dutch persecutors had driven from the true faith. Joseph, envisioning that this ministry would require a community of priests, joined a community of Goan priests whom Father Pascal da Costa had gathered in 1682. Soon, Joseph was named superior of the community, whose name he changed to the Oratory of Saint Philip Neri. In spring 1686, Joseph and a lay brother left Madras (now Chennai, India), and secretly entered Ceylon. Joseph disguised himself as a coolie slave, wearing only a loin cloth, and carrying a small bag which contained Mass vestments and vessels.

Father Joseph arrived at Jaffna, on the northern peninsula of the island in April 1687. Secretly, he celebrated the sacraments of baptism, penance, Eucharist, marriage, and the last rites. In 1690, Joseph expanded the mission to central and southern Ceylon. He walked to Puttalam and Kandy, where the local Buddhist king had allowed Catholic refugees to practice their faith. Joseph was mistaken for a spy, and spent the next four years in jail. After his release, he traversed the area establishing churches and forming catechists. When a drought occurred, the Buddhist priests prayed for rain, but to no avail. Joseph prayed, and the heavens showered down abundant rains. During a smallpox plague, civil officials abandoned the capital, but Joseph remained and ministered to the sick. The king, grateful for Joseph's interventions, invited him to bring other Oratorians into the kingdom, and urged the Ceylonese to convert to Christianity.

The Dutch Calvinists, furious at the Catholic revival occurring not only in the Buddhist Kingdom of Kandy, but also in the Calvinist capital of Colombo, captured Catholic laity and cut off their noses or ears. In 1696, a second Oratorian priest arrived at Ceylon. Fifteen years later, a total of fifteen Oratorians were ministering at Ceylon. In 1696, diocesan priests arrived to assist in the mission. Joseph strategically divided the island into geographical units for more efficient evangelization. The Church grew quantitatively and qualitatively.

To communicate the truths of the faith to his congregation, Father Joseph translated the Church's liturgical books, para-liturgies, and catechism into the native languages of Singhalese and Tamil. Joseph reached out humbly to communicate with the leaders and laity of Buddhism and Islam. He lived an ascetical, prayerful, self-sacrificing life for the benefit of his religion and his people.

In January 1710, Father Joseph became ill while ministering at Kottiyar, near Trincomalee. Villagers placed him on a bullock-drawn cart, and led him on an eight-day journey to Kandy. For a year, he remained too weak to leave his residence. Father Joseph never recovered; he died on January 16, 1711. "By the time he died, he was revered for holiness of life, and he was comforted by the awareness that more than seventy thousand openly professed the faith in Ceylon."[26]

22. ✠ Fernanda Riva, F.D.C.C.

Place: *Bombay (now Mumbai), India*
Fame: *Always kind in word and deed*

Fernanda Riva (1920-1956) was blessed by God with a winning personality: deeply sensitive, bright-eyed, humorous, intelligent, generous, kind in words and deeds.[27] This youngest of four children born to Italian Catholic parents demonstrated love of God and love of neighbor at every stage of her life, from childhood to sisterhood. All who knew her, loved her.

At eighteen, Fernanda felt called to the missionary vocation. The initial ardor grew into fuller flame while Fernanda was attending at the Cathedral of Milan the archdiocese's annual mission-sending ceremony for religious. Soon thereafter, after participating in the Missionary Congress at Vimercate, near her native town of Monza, the teenager announced her desire to serve Jesus and his Church abroad. A few days later, Fernanda writes to a Missionary Sister:

> The joy that this day brought to my heart cannot be imagined. I can assure you that your persuasive words have been engraved in my soul and that, with God's grace, they shall bear copious fruit. . . . I hope this day will mark a decisive victorious stage in the journey of my vocation. [Signed] In the heart of Jesus, F. R.[28]

Within a few months, Fernanda passed the Teachers Training exam, which permitted her to enter the Teachers Training College; and she entered the novitiate for the Missionary Institute of Vimercate in March 1939.

Mother Fernanda, which title all the Canossian Daughters of Charity bear, was missioned to India. She and Mother Rosa departed for India on October 18, 1939. The pair traveled from Milan, through Venice, across the Adriatic Sea and the Indian Ocean. Twelve days later, the religious sisters arrived at Bombay. The next day, the two Italian sisters traveled by train to Belgium, where they undertook their novitiate with the Indian sisters.

From December 1941 until 1950, Fernanda recorded in her journal her spiritual exercises. On Christmas Eve 1941, the day of her first profession of vows, she writes:

> It is absolutely necessary that Jesus be pleased with me. I will use all the creatures around me only in so far as they will help me to please God. There must be no sections in my life, but only one: to do the Will of God. Be generous, Fernanda, renounce [now] and forever all your inclinations, likings, tastes, preferences, in regard to the creatures with which God has surrounded you: your only liking, your only preference from henceforth must be: to do the Will of God.[29]

Throughout her life, Fernanda loved God and neighbor. As a child in elementary school, this bright student assisted slower-learning classmates, always with humility. In high school, when classmates did not fit in socially, Fernanda integrated them into academic and athletic activities. As a young religious, Fernanda's words and deeds were generous and kind. Her prayer was simple, as she meditated on the public life of Jesus. In religious community, and in schools where she taught, she drew out the best qualities from people by focusing on their potential. She earned her B.A. in education in 1947, and her M.A. in education in 1950. In 1947, she professed her perpetual religious vows.

Professionally, Fernanda manifested the same traits of loving service. From 1950-1953, at Mahim as headmistress, she treated all students and faculty with care. Latecomers were not punished, but were received patiently. Poor students during the monsoon season received dry clothing upon arriving at school. Joy pervaded the faculty meetings, and assignment of duties. When two cleaning ladies refused to clean the toilets in the school, Mother got down on her hands and knees and demonstrated that all work was dignified when it was for the love of God and neighbor. In fall 1953, she was appointed principal of Alleppy College. In Kerala, Mother studied and spoke the native Malayalam to communicate with construction workers at the school, and with donors who provided funding for the school. Another sister in the convent at Alleppy commented about Fernanda: "I have never seen such humility. Mother Fernanda was at the service of everyone."[30]

By September 1954, Mother's health had weakened. Suffering from stomach ulcers, she flew to Bombay, where she received a blood transfusion from a Hindu man. She kidded, "Before the operation I was a Christian but now with this non-Christian blood, who knows?"[31] In June 1955, Fernanda was appointed first assistant to the newly elected sister-superior. Fernanda worked diligently. By early January, however, a doctor discovered that the nun was suffering from lung cancer. In late January, she prepared for death. Visitors came to pray with her. Her last actions were to pray aloud the Acts of Faith, Hope, and Love. During the prayers, she whispered to the sisters surrounding her bed, "I'm going." They asked, "Where?" Mother responded, "The other side." To which she quickly added, "Don't leave me long in Purgatory."[32] The next day, she prayed aloud, "Jesus, Mary, Joseph," kissed the crucifix, and released herself into the love of God.

FEBRUARY

3. ✠ Takayama Ukon

Place: Osaka, Japan
Fame: Suffered exile for the faith

When Takayama Ukon (1552-1615) was five years old, his father Takayama Hida-no-Kami Zusho was appointed samurai for the feudal lord Matsunaga Hideyoshi of Yamato Province (now Nara prefecture).[1] The family moved into Sawa Castle, which overlooked the feudal lands at Settu (now Osaka).

TAKAYAMA UKON

Five years later, Hideyoshi assigned Takayama to lead an investigation into the teachings of the Portuguese Jesuit missionary Gaspar Vilela. In 1559, Vilela had founded the first Catholic mission at the capital Miyako (now Kyoto). Some Japanese Buddhist bonzes had complained to Hideyoshi about the new religion, and demanded that he expel the Catholic priest, his followers, and the native Japanese catechist Brother Lorenzo.

Takayama Zusho's investigation led him and two other members of the commission to convert to Christianity. These three officials had become enamored with the spiritual wisdom and intellectual depth of Catholic teachings. When returning to Sawa, Takayama Zusho brought along the catechist Lorenzo to preach the gospel. Many of Takayama Zusho's family, friends, and neighbors also converted to the Catholic faith. In 1563, the teenage Takayama Ukon, the oldest of five siblings, (c. 1552-1615) was christened Justin.[2]

During a battle between opposing warlords, Takayama Zusho was driven from Sawa Castle. A fellow samurai Wada Koremasa came to the aid of Zusho, and brought him into the service of Oda Nobunaga, the warlord of Miyako. Nobunaga gave Takayama Zusho responsibility for Takatsuki Castle. These two samurai hoped to achieve the return of the Catholic missionaries to Miyako. The oldest son of both of these samurai followed in their fathers' footsteps. In 1571, Takayama Zusho fought a series of military battles, during which his friend Wada Koresama was killed. Two years later, Wada's son Korenaga, who had fought alongside Takayama Zusho, challenged his father's friend to a duel. Takayama slew the challenger. Takayama Zusho, having been severely wounded in the duel, retired to convalesce, and to live well his Catholic faith. Takayama Zusho turned over to his twenty-one year old son Takayama Ukon the responsibility for defending Takatsuki Castle.

In 1574, Takayama Ukon Justin married Justa, another Christian. The couple was blessed with four children; two sons died shortly after birth, while another son and daughter survived into adulthood. Near Takatsuki Castle, the couple built a Catholic Center. The faithful gathered here for religious services, instruction, and meetings. A priest and lay brother visited regularly from Miyako. Takayama Ukon gained a reputation of an exemplary Christian.

In 1578, a dilemma arose for Ukon. The warlord Araki Murashige revolted against Odo Nobunaga. While Ukon's father still owed fidelity to Araki, Nobunaga had aided the Christian religion. Nobunaga surrounded Takatsuki Castle, and insisted that the Christian father and son surrender the castle, with the promise that Nobunaga would help the Church to flourish. Although the father refused to alter his allegiance to Murashige, Ukon, after having prayed for wisdom, chose to forgo helping his father and inheriting the castle and feudal estates. Instead, Ukon fled from the castle to support Nobunaga. Ukon chose what appeared best for the Church rather than for himself. Nobunaga kept his word. After Takatsuki Castle was taken, Nobunaga entrusted it to Ukon. Near Takatsuki, Ukon built twenty churches and a seminary. From the population of 25,000, the Church increased from 4,000 members in 1577, to 18,000 members by 1581. During the 1580s, many prominent Japanese converted to the Catholic faith.

After Nobunaga died in June 1582, Hideyoshi requested that Takayama Ukon would fight as his samurai. Ukon accepted the invitation, and fought successfully at Yamazaki, Omi, Tagami, and Shikoku. In 1585,

Hideyoshi bestowed upon Ukon the feudal estate of Akashi. There, like at Takatsuki, Ukon established a Catholic Center. Again Buddhist bonzes complained. Hideyoshi, however, allowed Ukon to promote the Catholic faith.

Suddenly in 1587, Emperor Hideyoshi reversed his position. Hideyoshi ordered warlords to renounce their Christian faith, or to suffer exile. Among the first persons to suffer persecution was Takayama Ukon. Hideyoshi's henchmen captured the Christian samurai, and took him to Miyako. Ukon was ordered either to give up his faith or his estates. Ukon opted to keep his faith rather than his property. The government exiled him to the island of Shodoshima (now Sadoshima).

On November 8, Takayama Ukon and 350 other Christians, half of whom were nobles, were placed on a dilapidated junk, and were sent from Nagasaki to Manila. "With his prayers, patience, and exhortations, Ukon was able to sustain the other exiles."[3] On December 21, the exiles reached their destination. On land, Ukon was diagnosed with a severe fever. He never recovered. After receiving the sacraments, he uttered the name of Jesus, and died on February 3, 1615.

4. ✠ Blessed Francis Pacheco, S.J.

Place: Nagasaki and Takaku, Japan
Fame: Martyr

From his youth, Francis Pacheco (1566-1626) became inspired to minister overseas from having read about the challenges of missionaries during the sixteenth century's era of global exploration, evangelization and colonization.

The youth attended a Jesuit school in Lisbon, Portugal, far removed from his hometown of Ponte di Lima, near Braga. Each year, he and other students participated in the ceremonies of Jesuits departing for the foreign missions.

In December 1585, Francis entered the Society of Jesus. After seven years of formation and education, his religious superiors sent him in 1592, to Goa and Macao to complete his preparation for priesthood. After being ordained in 1600, he was assigned to teach theology at Macao.

Japan became his home in 1604, where he remained until his death, except for a four year period as president of the Jesuit college at Macao beginning in1608, and a few months' absence at Macao after the Shogun expelled all foreign missionaries. In June 1615, after returning to Japan under the guise of a merchant, he set up shop at Takaku, and on the island of Amakusa. After the bishop died in 1614, Francis was named administrator of the Diocese of Nagasaki. In 1621, he re-located the provincial offices from Nagasaki to Kuchinotsu, in Arima, to foster better communications with outlying Jesuits.

FRANCIS PACHECO

Francis' ministry enjoyed success, albeit surreptitiously. From 1614 on, however, anti-Christian persecution grew in intensity. Soon, nearly two dozen Jesuits and hundreds of laity died for the faith, while thousands of other laity denied the faith.

On the evening of December 18, 1625, two hundred soldiers surrounded the home where Francis was staying. A former Catholic had succumbed to the temptations of money and political favor and informed governmental officials of the priest's hideout. The soldiers arrested the homeowner, his family, and the next door neighbor, in addition to two Jesuits and three catechists. The group was imprisoned in the dungeon at Shimabara. Other Jesuits and laity from other locales were arrested and swelled the ranks of the imprisoned.

In prison, Francis organized an "order of day" for rising, praying, and meditating. He led the group in supporting one another in spirit and spirituality. The catechists asked for and received admission into the Society of Jesus. Because the authorities had confiscated all religious articles, the priests could not say Mass, and all were without their rosary beads. For six months, in the cold of winter, their imprisonment continued.

On June 20, the inevitable occurred. The Catholics were marched to Martyrs' Hill. The authorities martyred the Jesuits, while the laity watched; it was the authorities' hope that some laity would apostatize. The Jesuits were burned over an open pit, and all died within fifteen minutes. Since none of the laity gave up their faith, they were marched back to prison. In the intervening three weeks, not one changed his mind; therefore, the government decapitated each of the laity on July 12.

The spirit of the laity was demonstrated by John Kisaku (c. 1605-1626). This youth from Kuchinotsu was in the neighbor's home when Francis Pacheco had been arrested. When the soldiers asked, "What does that young fellow do here?" One of the Jesuits replied, "He does housework here."[4] John, however, wishing not to abandon the Jesuits, admitted, "I've been with the Fathers for a long time and I do not intend to leave them now."[5] While in prison, Father Francis admitted John Kisaku into the Society of Jesus. John died as a Jesuit, for the sake of Jesus.

4. ✠ Saint John de Brittó, S.J.

Place: Madurai, Oriyur, Tamil Nadu State, India
Fame: Martyr

The mother of John de Brittó (1647-1693) supported his vocation to the Jesuit Order when he entered the Jesuit novitiate in 1662. She opposed, however, his missionary vocation when he volunteered for India in 1673. Fourteen years later, she welcomed him home after his arrest and torture in Marava land (now in Tamil Nadu state). In 1693, she thanked God that her son had become a saint after his martyrdom at Oriyur (now in Tamil Nadu state).[6]

John had been born and raised at Lisbon, Portugal, his parents' fourth and final child. When John was four, his father, the Viceroy of Brazil, died. At nine, John and his brothers were chosen as playmates for the Portuguese prince and future King Pedro II of Portugal. Two years later, John became deathly ill, and his mother prayed that if he recovered, she would dress him for one year in a cassock and cincture. John recovered, and his mother kept her promise. From this time on, John developed a devotion to Saint Francis Xavier.

John entered the Society of Jesus in 1662. Eleven years later, he was ordained a priest. On March 15 of that year, he sailed from Lisbon to Goa, where his 12,500 miles journey ended on September 4. He remained in that Portuguese stronghold for the next six months, studying the Tamil language and customs of the Indian people.

At that time in India, two famous Jesuit priests, Robert de Nobili and Balthasar de Costa, were advocating that Jesuits identify with the Indian people in dress, meals, and life style. Both men wore saffron robes, and gave up meat, eggs, fish, and alcohol. De Nobili directed his missionary activities to the high caste Hindus. De Costa, however, focused his energies on the low caste population. De Brittó, having observed that few high-caste Hindus converted to Christianity, opted to minister among the low-caste peoples. De Brittó adopted the native name Arulanandar. De Brittó began following local customs: "He preferred sitting cross-legged on the ground, drinking without the brass water vessel touching his lips, eating meals with his hands, walking barefoot, wearing a flowing shirt called 'anghi' and a turban on his head, and rings in his ears."[7] The Indian people regarded him not only as an ascetical *pandaraswami*, but also as a mystical *Sanyasi*, which Hindus regard as the fourth and final stage of human development, in which a person transcends the roles of youth, householder, and businessman in order to belong to the universal family of humankind.

From 1674 to 1686, Arulanandar served the Catholic populations at Kolei, Koothur, and Karayampatti. His opponents arranged Arulanandar's arrest at Vadakkankulam, but after one month, authorities released him because his opponents lacked jurisdiction.

Beginning in May 1686, Arulanandar instructed six catechists for Marava land. Within two months of ministry, over two thousand Hindus converted to Catholicism. Some Hindu religious and political leaders accosted the priest and members of his congregation, beat them with sticks, and subjected them to water torture whereby they were tied to a pole, and were dipped head-first into a well until almost drowned.

In 1687, the Jesuit provincial sent Arulanandar on a diplomatic mission to Rome. En route, the priest visited with his mother, and his boyhood friend, who now was the King of Portugal. The king urged the missionary to remain in Portugal. The priest replied, "I prefer the forests of Madurai to the palaces of Portugal."[8]

Back in India, trouble arose for Arulanandar in January 1693. The catechumen Prince Tadiya Teva had retained his first wife, but released his last four wives. The youngest of the wives complained to her uncle, a leading Hindu priest, who in turn complained to the powerful Raj of Marava about Arulanandar. On January 8, on orders of the Raj, Arulanandar was captured and jailed at Ramnad for preaching the gospel. Three weeks later, he was force-marched for three days over forty miles in the hot sun to Oriyur. On Ash Wednesday, February 4, 1693, soldiers led the prisoner to a sand dune. Arulanandar knelt before the executioner and exposed his neck. One swift stroke of the sword severed the priest's head. The lifeless head was thrust onto a stake where the birds of the air and wild animals devoured it.

5. ✠ Saint Gonzalo García, O.F.M.

Place: Bassein, India; Nagasaki, Japan
Fame: Martyr

This native Indian worked as a lay catechist with the Jesuits in Japan. Later, he went into business for himself at Macao and Manila, where he joined the Franciscans as a lay brother. Then he returned to Japan, where he suffered martyrdom.[9]

Gonzalo García (1557-1597) was born at Bassein, near Bombay (now Mumbai), India. It seems that his parents were Indian, although they had a Portuguese surname. After Gonzalo graduated from the Jesuit college at Bassein, a Jesuit invited Gonzalo, by this time an orphan, to assist the Jesuits as a catechist in Japan. For nine years, beginning in July 1572, Gonzalo worked at Nagasaki. "His natural linguistic ability was crowned with great success. It was said of him that he spoke Japanese like a native."[10] Many Japanese converted to the Catholic faith through the preaching of Gonzalo García.

In 1581, the youth repeated his request to join the Society of Jesus. For unknown reasons the lad's application was refused. Gonzalo left Nagasaki and headed fifty miles north to the island of Hirado. Shortly thereafter, he left Japan altogether and traveled to Macao, the busiest trading center in the Far East. He entered into business and enjoyed financial success. After three years, he moved to Manila, another major port in the trading network. While working there, Gonzalo attended daily morning prayer and Mass with the Franciscans. After one year, he applied to and was accepted by the Franciscan Order. He made his first vows as a lay brother on July 3, 1588.

In 1593, the Franciscans joined the Jesuits in missionary work in Japan. Four Franciscans, led by Friar Pedro Bautista and assisted by lay brother Gonzalo García, departed Manila and arrived at Hirado harbor on July 8. During the group's audience with Emperor Hideyoshi, he delighted in Friar Gonzalo's fluency with the Japanese language. The Emperor donated to the Franciscans land and a building in which to conduct their missionary ministry.

For the next four years, the Franciscans involved themselves in preaching, teaching, baptizing, and serving the sick. At Osaka, the mission flourished until some over-zealous Christian converts destroyed Buddhist shrines. The general populace, the Buddhist bonzes, and the Emperor himself became infuriated against these excesses of the Christians, who by 1587, had increased to two hundred thousand believers.

In 1587, Emperor Hideyoshi, urged on by his physician-advisor Seyakuin Hoin, decreed that all Jesuits immediately must leave Japanese soil. Some Jesuits left, and some remained, albeit surreptitiously. In December 1596, Hideyoshi decreed that all Christians were subject to execution. On December 8, two dozen clergy and lay Christians were arrested at Osaka. Three weeks later, the prisoners were marched to Macao, where they had their left ear lobes cut off.

The Emperor decided to execute these Christians at Nagasaki. The five hundred mile journey by land and sea would demonstrate to other Christians what punishment awaited those who contradicted the Emperor's prohibition. On January 4, 1597, the journey began. The twenty-six prisoners included three Jesuits, six Franciscans, and seventeen lay men including three boys between ten and thirteen years of age. All the Jesuits and laymen were Japanese; Gonzalo was the only native Asian among the Franciscans.

"On Nagasaki Hill twenty-six holes had been dug in a long straight row, four feet apart. Twenty-six crosses were lying on the ground, waiting for their victims, each of whom was attended to by two executioners."[11] The executioners fastened the prisoners to their respective wooden crosses by placing iron hooks over the prisoners' hands, feet, and necks, and tying their upper arms and torsos to the intersecting beams.

> The two executioners, probably helped by others, held the upper transverse beam and dragged the cross with its burden till the lower end of the vertical stake was right over the hole into which it had to be fixed. They tilted the cross and dropped it with a thud into the hole and fixed the loose soil around the lower end of the cross so as to hold it firmly erect. The dropping of the cross into the hole was probably the most painful ordeal for the victims and they moaned with pain.[12]

In a single instant, each of the pairs of executioners thrust their lances up into the chest of their respective prisoners. The lances intersected to assure the death of the victims. Gonzalo Garcia died as one of the first twenty-six martyrs of Japan.

6. ☩ Martyrs of Japan

Place: Nagasaki, Japan
Fame: Martyr

In the half-century 1597 to 1650, Japanese Catholics suffered martyrdom virtually every year with spikes in the number of those killed in 1597, 1622-1634, and 1637.[13] Tens of thousands of Catholics died, of whom the Church counts strictly 3,125 as martyrs.

After Portuguese sailors had arrived at southwestern Japan, local officials invited the foreigners to select a site for a harbor. The Portuguese chose Nagasaki, which enjoyed a nearly enclosed spacious harbor and a proximity to the Portuguese ports at Macao and Manila. After the sailors, Jesuit (1549), Franciscan (1593), Augustinian (1602), and Dominican (1605) missionaries arrived from Portugal beginning in 1549 and from Spain beginning in 1593.

The mission enjoyed immediate success. Saint Francis Xavier arrived at Kagoshima on the Island of Kyushu in 1549. His two-year ministry extended geographically from Kyushu in the south to Miyako (now Kyoto) in central Japan. He writes eloquently about the qualities of the Japanese people. In 1563, the local daimyo Omura Sumitada sought and received baptism. In 1576, the first church in Japan was built. By 1587, two hundred thousand Catholics lived in Japan; and by the end of the century, the number had burgeoned to three hundred thousand. Some local daimyos, however, opposed Christianity and sporadically persecuted members of the new religion.

The mission's growth did not last; internal and external disputes erupted. Internally, the Jesuits and Franciscans disagreed about missiological methodologies: the Jesuits were discreet in their manner and respectful of the local culture, whereas the Franciscans boldly presented their religion without reservation. Also, Portuguese and Spanish political administrators competed against each other, and impeded the success of the other nation's clergy. Externally, because Buddhism had suffered losses in membership, income, and influence, the monks felt threatened by the new religion. The Buddhist monk Nichijoshonin complained to Emperor Hideyoshi, who in 1587 promulgated an anti-Christian edict, declaring that Shintoism and Buddhism were the national religions of Japan and prohibiting the practice of Christianity. Although Christians suffered no physical attacks on their person, one hundred forty churches and twenty-six Christian residences were destroyed. Some clergy left the country, but many more fled to the hillsides whence they continued their ministry.

Ten years later, Japanese authorities unleashed a bloody persecution. The Spanish ship San Felipe had run aground at Urado in Shikoku, and officials discovered that the ship's cargo included guns and ammunition. The ship's captain boasted to Japanese port authorities that just as Spain had conquered Mexico and the Philippines, so too Spain would conquer Japan. When pressed as to how this might happen, the arrogant captain reported that the priests would prepare the way for the victory. A bonze reported this information to Hideyoshi, who ordered a census of Catholics living in Miyako.

After the initial persecution, Catholics enjoyed a respite in persecution, and growth in numbers. Suddenly, in 1614, the shogun Ieyusu ordered the prohibition of Christianity, the expulsion of foreign clergy, the destruction of churches, and the execution of all who disobeyed his order.

In the next two decades over 1,600 Japanese were killed for the faith. During this era, the period of "hidden Christians" originated as the faithful fled from the cities into the countryside.

A few years later, a socio-economic revolution led by farmers from the highly Catholic Kyushu region came to be perceived as a religious war. This Shimabara Rebellion, which lasted from mid-December 1637 until mid-April the following year resulted in the deaths of over thirty thousand peasants. From this date on, the government closed its borders to Christians, whether merchants or missionaries.

For more than two hundred years, foreign missionaries were prohibited from entering Japan; in 1643, foreign missionaries left Japan and didn't return until 1854, when Commodore Perry forced Japan under threat of military attack to open its ports to international trade. When French missionaries entered Japan, Catholics there stepped forward and greeted the priests. The two groups rejoiced: the lay Catholics for again having priests; and the missionaries in their astonishment at the people's two-hundred-year preservation of the Catholic faith and community.

6. ✠ Saint Paul Miki, S.J., and Companions

Place: Nagasaki, Japan
Fame: Martyr

Paul Miki (1562-1597) was born near Osaka to deeply committed Christian-convert parents. Young Paul received an excellent education from the Jesuits at the College of Azuchi. He entered the Society's seminary in 1584, and two years later, entered the Society. While a student, this native Japanese became an eloquent evangelizer, and led many Japanese to convert.

SAINT PAUL MIKI, S.J.

Shortly before his ordination to the priesthood, Paul was captured with two other Jesuits. Despite intense interrogation, the three remained firm in the faith. They were marched over a thousand miles from Kyoto to Nagasaki. Along the way, Paul sent letters to his provincial and family describing his deep faith and feelings as he approached inevitable martyrdom. At Nagasaki Hill, the trio was joined with other religious and lay prisoners. Paul Miki, in the words of an eyewitness, perceived his position on the cross as "the noblest pulpit he had ever filled."[14] From his cross, Paul preached the following.

> As I come to this supreme moment of my life, I am sure none of you would suppose I want to deceive you. And so I tell you plainly: there is no way to be saved except the Christian way. My religion teaches me to pardon my enemies and all who have offended me. I do gladly pardon the Emperor and all who have sought my death. I beg them to seek baptism and be Christian themselves.[15]

Some of the other martyrs started praying, "Jesus, Mary!"[16] When the soldiers raised their lances to pierce the heart of each prisoner, the crowd's voice swelled into a rousing chant of "Jesus, Mary!"[17] The four executioners systematically slew the Twenty-six Martyrs of Nagasaki.

8. ✠ Francis Convertini, S.D.B.

Place: *Krishnagar, Bengal, India*
Fame: *Unassuming missionary*

A simple soul, Francis Convertini (1898-1976) inspired people by the quality of his person rather than by any measurable achievement.

Francis was born the second son of humble farmers near Apulia, in southern Italy. Francis' father died when he was two months old, and his mother, who had remarried, died when he was ten. Two weeks after his mother's death, his stepfather, finding it impossible to care for two boys, took Francis and his brother to a market area, where he hired them out as live-in laborers for an elderly couple. From this couple, the boys learned to read, write, and pray the rosary daily.

After the World War broke out, Francis was drafted into the Italian army in 1917. Twice, he tried to desert the army, but he was captured by his own. Finally, he was captured by the enemy, and was sent to a Prisoner-of-War camp on the Baltic Sea. In 1918, he was released, only to contract meningitis, for which he was hospitalized. Having recovered his health, he worked at farming, as a customs officer, and as a factory worker. Once, a priest asked him, "Would you like to become a missionary?"[18] Shocked, Francis pondered the question. Later, providentially, the priest and young man again bumped into each other in the streets of Turin. The priest repeated his question, and the youth answered affirmatively.

In December 1923, Francis entered the Salesian Fathers formation program at Ivrea. This minimally educated twenty-five-year-old sat in class with bright fourteen-year-olds. A teacher described Francis' situation, saying, "He was like a rusty old tractor competing with the latest cars, yet he kept moving all the same."[19] Francis required twice as much time as his classmates to complete studies; he had failed and repeated virtually every subject he took. At the same time, he was exemplary in prayerfulness and generosity. A teacher observed, "Francis learnt more on his knees [in front of the Eucharist] than at his desk."[20]

In December 1927, Francis sailed for the Salesian mission at Assam, India. He completed the novitiate in 1929 and philosophical and theological studies, his two-year regency, before being ordained a priest in 1935. Throughout his student days, Francis emanated the love of God wherever he went. One may inquire, "How could he who was intellectually the poorest and had such a scanty knowledge of the local language, achieve much more than his brilliant companions? The answer was to be found in his fasting and prayer before each weekend visit to the villages."[21]

In priesthood, Father Francis served for forty years at Krishnagar, Bengal, which was located in northeastern India until Bengali independence in 1947. Whether in the rural villages or the cathedral parish, Francis treated with the greatest kindness all whom he met, whether in extraordinary times such as the Great Famine of 1947 when millions starved to death, the death of Mahatma Ghandi in 1948 when millions mourned, during the Pakistan-Bengali War in 1971 when millions were killed, or in the daily ordinary events of people. He was beloved by people of all classes and religions. This man of God lived simply; he was "poor by birth, poor by calling, and poor by choice."[22]

Despite his advanced years and failing health, his limitations of language and education, Father Francis brought the gospel of Jesus to as many people as possible.

17. ☩ Saint Francis Régis Clet, C.M.

***Place:** Kiang-si and Hou-Kouang in Hopei (now Hubei) Province, China*
***Fame:** Missionary martyr*

Francis Régis Clet (1748-1820) had been born at Grenoble in southwestern France, the tenth of fifteen children.[23] He received his baptismal name in honor of the Grenoble native and Jesuit missionary Jean Francis Régis, who had been canonized in 1737. Francis grew up on the family farm, with pious parents and an older brother and sister who had entered religious life.

Francis received his secondary education at the local Jesuit Royal College and his philosophical-theological education at the Oratorian-administered diocesan seminary. On March 6, 1769, he entered the Vincentian novitiate at Lyons, and four years later, he was ordained a priest.

His first sixteen years of priesthood were spent in the formation of seminarians, as teacher, director of novices, and rector of the Vincentian major seminary. Students nicknamed Francis Régis "the walking encyclopedia" because of his wealth of knowledge.

Saint Francis Régis Clet, C.M.

At forty-three, Francis Régis volunteered for the foreign missions. In March 1791, he left from Marseille and six months later, he arrived at Macao. He spent one year on the island learning the Chinese language and customs.

In October 1792, Francis Régis arrived at Kiang-Si, where he spent one year ministering to the Christians in this most destitute of cities. The next year, he was transferred to Hou-Kouang, where he spent twenty-seven years as the superior of the two dozen circuit-riding Vincentians. Francis lived alone in his home, the only European in an area of 270,000 square miles for which he held pastoral responsibilities.

Anti-Christian persecutions erupted in 1811. The next year, Chinese officials burnt the church and school which Father Francis and his local congregation had constructed. In 1818, a new persecution began. The following year, a reward was offered for the capture of Father Francis. For three months, Francis hid in the mountains by day and ministered to his people at night.

On June 16, 1819, soldiers arrested Father Francis. A Catholic informant had betrayed the priest to the authorities for a large sum of money. For five weeks, Francis was beaten and tortured in prison. After being transferred to another prison, he met a Chinese Vincentian priest who heard Francis' confession. During his eight months of incarceration, Clet was confined in twenty-seven prisons; some officials treated him well, and others mistreated him terribly.

On January 1, 1820, the emperor decreed the death sentence upon the Catholic priest. On February 18, Father Francis Régis Clet was tied to a cross, and, in typical Chinese fashion, was strangled three times: the first two times up to the brink of death and the last time until death.

18. ✠ Saint Agatha Lin Zhao

Place: Qinglong County, Guizhou Province, China
Fame: Lay catechist, Martyr

The parents of Lin Zhao (1817-1858) practiced their Catholic faith despite the prohibitions of Emperor Hien Fung. Shortly before the girl was born, Lin Zhao's father was captured. Three years later, after the father's release from prison, Lin Zhao received baptism.[24]

Bright and beautiful, Agatha grew up with significant self-confidence. She had a mind of her own and the courage to express her mind.

When Agatha was young, her parents secretly betrothed her to a young man of a family named Lin. Meanwhile, Agatha kept growing in the desire to dedicate her life to God as a virgin. At eighteen, Agatha announced her desire to her parents; they in turn informed her about the long-standing betrothal. The young girl successfully pleaded with her parents to respect her desires. A friend of the family, Father Matthew Liu, arranged that Agatha would enter a girls' school in Guiyang.

In 1837, a new persecution erupted against Christians. Agatha's father was arrested again. In jail he was beaten so severely that upon release he no longer could perform physical labor. The situation occasioned Agatha's returning home to support the family financially. At home, she taught catechism to children.

After the father died, and her mother moved in with a son by a previous marriage, Agatha pursued her religious vocation. At twenty-five, she pronounced her vow of perpetual virginity. At Father Liu's request, she became the directress of his girls' school. A year later, at the request of the diocese's Apostolic Administrator, she became the superior of a convent, whose members taught children and cared for the sick.

In 1857, Agatha and two male catechists, Jerome Lu Tingmei and Laurence Wang Bing, were arrested for being Christians. At their trial, the trio defended their religion, and she, the right to remain a virgin. The judge ridiculed her for pretending to be a virgin, which physical state was confirmed by a post-mortem autopsy. The judge condemned to death by beheading all three Christians. They suffered martyrdom on January 28, 1858. The three are known as the Martyrs of MaoKen.

18. ✠ Saint Agnes Lê Thị Thành

Place: Bai Dien, West Tonkin (now Vietnam)
Fame: Martyr

The sole woman among the 117 canonized Martyrs of Vietnam, Agnes Lê Thị Thành (c. 1781-1841), suffered and died in prison rather than relinquish her Catholic faith.[25]

Born at Bai Dien, in the province of Thanh-hoa, in West Tonkin, she grew up under the guidance of her fervent Catholic parents. At seventeen, Agnes married a farmer from the village of Phue-nhac. Together they bore and raised two boys and four girls. At home, Agnes prayed with her children each morning and evening, took them to church for frequent visits, included them in her assisting the poor, instructed them in the catechism, enrolled them in a children's Marian Society, and prepared them for reception of the sacraments. As each child successively left home and married, Agnes continued to inquire about each one's attendance at Mass and practice of devotions. One daughter recalls Agnes' marital advice to the young couple: "Inspired by God, you have become married; it is a responsibility. Be good; do not quarrel. Accept generously whatever cross God might send you. Live in union, in peace. Let no one see you arguing."[26]

Early in 1841, the government promulgated a law that persons who aided and abetted foreign clergy would be subjected to the death penalty. Agnes, nonetheless, accepted into her home in March 1841 two recently-arrived French missionaries, Fathers Berneux and Galy. During the day, the missionaries secretly studied the Vietnamese language at the convent of the Sisters Lovers of the Holy Cross. At night, the pair discreetly returned to Agnes' home. One day, a catechumen heard that priests were hiding in Agnes' home. The pupil reported this information to the governor of the province of Thanh Hoa.

On April 11, 1841, the governor ordered five hundred soldiers to surround Agnes' home. Inside, the military discovered religious materials and foreign money that belonged to the two priests. Outside, the soldiers noticed Father Galy running through the garden, and jumping into an empty cistern on Agnes' property. The soldiers chased after the priest, captured and bound him, and brought him back to Agnes' home. Investigating further inside the home, the soldiers discovered the missionaries' mail which Agnes was about to smuggle overseas to the clergy's religious community. Agnes was arrested along with her two sisters, the two missionary priests, and eight other villagers.

The thirteen prisoners were force-marched an entire day's journey to the provincial capital Thanh Hoa. During this travail, Agnes succumbed to beatings and fell several times. A few days after their arrival, Agnes was brought before the mandarins. They ordered her to apostatize. Agnes replied, "I worship the Lord of heaven; never will I renounce the religion of the sovereign Lord."[27] Repeatedly, Agnes underwent interrogation. She reported to one of her daughters during a visit, "They treated me cruelly, that is true. The amount of force with which they tortured me is inhumane. But I have been aided by the Blessed Virgin and have not resented these sufferings."[28]

The mandarins ordered the Christian prisoners to trample on the crucifix to demonstrate rejection of the foreign religion. Eight captives walked on the cross and were released. Agnes and her two sisters, however, refused to desecrate the cross, for which they were beaten with rods countless times. A second time and a third time, Agnes and her sisters were ordered to walk on the cross. They refused. The furious governor threatened to burn the women to death. When the trio remained faithful, the governor ordered the women to be stripped naked. He then asked if the women prisoners felt ashamed. Agnes replied that they did, and noted that the governor's wife too was ashamed for what he had done to them. The governor's wife nodded in agreement, and the governor ordered the torture to cease.

A couple of days later, the governor ordered soldiers to place snakes inside the clothing of the three prisoners with the expectation that the snakes would bite and poison the women to death. The women lay motionless, and the snakes harmlessly crawled away from them. The frustrated governor tried to trick the women into signing documents denying their faith. Agnes' two sisters were duped into signing and were released. Agnes refused, and she remained in jail.

Three more months passed. Family and friends visited Agnes, and became heart-broken at seeing her bloodied garments and filthy quarters. Agnes urged her distraught daughters to stay at home in order to take care of their families. Agnes remained in jail praying her repertoire of prayers and meditating on the cross of Jesus.

Fifteen days before she died, Agnes became very ill. In disguise, a priest came to hear her confession. Agnes murmured, "My God, you wished to be crucified for me. I accept with my whole heart your holy will. I place my soul and my body in your hands. Lord, pardon my sins."[29] Agnes died peacefully on July 12, 1841.

Family and friends placed the corpse of Agnes Lê Thị Thành in Nam Mau cemetery. Six months later, her sons exhumed the body and discovered that her body had not deteriorated. They placed limestone on the body and returned it to the grave, after which they returned and gathered her bones. Forty years later, in 1881, the pastor of Phuc Nhac parish gathered the bones of Agnes and seven other martyrs of Phuc Nhac and buried their remains in the parish cemetery.

25. ☩ Rani Maria Kunju Vattalil, F.C.C.

Place: *Uttar Pradesh and Madhya Pradesh, India*
Fame: *"Mother of the poor," social worker, and martyr*

Sister Rani Maria (1954-1995) was riding on a crowded bus when a man began stabbing her. Two accomplices helped to pull her off the bus, where the attacker killed her.[30] The forty-one-year-old Franciscan Clarist Sister suffered fifty-four stab wounds.

News of her death spread like wildfire around Udainagar in the central Indian state of Madhya Pradesh, where she had been working for three years. As in her previous missions at Bijnor in Uttar Pradesh (1976-1983) and at Odgadi in Madhya Pradesh (1983-1992), Sister Rani had served the poorest of the poor.

The murder occurred on February 25, 1995. The funeral was delayed until February 27 to allow Sister's father and family to travel from Kerala in southern India to Udainagar; her mother was out of town and could not be contacted in time to attend the funeral. Seven bishops and over one hundred priests concelebrated the Mass of the Resurrection in the cathedral at Indore. Thousands of Christians, Hindus, and Muslims lined the hundred mile route from the cathedral to the burial place at Udainagar. A motorcade of one hundred twenty-five cars followed in a solemn "procession of anguish and triumph" carrying Sister's casket.[31] The poor wept and wailed about the loss of this Sister who had been their servant, spokesperson and spiritual guide. The Bishop of Indore circulated a letter in which he lauded Sister Rani:

> Sister Rani Maria is a martyr. The funeral procession from Indore to Udainagar has been a pilgrimage. Her tomb will become a centre of pilgrimage. Sister Rani gave up her life witnessing for Christ. By shedding her blood, she has become a martyr. She

preached the Good News of salvation to the poor. She served the sick and the afflicted, consoled the needy and the outcasts.[32]

Sister Rani Maria had gained the enmity of money-lending landlords by advising illiterate Adivasi tribal members that they did not have to borrow money at exorbitant rates. She taught the poor to pool their meager resources in banks and to obtain loans at minimal rates. She instructed them to form cooperatives to purchase machinery for a flour mill and oil extractor. All along, the state had been offering low-rate loans for purchasing seeds and fertilizers, but the poor could not complete the complex application forms until Sister Rani assisted them. For the women, Sister organized programs of cottage textile industries, good hygiene, and home-making. Sister gathered the poor into village councils to discuss problems and possible solutions, to develop village leaders, and to hear governmental speakers inform the poor about their rights. In addition to "helping people to help themselves," she organized food and clothing distribution centers and promoted the education of boys and girls. In order to better assess the people's social needs, she earned bachelor's and master's degrees in sociology. All this she did for Christ and his poor. Many poor subsequently inquired about becoming Catholics. A Sister companion and co-worker comments:

RANI MARIA KUNJU VATTALIL

> Sister Rani Maria, inspired and infused with the Franciscan ideals and charism, fell in love with the poor, regardless of caste and creed, age and sex, and firmly believed that she encountered the crucified Christ in the suppressed and oppressed of society. And as she matured in this conviction day by day, she was totally immersed in thinking, working, praying for the poor, and living as one of them.[33]

Sister Rani Maria had grown up at Pulluvazhy in central Kerala. Her parents named their second child and first girl, Marykunju, i.e., "Little Mary." In time, five more children followed. The Vattalil family owned a large plot of farmland, on which worked lower-caste Pulayas; Mary interacted very comfortably with these workers, and with the poor who came to the door begging. She received an excellent education at local and regional schools.

Mary left home on July 3, 1972, and joined the Franciscan Clarist Congregation. After professing temporary vows on May 1, 1974, Mary was assigned to the juniorate program at Aluva in Kerala.

On February 25, 1995, Sister Rani Maria left her convent, named Snehasadan (Abode of Love) and caught the morning bus from Udainagar to Indore. As the bus passed the Nochembur Mountain forests, a hired killer left his passenger seat and approached Sister. He lunged at her with a knife, slashing her face. As she raised her hands in self-defense, he slung the knife at her hands. He thrust the knife into her side. The hired killer and two accomplices tried to pull her off the bus. Sister grasped the bus railing to try to remain inside. The leader of the murderous trio shouted to the killer, "Cut her hands off."[34] Sister yielded to the continuing thrusts and the attackers carried her off the bus and threw her onto the ground. As the killer continued stabbing her, Sister Rani kept praying aloud, "Jesus."[35] Some passengers attempted to help the religious woman, but these would-be rescuers were driven back by the trio's threats. The three ran away. Within two days, however, the landlord who had devised the plan and the three hired killers were captured.

MARCH

16. ✠ Aloysius Schwartz

Place: Pusan, South Korea; and Manila, Philippines
Fame: Founder of the Sisters of Mary, and the Brothers of Christ

ALOYSIUS SCHWARTZ

Born in Washington, D.C., the third of seven children, Aloysius Schwartz (1930-1992) attended Holy Name Grammar School, Saint Charles Seminary near Baltimore, advanced to Maryknoll College at Lakewood, New Jersey and Glen Ellyn, Illinois; and matriculated in theology at Louvain University, in Belgium.[1] After visiting the shrine of the Virgin of the Poor at Banneux, Belgium, he dedicated his life to serving the poorest of the poor.

After ordination on June 29, 1957, Father Al was assigned to Pusan, South Korea, where he arrived on December 8. Evidence of post-war poverty abounded, especially among orphaned or abandoned street children. These children lacked the necessities of life. For these innocent victims, Father Al conceived and oversaw the construction of a Children's Village to provide the poorest youth with basic necessities. To assist him in this mission, he founded two religious congregations: in 1964, the Sisters of Mary; and seventeen years later, the Brothers of Christ.

In 1985 and 1990, he extended his ministry to the Philippines and Mexico respectively. His focus remained the poor, and especially children. He founded Children's Villages in South Korea at Pusan (1964) and Seoul (1975); in the Philippines at Manila (1985), Talisay (1990) and Silang (1991); and in Mexico at Chalco (1990).

In November 1989, this servant of the poorest of the poor was diagnosed with ALS, known popularly as Lou Gehrig's disease, and medically as Amyotrophic Lateral Sclerosis. As his muscles gradually weakened, his mobility lessened, and he became increasingly dependent on the use of a walker, and wheelchair. As his voice weakened, he no longer preached to large crowds, but to small groups, and eventually, his spoken word gave way to written messages. He, nonetheless, continued his ministry. As his activities diminished, his prayers increased; he spent hours praying in front of the Blessed Sacrament, also saying the rosary, and hearing confessions. He writes in an autobiography:

> Pain is pain and suffering is suffering no matter how deep the faith, how bright the hope and how pure the love. At the same time, in the depths of the pain there is this oneness of spirits, and in the heart of the suffering there is this union of souls. And from this oneness and this union there rises a very pure, spiritual peace — this peace of God which surpasses all human understanding.[2]

In recognition of his extraordinary contribution to society, he was nominated twice for the Nobel Peace Prize — in 1984 and 1992.

On March 16, 1992, he died at Manila. The funeral procession took several hours to wind its way through Silang as the poor poured out of their hovels to line the streets in demonstration of their affection for their advocate. Dignitaries followed the cortege in grateful recognition of all that this priest had done for the church and the community. His remains were buried at the Children's Village at Silang, in Cavite Province, Philippines.

23. ✠ Felice Tantardini, P.I.M.E.

***Place:** Taunggyi, Burma (now Myanmar)*
***Fame:** Lay missionary; "God's blacksmith"*

Happy and hard-working, Felice Tantardini (1898-1991) labored as a lay missionary in Burma (now Myanmar) for seventy years, assisting the P.I.M.E. Fathers.[3] In an autobiography which his religious superiors asked the iron-worker to write, Felice described himself as "God's blacksmith."

Felice was born at Introbio, in the Lombardy region of Italy. This sixth of eight children was raised by devout Catholic parents. Felice attended school until third grade; at ten, he became apprenticed to a blacksmith. Felice loved his first name, which means happy. Companions called him "Brother Happy," not only because of his name, but also because of "his way of being: he was happy, content, full of joy and optimism."[4] Ever since childhood, and throughout his life, faith-filled and happy Felice maintained the practice of lighting two candles before Our Lady and praying for her help and protection before he undertook any major project.

FELICE TANTARDINI

After World War I erupted, Felice left his job and joined the Italian army. In January 1918, he was sent to the front lines at the Piave River. Two days later, he was captured, and was sent to a German Prisoner of War work camp. POW's received only bread and water, and almost no clothing or blankets despite the cold weather. During these deprivations, Felice's faith served as his greatest consolation. In October 1918, Felice and four other prisoners escaped from imprisonment by crawling under a fence. Felice hitched train rides from Yugoslavia to Bulgaria to Greece. He slept and ate with farm animals in barns and open fields. In November, the war ended. In December, Felice arrived at Salonica, Greece, where he found refuge in an Italian camp for former POW's.

In June 1919, Felice returned home. The first thing his mother told him to do was to go to confession. As was his practice, he prayed the rosary daily, and regularly read *All For Jesus*, which book inspired him to become a missionary.[5]

On September 20, 1921, Felice entered the P.I.M.E. seminary at Milan. One year later, the young lay handyman departed for Burma along with two P.I.M.E. priest missionaries.

For the next seventy years, Felice Tantardini demonstrated his love for God and neighbor, traversing all of Burma, and assisting the clergy and natives in all the ways which he knew how. Felice worked in all five dioceses of Burma. His origins on a farm had given him the experience for showing others how to cultivate plants and trees. He dug wells and built cisterns. He produced the bricks and forged the nails. Herbal medicines, this simple man taught to the local populace. With damaged armament left behind after Japanese military attacks, this experienced iron-worker cast bells for church towers. He repaired, designed, and constructed homes, schools, orphanages, aqueducts, and hospitals. He oversaw the construction of a dominating cross on two mountain-tops; each cross measuring more than forty feet high and fifteen feet wide. This multi-talented layman learned to speak the native language, and developed a written script for the language. While some churchmen restricted themselves to the population centers, Felice ventured far into the forests where he worked with remote tribes, some of whom practiced cannibalism and occult religion.

Because of his eighty-five years and partial blindness, Felice was ordered by his superiors to retire from active ministry. Having been recalled to Milan, he resisted retirement, and daily prayed three rosaries and lit a candle before the Blessed Mother in the hope of being healed sufficiently to return to Burma. And if he were not healed, he prayed that "with or without my leg, I might be able to go back to Burma," which he did after just five months in Italy.[6] When opponents of his return to the wilds warned him of possible illnesses from disease-carrying mosquitoes, leathery-skinned Felice replied, "Any mosquito that bites me, will die instead of me."[7]

When he died at ninety-three, this happy and hard-working lay volunteer remained in Burma, having been buried at Paya Phyu.

23. ✢ Saint Rafqa de Himlaya

Place: Bikfaya, Lebanon
Fame: Blind Mystic

In the village of Himlaya in the Lebanese Mountains, new parents baptized their daughter Boutrosiya (1832-1914).[8] Soon, the girl acquired the affectionate nickname of Rafqa. When Rafqa was seven, her mother died. Soon, her father re-married. When the nation's civil war resulted in economic hardships, the father let the girl work as a maid in the home of a wealthy couple, first at B'Abda, Lebanon and later, at Damascus, Syria. After three years, the father called his daughter to return home so that he could arrange a marriage for her. One day, Rafqa overheard a loud quarrel between her stepmother who wanted Rafqa to marry her stepbrother, and her aunt who wanted Rafqa to marry the aunt's brother. Rafqa already had set her soul on becoming a nun.

On her twenty-first birthday, against the wishes of her father and stepmother, Rafqa entered the convent of the Marian Order of the Immaculate Conception at Bikfaya. After postulancy and novitiate, she took religious vows and the religious name Anissa (Agnes). For seven years, she worked in the convent's kitchen during the day, and studied at night. For the next eleven years, she taught in the religious community's schools at Deir-El-Qamar, Jbeil (ancient Byblos) and Ma'ad. During the anti-Christian massacres, she once hid a young boy under her ankle-length religious habit, and another time, she hid with other sisters in a stable.

In 1871, at thirty-nine, the Marianite Sisters merged with Sisters of the Sacred Heart of Jesus. Each sister was given options: either to join the new order, or to join another order, or to be released from vows. Sister Anissa, who recently had experienced a vision of Saint Anthony the Monk, chose to leave the apostolic life and to enter the monastic life. At the monastery of Saint Simon in Aitu near Ehden, she adopted the new religious name of Rafqa in honor of her mother. In 1873, she took permanent vows as a monastic sister.

At fifty-three, Sister Rafqa thought that God had made her life very pleasant, and in the process he had deprived her of much suffering. Believing that suffering provided a safer way to sanctity, she prayed, "O my God, why are you distant from me and have abandoned me? You don't visit me with sickness. Have you perhaps abandoned me?"[9] That very night, Rafqa experienced a sharp pain in her head that — a pain that shot into her eyes.

Many doctors tried to relieve the suffering. One doctor removed her eye without applying anesthesia. She viewed the experience as being "in communion with the Passion of Christ."[10]

A dozen years later, Sister Rafqa's sufferings worsened. After transferring to the convent of Mar Youssef of Jrabta in Batrun, she lost weight and developed a paralysis in the joints of her body. A posthumous medical report in 1981, diagnosed the illness as "tuberculosis with ocular localization and multiple bony excrescencies. This disease causes the most unbearable pain."[11] On March 23, 1914, Sister Rafqa died. She had endured excruciating pain for twenty-nine years. Throughout this period of suffering, crippled and blind Rafqa continued to perform menial chores in the convent, especially spinning wool and knitting, and always without complaint about her disability or pain.

APRIL

2. ✝ Blessed Pedro Calungsod

Place: Cebu, Philippines; and Tomhon, Guam
Fame: Teenage catechist and martyr

Pedro Calungsod (c. 1655-1672), a young catechist working with the Jesuit missionaries, sailed from Cavite, twenty miles south of Manila en route to Guam.[1] The ship left the Philippines on August 7, 1667; arrived at Acapulco, Mexico on January 6, 1668; and two months later, embarked from Acapulco, and arrived at Agana, Guam on June 15, 1668. Fifty men arrived on that ship: five Jesuit priests and one Jesuit seminarian, thirty-four soldiers, and ten Filipino youths, some of whom would work as catechists and others as cooks.

BLESSED PEDRO CALUNGSOD

Almost four years later, on April 2, 1672, the local native chief and companions with machetes and spears killed young Pedro. A minute later, the chief and companions killed Father Diego. Pedro died from a spear having been thrust into his chest, and a machete having been whipped across his head. The attackers took the two victims' corpses, and hurled them into the sea at Tomhon Beach, near Agana. Pedro is included among the martyrs honored as "Father Diego Luis de San Vitores and Companions."

Pedro Calungsod had come from a village in the Visayas region of the Philippines. Pedro was among the boys whom the Jesuits recruited in 1668 to assist in the evangelization of the Chamorros; the boys ranged in age between twelve and fourteen. The Jesuits had discovered that these boys learned foreign languages quickly. These youths possessed a strong basic understanding of the faith, and came from good Catholic families.

Franciscan, Jesuit, and Augustinian missionaries had brought the faith to the Philippines almost a hundred years before, beginning in 1577.

No painting or written description of Pedro exists. A Jesuit source, contemporary with Pedro, reports that typical Visayan males were "usually more corpulent, better built and somewhat taller than the Tagalogs in Luzon; that their skin was light brown in color; that their faces were usually round and of fine proportions; that their noses were flat; that their eyes and hair were black; that they — especially the youth — wore their hair a little bit long."[2] Twentieth-century promoters of the cause of Pedro Calungsod chose a youth whose visage they perceive typifies Visayan youth as the image used popularly to present the imagined image of Pedro Calungsod.

Pedro and his fellow catechists had to be adventurous and courageous. They willingly left home to labor in the Marianas Islands — 1,500 miles due east of Manila. Their destination was the string of fourteen Northern Marianas Islands, which stretched for almost fifty miles, with Guam being the southernmost and largest.

6. ☩ Saint Paul Lê-Báo Tịnh

Place: *Thanh Hoa Province, West Tonkin (now Vietnam)*

Fame: *Martyr, wrote a death-row letter describing the sufferings of prisoners*

As a youth, Paul Lê-Báo Tịnh (1793-1857) entered the seminary, but left after a brief stay. As an adult, he again entered the seminary, and was ordained a priest at age fifty-six.[3] He ministered for eight years, before being arrested and decapitated.

At Trinh-Ha village, in Thanh hoa Province, Paul was born of wealthy parents, who practiced a syncretism of Catholic worship and native sacrifices. As a child Paul studied under a local Confucian scholar, until his parents sent him at twelve to the Catholic seminary at Ke-Vinh. The faculty and students described Paul as prayerful, ascetical, and studious. He enjoyed reading the lives of the saints, and reminded his peers that everyone's Christian vocation was to become a saint.

In search of the eremetical life, Paul left the seminary. Having traveled to Bach Bat Forest, Paul lived in a cave, survived on rice and fruit, and passed his days in prayer and mortification. Bishop Havard, having kept in communication with the former seminarian, requested in 1837 that Paul travel to Macao to secretly bring back missionary priests for Tonkin and Laos. Paul accepted the challenge, and twice brought back priests including the future Bishop Retord. Paul settled down in the mountains of Laos, where he integrated the eremetical and evangelical missions.

After Bishop Havard died in 1840, his successor Bishop Retord contacted Paul in Laos. The new bishop requested that Paul again might travel to Macao to lead additional priests to West Tonkin. Paul accepted the request.

The next year, governmental officials arrested Paul at Ke-dam village. The next seven years he passed in prison at Hanoi. Shortly after receiving the death sentence, Paul wrote on April 20, 1843, to the seminarians at Ke-Vinh describing his experience of prison.

> I, Paul, bound in chains for the sake of Christ, send to you from prison, salutations which are many and final.... This prison is truly a living example of hell; to chains, shackles, and manacles, are added anger, vengeance, lies, obscene conversations, brawls, evil acts, swearing, slanders, plus boredom, sadness, mosquitoes, flies and smelly animals.... I write these things to you not to frighten you or weaken your spirit, but that you might unite yourself to me, inspired by mutual charity, and that you might pray with fervor for me.... I write these things so that your hearts might burst with the desire to be martyrs, and that your prayers might strengthen me, who lives in the arena of combat. For yourselves, good friends, remember that the Blessed Mother is proclaimed the Queen of Martyrs, without having felt the blade of the sword. You also are able to be martyrs in the same way, that is to say, martyrs of love, by desire, and in suffering with Christ. ... Good-bye to each and everyone of you, and pray for me.[4]

Emperor Thieu Tri in 1848, commuted Paul's sentence from death to perpetual exile in Phu Yen province. At the end of the same year, the new emperor Tu Duc, granted amnesty to all exiles. Paul traveled to Ke-Vinh Seminary, where he renewed his studies, and in 1848, was ordained a priest.

Paul's priestly assignments included teaching in the seminary, and serving as superior from 1849-1852 and again beginning in 1855. On February 27, 1857, some mandarins complained to the governor of Nam

Dinh Province about the Christians. The governor arrested Paul. Fortunately, back in 1841, at Hue, Paul had healed this governor from a terrible sickness. The governor had the highest respect for Paul, and helped Paul to prepare his defense.

On April 5, 1857, after Paul had served thirty-seven days in jail, the emperor rejected the governor's request for leniency. Instead, the emperor wrote, "Le bao Tịnh, who had been guilty before and had received the emperor's amnesty, now continued to do the priest's job. So this relapsing criminal is to be decapitated immediately."[5] Early the next day, Paul was led to the place of execution. His last words were, "The religion of the Heavenly Master is perfectly true, even though our king and the sovereigns of other nations persecute it and wish to destroy it. But this religion will be victorious, and in the future it will count more adherents than it ever has had in the past."[6]

The executioner approached Paul. The soldier raised his sword and chopped five times at Paul's neck before successfully separating the martyr's head from the body. Paul's remains were buried at the church in Vinh-Tri.

Overall, Paul's spirituality had centered on the cross of Jesus, devotion to Mary, and the practice of prayer and asceticism. Regarding devotion to Jesus, Paul carried a crucifix with him always. He would touch the cross and experience a spiritual strength. Regarding Mary, he prayed the rosary daily, and fasted on the vigil of all Marian liturgical feasts. He pondered often the dictum: "First, love God. Second, love Mary." In celebrating Masses, preaching, and converting, Paul relied on prayer to inspire his actions and words, trusting that good would flow from God, rather than from Paul's limited abilities.

22. ☩ Mario Borzaga, O.M.I., and Thoj Xyooj Paolo

Place: Laos
Fame: Missionary martyrs

Many times, Mario Borzaga (1932-1960) had written in his diary that he wished to serve God as a "priest, apostle, missionary, martyr."[7] After serving twenty-three months in Laos, Father Mario and his native Hmong catechist Thoj Xyooj Paolo (1941-1960) disappeared while returning from a sick call at Pha Xoua in the remote forest along the northern border with China. Investigators learned from witnesses that the pair had died at the hands of the Pathet-Lao Communist soldiers. Forty years later, information surfaced to confirm these original testimonies.

MARIO BORZAGA

Mario had grown up in the suburbs of Trent in northern Italy. His five older siblings and he had benefited from a joyful faith-filled home. Their carpenter-father and seamstress-mother prayed the rosary with the family each evening.

THOJ XYOOJ PAOLO

At eleven, Mario expressed to his mother his desire to enter the seminary. She hesitated to approve, thinking he was too young. He assured her that from his earliest days he had wanted to become a priest, and that his days of playing at "saying Mass" under the kitchen table had been an expression of his faith-filled desire. The parents conferred with the seminary director and respected relatives, and gave an affirmative decision.

At every level of the seminary, Mario performed well. Faculty and classmates respected and accepted him. He studied diligently and received good grades.

While at the major seminary, Mario felt called to serve as a missionary in foreign lands. During his daily thanksgiving after Communion, "he persistently asked to be 'priest, apostle, missionary'."[8] Through his reading of missionary magazines, the "vocation within a vocation" to serve as a missionary kept growing. Five years before ordination, he wrote to his mother, "I feel the Lord is calling me to labor in far away missions, beyond the sea, where there are so many souls who still don't know God. In our own diocese there are already very many priests and religious."[9]

Part-way through the major seminary, Mario transferred from the diocese of Trent to the Oblates of Mary Immaculate. He describes the community's novitiate in these words: "It's a year in which our potential for complete giving of self to the Lord is tested, a year which requires us to renounce, to empty ourselves completely of ourselves."[10] Shortly before completing the major seminary, he wrote in his diary, "I am convinced that the Madonna has a prominent part in my priesthood. The Immaculate Conception will make my soul like hers, because in her there rests more easily the Heart of her Son Jesus."[11] Mario was ordained a priest on February 24, 1957.

After volunteering for the mission in Laos, Father Mario and five other Oblates sailed on October 31, from Naples for Southeast Asia. One month later, the group arrived at Paksani, Laos. Immediately, Mario applied himself to learning the natives' culture, customs, and languages: Laotian; and Hmong. By May 1958, he ventured into the mountain regions of Phon Hom and Pak Kadine. In his diary he penned, "All these brethren are entrusted to my sanctity, to my fervour."[12] A few months later, he climbed into even more remote heights: Keng Sadok and Kiucatian. He overcame occasional diffidence by praying, "Jesus loves me all the same, and I love him."[13]

In May 1959, at Long Vai, he encountered Pathet-Lao soldiers. This leftist militia had joined forces with the Vietnamese Communists to topple the French colonial government. The Laotian rebels hid along the mountain trails and posed a constant threat of ambush against passersby and their property.

In April 1960, Father Mario received news that a desperately ill Catholic wished to see him. Mario, the committed priest, apostle and missionary, set out with his catechist, nicknamed Shiong. The priest shouted to his confreres as he departed, "I'll be back in two weeks. See you at Luang Prapang."[14]

After two weeks, neither Mario nor Shiong had returned home. The OMI priests and lay leaders made inquiries of the pair's whereabouts. Villagers along the route reported that Father Mario and his catechist had passed through their villages but had not returned; that the pair had reached their destination and administered the sacraments, and had departed from the village of the sick person. The pair, however, was never heard from again.

Just before having taken religious vows, Mario had written repeatedly in his diary, "We are always ready, Lord, at all times, to be butchered, considered as slaughter lambs."[15] Mario Borzaga died as he had lived and prayed: as priest, apostle, missionary, and martyr.

24. ✠ Venerable Anastasius Hartmann, O.F.M., Cap.

Place: Bombay (now Mumbai) and Patna (now Allahabad), India
Fame: Vicar Apostolic

Anastasius Hartmann (1803-1886) had been born the seventh of ten children, and was baptized Joseph Lewis.[16] The family lived in the Altwis Canton near Lucerne, Switzerland. Young Joseph possessed not only a religious fervor, but also a stutter which frustrated his communications.

ANASTASIUS HARTMANN

At eighteen, Joseph entered the Capuchin Novitiate at Baden. His superiors chose for him the religious name Anastasius. On September 24, 1825, Anastasius was ordained a priest.

Early in priesthood, Anastasius served successively as a curate, novice director, and teacher of philosophy and theology. In 1841, he was transferred to Rome to teach at the International Saint Fidelis College, which prepared priests for ministry in foreign missions. In 1858, the Congregation for the Propagation of the Faith appointed Anastasius the rector of the College, in addition to his role as director for the Capuchin Foreign Missions.

Anastasius yearned to serve in the foreign missions. He writes to his superiors, "I wish to express an interior desire which I felt for many years and which I consider as God's will. . . . All kinds of sufferings and persecutions and even martyrdom may be waiting for me, . . . but of all these I am not frightened, but only attracted and I cannot doubt that God himself gave me this vocation."[17] After many failed requests, Anastasius received an assignment for India.

Embarking for India on November 24, 1843, Anastasius and two other Capuchins arrived at Bombay on January 15, 1844. They began the eight-hundred mile journey by ox cart to Agra, where they arrived on March 6. In less than six months, Anastasius learned enough Hindi and

English to begin evangelizing the local population and the neighboring tribals. He celebrated the sacraments for Catholics, founded schools for children of all religions, and constructed a shelter for reformed prostitutes, which occasioned slanderous rumors about him.

The Vatican appointed Anastasius the first Vicar Apostolic of Patna. He was ordained bishop on March 15, 1846. When Anastasius arrived in the city of 300,000 inhabitants, he saw that the mission house and cathedral were dilapidated. The mission territory extended for 150,000 square miles and a civil population of twenty million. The vicariate had 2,700 Catholics and four missionaries.[18] There were no schools, no Sisters nor Brothers.

The zealous bishop responded enthusiastically to these challenges. Throughout the vicariate he constructed churches, chapels, schools, priests' residences; and renovated the cathedral. He traveled to Europe to recruit religious communities and to raise funds. To promote native vocations, he converted part of his residence into a seminary. Despite the difficulties of travel by ox-cart, horseback, and train, Bishop Anastasius visited his flock in their distant towns and villages.

The bishop's road to revivifying the vicariate suffered many bumps. In a court of law, a fraudulent clerk succeeded in having the bishop convicted on charges of fraud and simony. "It turned nearly all the Catholics against him."[19] On appeal, the High Court reversed the decision, after which the bishop's accuser admitted he had falsified the allegations. Other lawsuits regarding ownership of church property consumed the bishop's intellect and energy. One priest of the diocese had been teaching false doctrines, and the bishop had to confront him. Lack of sufficient funds constantly burdened Bishop Anastasius.

In 1849, Rome named Anastasius the Administrator of the Apostolic Vicariate of Bombay, and in 1854, appointed him the Apostolic Vicar for Bombay and Patna. At Bombay, the bishop dealt with seemingly endless internal conflicts between: supporters of the Spanish *Propaganda Fide* and the Portuguese *Padroado*, English and Italian priests, religious and diocesan clergy, Irish and Italian nationals, and among laity some of whom wished to own the church buildings which the laity had built through lay funds. While fighting these battles, the bishop founded the still-extant church newspaper *Bombay Examiner*, translated the New Testament into Urdu, and produced a catechism in Hindi, which he translated into Latin, Persian, and Devangari.

In 1860, the Holy Father re-appointed Anastasius the Vicar Apostolic of Patna. "The reception given to him by the sisters, clergy and the laity cannot be described in words. It was like a hearty and royal welcome to a friend, who had been missed for a long time and who had now returned home, crowned with glory and with the marks of venerable old age."[20]

The bishop divided his time between both vicariates. Shortly before he died, he made the thousand mile journey from Bombay to Patna. He celebrated Holy Week at Bankipur, led a construction meeting for a church at Jaimapur, and returned home to Kurjee, where he contracted cholera. Unable to recover, the octogenarian prepared for death; he made his confession, received the Last Rites and the Eucharist. Two days later, the revered churchman succumbed.

Words which he had written on his anniversary of episcopal ordination describe well his experience of service in the Church: "I do not wish to be sheltered from storms and to be exempted from trials. All that I beg of God is that I may bear them in a Christian manner and render them beneficial to the missions."[21]

28. ✠ Saint Peter Chanel, S.M.

Place: Island of Futuna, Oceania
Fame: First martyr of Oceania

In the South Pacific, thirteen hundred miles northeast of New Zealand, and twenty-six hundred miles southwest of Hawaii, lies tiny Futuna Island (about the size of Washington, D.C.). In 1837, Father Peter Chanel (1803-1841) and Brother Marie Nizier Delorme, members of the recently approved Society of Mary, arrived at Futuna as the island's first Christian missionaries.[22] A Protestant English-speaking sailor, Thomas Boag, disembarked on Futuna to assist the two missionaries.

Though Futuna had only a thousand people, it was divided into the two rival kingdoms of Sigave and Tua, which were at war when Chanel landed. The religion he found there consisted of a fearful respect of the *'atua muli*, malevolent spirits who were not to be angered, lest people would become sick and crops would fail. Chanel labored zealously amid the greatest hardships. He learned the local language, cared for the sick, baptized the dying, and received the sobriquet of "the man with the kind heart." Niuliki, the king of Tua, happily received Chanel and Delorme. The king ordered a hut to be built for them, and even declared them "taboo" or inviolable. In 1840, however, Niuliki grew hostile toward Chanel, after the king heard about many conversions to Catholicism on Wallis Island, about 120 miles away. The local situation worsened when Meitala, Niuliki's son, decided to embrace the "foreign" religion.

SAINT PETER CHANEL, S.M.

On Sunday, April 25, 1841, Chanel went to visit Meitala, who took hold of the cross hanging around the priest's neck and placed it on his own, indicating definitively that he was embracing the religion of the crucified Jesus. Afterwards, the priest returned to his hut. The next day, Meitala went with six other catechumens to see the Englishman Boag. They carried fruit which had been declared taboo, i.e., forbidden to be touched. To show their disdain for the old beliefs, they asked the sailor to cook the fruit for them. During the meal, the prince's mother arrived. She begged her son not to eat the forbidden fruit. Furious at his misconduct, she ran to tell the king what their son had done. The next day, during an hour-long conversation, Niuliki tried to change his son's mind regarding the new belief, but the son remained firm.

Aware of the king's anger, Musumusu, another chief, and probably Niuliki's son-in-law, suggested to Niuliki that they get rid of Chanel. Niuliki seemed to give tacit approval.

The conspirators traveled to the village where Chanel lived. On the morning of April 28, one of the men went into the priest's house and asked him to bind a wound. While the good Father was tending to the patient, another conspirator struck him on the forehead with a club, while a second attacker hit him with a stick. When Chanel sat down, a third man thrust a bayonet through the priest's shoulder; the victim pulled out the blade without saying a word. Suddenly, the house was swarming with attackers, who seemed more intent on stealing. Musumusu gave the order to kill the priest, but no one paid attention. Musumusu himself took an adz and split open the priest's skull, killing him. Chanel was alone at the time. A woman from a nearby valley washed the martyr's wounds, wrapped his body in a tapa cloth, and, with her husband's help, buried him nearby.

At this point only a handful of natives had been converted, and another handful were receiving instructions for Baptism. Within two years of Peter Chanel's martyrdom, however, the entire island converted to Christianity. To this day, the populace of Futuna Island remains entirely Catholic.

Peter had been born in the hamlet of La Potière, near Cuet, France. He studied for the Diocese of Belley in its seminaries. After ordination for the diocese, he served admirably in two successive parishes: Amberieu and Crozet. In 1831, Peter became a part of the Marist project. After serving as professor and spiritual director at Belley College, he was appointed in 1834, the school's assistant superior. In 1833, Chanel accompanied the Marist founder, Jean-Claude Colin, to Rome to present the proposal for the new congregation. After Pope Gregory XVI approved the Society of Mary in early 1836, Peter professed his vows in the young community on September 24, 1836.

Peter's boyhood dreams became realized when his superiors accepted his request to labor overseas. On December 24, 1836, Peter and six other Marist missionaries sailed for the South Pacific. On November 8, Father Chanel and Brother Delorme disembarked at Futuna Island. The other Marists traveled on to Wallis Island and New Zealand. The life at Fortuna was lonely, and Peter welcomed the occasional visits from his confreres at Wallis Island.

MAY

10. ✝ Blessed Damien de Veuster, SS.CC.

Place: Honolulu and Molokai, Hawaii
Fame: Apostle among those afflicted with leprosy

Joseph de Veuster (1846-1889), the seventh of eight children, interrupted his education to help out on the family farm.[1] At twelve, the boy returned to school to study commercial farming. At the college, a Redemptorist preacher inspired Joseph to become a priest. Like his older brother Auguste, named Pamphile in religious life, Joseph joined the Congregation of the Sacred Hearts of Jesus and Mary. One month after his thirteenth birthday, Joseph became a novice and received the religious name Damien.

In spring 1863, the provincial of the Congregation of the Sacred Hearts invited priests to evangelize the inhabitants of the Sandwich Islands (now the Hawaiian Islands). Both Pamphile and Damien volunteered. The older brother, but not the younger, was chosen. When Pamphile became ill, however, Damien was allowed to take his brother's place. Damien left Bremerhaven on October 23, 1863, and arrived at Honolulu on March 19, 1864.

Two months after his arrival, and the completion of his theological studies, Damien was ordained a priest. His superiors assigned him to the eastern part of Hawaii. For eight months, he ministered at Puna, and for the next eight years, in the neighboring districts of Kohala and Hamakua. Damien became a circuit-riding missionary, with each circuit requiring six weeks.

In spring 1873, the Bishop of Honolulu requested priest-volunteers to serve the population afflicted with leprosy, who, in 1865, the government had segregated at Kalaupapa on the island of Molokai. Four priests stepped forward. They planned to rotate turns every few months. Damien took the first rotation, arriving on May 10, 1873. At the end of the first week, Damien wrote that he would be happy to remain forever among those suffering from leprosy. The other three priests never served at Molokai. Damien never left this apostolate; sixteen years later, he died at Molokai.

Damien received instructions on how to preserve himself from contracting Hansen's Disease. He was advised to neither breathe the air emitted by the lepers nor touch anything used by them and to wash his hands repeatedly every day. To implement these procedures, however, would prove impossible. How could this dedicated priest not risk contamination in breathing the same air as his parishioners when he was visiting and talking with them? How could he avoid risk of contamination when eating the food which his hosts had prepared with their leprous hands? How could he as priest anoint his people without touching them? How could he wash frequently when the community's only water source lay hundreds of yards away?

Damien busied himself serving the people's basic spiritual and material needs. Among the colony's six hundred inhabitants, he ministered to the two hundred Catholics by baptizing, catechizing, confessing, counseling, and celebrating Eucharist for them. He celebrated Benediction and provided Adoration for his flock. For the citizens of Kalawao Settlement, Damien repaired and built homes, dug out streets, developed a sanitary system, and constructed a pipeline to bring water into the middle of the community. This former farm boy taught his new companions how to raise chickens and cows. "[For the sick] he washed their bodies, bandaged their wounds, tidied their rooms and made them as comfortable as possible."[2] For the dying, Damien built coffins, dug cemetery plots, ritualized funerals, and organized a musical band to process to the cemetery. At the Kalawao Settlement, in the midst of the flagrant drinking, stealing, and sexual attacks, Damien instituted separate quarters for men and women, an orphanage for children, and a security force for the protection of all inhabitants. "To the lepers of Molokai, Father Damien was priest and doctor, carpenter and plumber, but above all he was the tangible evidence of God's love among them."[3]

After thirteen years without peer companions, Damien was blessed with two special guests: in July 1886, Ira Barnes Dutton, recently converted and baptized Joseph, arrived as a lay volunteer from Vermont to help at Kalawao. "They [Damien and Ira] labored marvelously together and Joseph, now dubbed 'Brother Joseph' became Father Damien's closest and most cherished associate."[4] In November 1888, Mother Marianne Cope, who had arrived five years earlier with four other Sisters of the Third Order of St. Francis from Syracuse, New York, transferred from Oahu to Molokai to assist Father Damien.

Ever since the end of 1873, his first year at Molokai, Damien had experienced the burning sensations symptomatic of Hansen's Disease. Five years later, the symptoms disappeared. In 1881, however, symptoms resurfaced. In 1884, he noticed that while bathing his feet in near boiling water he felt no heat, although his feet had blistered. In 1885, he was diagnosed medically with Hansen's Disease. To his provincial's suggestion that Damien be transferred to receive treatment, the priest replied, "I would not be cured if the price of my cure was that I must leave the island and give up my work."[5] In July 1886, he traveled to Honolulu to receive aid from a renowned Japanese doctor, but the salutary effects lasted only a few months. On March 19, 1889, Father Damien celebrated twenty-five years of service in the Hawaiian Islands, on March 27, he became bedridden at home, and on April 15, he died.

10. ✠ Matteo Ricci, S.J.

Place: Chao-k'ing, Nanking, and Peking, China
Fame: Founder of the modern Catholic Church in China

Until the Chinese met Matteo Ricci (1552-1610), Chinese leaders believed that they had little or nothing to learn from non-Chinese. Ricci, however, aroused the curiosity and excitement of the Chinese to learn more about this man "from the God of the West."[6]

Having been born at Macerata, Italy, Matteo Ricci left home at sixteen to study law at Rome. One year later, in 1571, contrary to the wishes of his father, the youth entered the Jesuit novitiate. The following year, he undertook studies in mathematics, philosophy, and theology. In spring 1577, he traveled to Portugal, and the next spring, for Goa, where he arrived in mid-September 1578. While continuing his theological studies, he was ordained a priest on July 25, 1580; and in early 1582, Matteo Ricci completed his academic and spiritual formation.

Meanwhile Alessandro Valignano, who oversaw the Jesuit missions in the East, set his sights on bringing the gospel to China. Until this time, China had isolated itself from non-Chinese political, economic, and cultural influences. Christian missionaries had entered China many centuries earlier: initially, during the Nestorian movement from Syria to China during the fifth to seventh centuries, and later, during the Franciscan missions from Assisi to China in the thirteenth and fourteenth centuries, until the Black Death wreaked its havoc. Neither of these ventures resulted in broad or deep impact. Between 1555 and 1582, Augustinian, Dominican, Franciscan and Jesuit missionaries attempted a half-dozen times to enter China, but each of these efforts lasted little more than a month and all proved fruitless.

Valignani imagined that if Catholic missionaries would challenge on equal ground the esteemed intellectual aristocracy among the Chinese, then missionaries would be accepted. The Jesuit director reasoned that if the Chinese elites would accept the religion, then the hierarchically ordered Chinese masses would embrace the new religion; "because the cult of officialdom was everywhere deeply inbred, the masses would inevitably be drawn to the faith."[7] In 1579, Valignani advised his confrere Michele de Ruggieri to go to Macao to learn the language and customs of the educated Chinese, and three years later, Valignani directed Ricci to do the same.

On September 10, 1583, Fathers Ruggieri and Ricci received permission from the viceroy of the province of Canton to establish a residence at the administrative capital of Chao-k'ing. The two priests explained that they wished to experience the country's good government and to serve the Lord of Heaven. As a means of passive evangelization, the two Churchmen decorated their home with religious paintings and books. The pair anticipated that the curious Chinese would inquire about the portrayals of Jesus, Mary, and Joseph; the saints, churches; and about the Bible and other religious writings. The Westerners displayed also in their home scientific advances which the Chinese had never seen: "Venetian prisms, European books, paintings and engravings, sundials, clocks, and projections of maps."[8] Perhaps the most intriguing artifact was a map of the world, which portrayed all the known countries in quite accurate proportions, unlike the Chinese map of the world which presented China surrounded by the rest or the world consisting of many smaller countries, whose entire land mass did not equal the land area of China.

As expected, the Chinese expressed interest in the religion of the West. Ricci and Ruggieri with the assistance of fellow Jesuits produced a Chinese translation of the Ten Commandments, a summary of the Christian moral code based on doctrinal teachings, and a small catechism written in the format of a dialogue between a curious Chinaman and an attentive European priest. The catechism was distributed to hundred of thousands of Chinese. Mandarins and commoners prided themselves on having received these esteemed works. Ruggieri and Ricci enjoyed increasing popularity, and interest in the scientific and religious contributions of the West.

In 1588, Valignani sent Ruggieri on a mission to Rome to gain the support of the Holy See for the methodology of the Jesuit mission in China. Ruggieri never returned; he died at Rome in 1607. Ricci was left alone with a young priest missionary apprentice. Stalwartly, Ricci continued the method of appealing to the intellectual curiosity of the officials and educated elites. From 1583 until 1589, Ricci lived in Chao-k'ing, where he had adopted the Buddhist garb at the recommendation of the local mandarin. A political change of viceroys led to the ouster of Ricci from Chao-k'ing to Shaochow, farther north in the same province of Kwangtung. Here Ricci adopted the square bonnet and the silk robes of a Chinese scholar, which resulted in his being invited to lecture, and his being accepted on equal level with native scholars. He became regarded as the Doctor from the Great West Ocean. After one year at Shaochow, Ricci happily moved to the intellectual and political capital of southern China, namely, Nanking. About a decade later, 1601, Ricci left Nanking and arrived at Peking, the nation's capital and seat of the imperial court.

Ricci and his Jesuit companion, whose reputations had preceded them, presented to the emperor numerous gifts, and received in return permission to reside in the city, and to pursue their mathematical and astronomical investigations. Ricci describes the reception: "not only do we reside in Peking, but we enjoy here an incontestable authority."[9] At this time ministering in China were eight priests and eight Chinese lay brothers, serving about two thousand converts at four mission centers including the two capitals.[10]

After twenty-seven years in the Middle Kingdom, with the last nine years having been spent at Peking, sixty-two year old Ricci felt his body wearing down, and he soon died. "This missionary scholar from the West became and has ever remained the most respected foreign figure in Chinese literature." He ranks as "one of the most remarkable and brilliant men in history."[11]

22. ✠ Saint Michael Hồ Đình Hy

***Place:** An-Hoa, near Hue, Vietnam*
***Fame:** Martyr*

Born at the village of Nhu Lam in Thua Thien Province, into a family of Christian nobility, Michael Hồ Đình Hy (c. 1808-1857) grew up as the youngest of five surviving children.[12] He benefited through education and royal relatives to become a governmental official. At twenty, he married Lucy Tan, and together they raised three boys, one of whom became a priest. Like his catechist father, Michael Hồ Đình Hy became a leader within the Catholic community.

In his professional career, he rose rapidly through the bureaucratic ranks because of his capability and kindness. He attributed his faith as his inspiration and guide in treating people, and conducting business. People regarded him highly for his honesty and justice.

After thirty-one years of governmental service, Michael was appointed by King Tu-duc to the third highest rank of mandarin. Michael's responsibility consisted in overseeing the operations of the royal silk mills. He associated regularly with the royal family, and traveled extensively on royal business. For a period of three years, he became lax in his practice of the faith. Recovering from this period of lassitude, he returned more strongly to his praying and resting on Sunday, reading the lives of the saints and spiritual authors, and confessing his sins. He became renowned for practicing heroic charity with everyone regardless of class.

In 1856, a mandarin of lesser rank, named Phan Y, approached Mandarin Hy and requested silk products to give to the king. The lesser mandarin, however, according to custom, was undeserving of the highest quality silks. Mandarin Hy refused the request. Mandarin Phan Y promised revenge. He informed governmental authorities that Mandarin Hy belonged to the Catholic faith, which the emperor had banned since 1841.

On November 8, 1856, soldiers surrounded the home of Mandarin Hy. They arrested him for on the charge of "having practiced a perverse religion," and "having adhered to an evil and forbidden cult."[13] The mandarin remained in jail for six months, during which time he suffered frequent interrogations and cruel tortures. On December 19, he received the sacraments of Penance and Communion. Throughout his half-year imprisonment, friends and fellow-mandarins begged him to forsake his faith. He replied to one colleague, "My life is nearing its end. I wish, up to the moment of death itself, to remain faithful to my religion."[14] On May 1, 1857, he was sentenced to death by decapitation. The king's decree reads:

> We order, therefore, that five mandarins and fifteen soldiers bind . . . Hy and lead him around the Citadel [at Hue] past all the roads, i.e., all those places which are teeming with people. This is to be done three times for three successive days. At each intersection, it is ordered that he be beaten thirty times and it is be to be proclaimed loudly that: "Hồ Đình Hy is a criminal because he follows the heretical Catholic religion that he dares to act contrary to national law, and fails to adhere to ancestor worship. For these reasons, the emperor condemns him to death.[15]

On May 15, 18, and 21, Mandarin Hy was paraded and beaten with a stick through the streets of Hue. On May 22, the prisoner was marched to the place of execution at An-Hoa, one mile outside of Hue.

Michael Hồ Đình Hy remained chained in the public square for three hours, during which time he prayed while the public reacted with the gamut of emotions. Bystanders observed that Mandarin Hy had been a most responsible, honest, and kind public servant, and that the only cause for killing him was the mandarin's religion. The executioner informed Hy that after three intervals of drum beatings and trumpets blaring that the prisoner would be killed. The prisoner made the sign of the cross, and received the same from a priest in the crowd, indicating God's forgiveness for whatever sins the mandarin may have committed. The executioner slashed twice at the neck of Mandarin Hy, separating the head from his body.

23. ✠ Matthew Kadalikkattil

Place: Kannadiyurumpu, Kerala, India
Fame: Apostle of the Sacred Heart, founder of Sisters of the Sacred Heart

Like almost every founder of a religious congregation, Matthew Kadalikkattil (1872-1935) experienced great suffering in the birthing process of the community.[16]

Matthew grew up at Edappadi, Kerala, as the second of four children. From childhood, he manifested a predilection to help the needy. This trait developed further when seven year-old Matthew saw his hard-working farmer-father fall from a tree. The man suffered a severe spinal cord injury, which resulted in physical sufferings for the father, and financial sufferings for the family. The already sensitive lad became inspired to do all he could to lessen the sufferings of others.

MATTHEW KADALIKKATTIL

At eleven, Matthew, having completed introductory studies with a local tutor, advanced to the parochial school at Thanoli. There, the parish priest noticed the boy's natural giftedness and spiritual goodness, and offered to instruct the lad in the Syriac language and other subjects essential for seminary studies. After two years at Thanoli, Matthew entered the seminary. Unfortunately, the priest-director of the seminary belonged to a schismatic church. After two years of study at the seminary, Matthew appealed to the Catholic bishop, who interviewed the student, and assigned him to the seminary at Mannamam. Four years later, Matthew was ordained a priest on February 11, 1901.

For the next two dozen years, Father Matthew served in numerous parishes: Pala (1901), Karoor (1903), Lalom (1906), Pala (1910), New Lalom (1914), Kannadiyurumpu (1917), New Lalom (1921), and Kannadiyurumpu (1922-1935). In each place, the priest demonstrated special care for the destitute: widows, orphans, the sick; and the promotion of devotion to the Sacred Heart through his preaching, teaching and enthronement of the Sacred Heart in every home.

To assist him with the destitute, Father Matthew wondered if God might be calling him to establish a women's religious community dedicated to the poor. At the beginning of 1911, Father Matthew rented a home for the women with whom he had spoken about this religious community. Within six weeks, ten women joined this venture. Because of increasing numbers, larger quarters had to be rented in each of the next three years. Although Father Matthew and his community members desired to be recognized as an independent foundation of the community, the local bishop and Vatican officials did not permit this. These administrators requested instead that Father Matthew's community be subordinated under an already established religious community. The Clarist Sisters were willing to receive Father Matthew's sisters as a Clarist Third Order.

The uncertainty about not only the community's approbation, but also its charism created unrest among community members. Complaints arose about the founder, and his inability to satisfy the sisters' desire for legal and religious status. As the community grew in members and sites at Pala, Punnathura, and Ramapuram, a certain disparateness of vision and communication developed. Conflicting points of view without adequate avenues for face-to-face communication resulted in conflicts among the sisters and founder. Clergy and laity frequently criticized the priest. Father Matthew accepted patiently the calumny and slander to which he was subjected. One sister who complained to him reports this response from him:

> My daughter, this is what is due from the world to all those engaged in public undertakings. Otherwise we will all become proud. If we are rewarded with love and gratitude here, then there will be nothing left over for us when we reach there. What do you want? Reward here or there? What has Jesus not done for us?[17]

At Kannadiyurumpu, the zealous priest's health worsened as years of selfless service to the poor took their toll. And still his community had not yet been approved.

Finally in 1917, the bishop permitted Father Matthew's community to receive candidates. In 1931, the bishop recognized the sisters as an independent community called Sisters of the Sacred Heart. Four years later, the

Vatican authorized the bishop to approve the congregation. Ironically, Father Matthew died just a few hours earlier on the same day when papal approbation was granted.[18] At the end of his life, all that Father Matthew owned consisted of "two silver rupee coins and a few coppers."[19]

23. ✠ Zacharias Salterinte, O.C.D.

Place: Ernakulam, Kerala, India
Fame: Seminary Professor for 44 years

ZACHARIAS SALTERINTE, O.C.D.

Zacharias Salterinte y Viskara (1887-1957) was born in Biscay Province in the Western Pyrenees of Spain.[20] He received his education locally until he joined the Carmelites at Larrea, Spain in August 1903. One month later, he received the religious name Zacharias of Saint Teresa. He took his philosophical and theological studies in Spain at Bilbao, Vittoria and Pamplona. In his fourth and final year of theology, Zacharias was selected to teach in the seminary at Puthenpally, in Kerala state, southwest India. Before traveling to India, he studied programs of seminary formation and education at Rome for many months beginning in 1911. Zacharias was ordained on July 11, 1912, and left for India two months later.

Zacharias spent the next forty-five years of his life in India teaching and forming seminarians, promoting the Catholic Christian faith by his writing and publishing; and pastoring the sick and poor. He edified the seminarians by his manner of praying at Mass and meditation, his observance of the community and seminary rules, patience with penitents, congeniality with the seminarians, and generous support of and defense of the poor. Father Zacharias remained with the seminary until it was moved from Puthenpally to Alwaye in 1932.

In the seminary, he introduced into the curriculum the study of Indian philosophy and theology, which all dioceses of India later required of all seminarians. He inspired and organized missionary-minded seminarians to go beyond their native Kerala to work in other states of the vast subcontinent. He formed a Mission Circle within the seminary, whereby he and interested seminarians shared their correspondences with missionaries from around the world, and recruited members willing to serve in mission lands, both inside and outside of India.

To promote the faith, he published dozens of pamphlets and articles explaining the Catholic faith to his audience of Hindus. He originated a mission magazine, "Preshita Kerala." To pay expenses for the printing house, he traveled abroad on fund-raising tours. He wrote three books, *Religio-Philosophic History of India* (1921; revised edition, 1930), *Christianity and Indian Mentality* (1952), and *An Outline of Hinduism* (1956). He earned a reputation as an expert Indologist.

Prodigious in efforts to promote the faith, he served as advisor to a local branch of the Catholic Students University Federation, the St. Vincent de Paul Society, a member of a three-man committee appointed by Indian bishops to develop the curriculum for all seminarians, and organizer of the Kerala Round Table whose participants discussed economic and social issues.

Highly respected, he was appointed to numerous positions in the seminary and the Carmelite community.

After forty-four years in the seminary apostolate, Father Zacharias, who had suffered during much of his active life with stomach ailments, became increasingly ill. He underwent an operation, but he never recovered, and died serenely on May 23, 1957. At the funeral Mass, "twelve bishops, three-hundred priests, four-hundred seminarians, many Sisters and many prominent lay people participated."[21] Father Zacharias was buried in the cemetery chapel of the seminary at Mangalapuzha, Alwaye.

24. ✝ Saint Lucy Pak Hŭi-sun

Place: Seoul, South Korea
Fame: Courtly lady among the Korean Martyrs

Lucy Pak Hŭi-sun (1800-1839) was born into a wealthy family.[22] Blessed with natural gifts of intelligence, warmth, gentleness, and maturity, this young teen was invited to become one of the ladies in waiting to the queen at the royal court. Because of her refinement and education, she was chosen to instruct the other court ladies in Korean and Chinese literature. When Pak was fourteen, the sixteen year old king attempted to seduce her; she successfully resisted.

When she was about thirty, Pak first learned about the Catholic religion. Wishing to learn more and valuing truth more than position, Pak feigned an illness which excused her from service in the palace. Because her father disliked Catholics, she moved intoher nephew's home.

Pak prayed and studied, and chose to be baptized a Catholic. She even converted her nephew and his immediate family. Years later, when persecution erupted in 1839, Lucy moved to Seoul, where she took up quarters with other pious Catholic women. On April 15, Lucy and her house-mates were arrested. Before leaving home, Lucy treated her captors to food and drink, and distributed to them whatever money she had. She expected that she would not return home.

In jail, the police chief questioned Lucy, who replied clearly to each question.

> "As a court lady you are different from other women. How can you believe such a low religion?"
>
> "Our religion is not a low religion. Everybody should worship God, Who is the Creator of heaven and earth, and the Giver of life."
>
> "Deny your religion and reveal the names of your fellow Catholics."
>
> "I cannot deny God, Who is my Lord, and I can do no harm to my fellow Catholics."[23]

The chief ordered Lucy remanded to Criminal Court. During detention, she suffered beatings on three occasions: each beating consisted of thirty blows with a stick. One blow was delivered so forcefully that it broke her leg. As she grasped her leg, she cried out, "Now I think I can feel the pains of Our Lord Jesus and Mary."[24] Called into the courtroom, Lucy hobbled with her broken leg. Her injury occasioned a display of sympathy from on-lookers including those who remembered her as one of the queen's ladies in waiting. "Lucy explained the Catholic doctrines so eloquently that even the judges could not refute her."[25] Nevertheless, she was condemned to death. While waiting in prison for her execution, she passed her time praying and caring for other prisoners. On May 24, 1839, Lucy was called to the courtyard, where with eight other Catholics, she suffered decapitation. "It is said that Lucy didn't lose her peaceful composure and kept praying while she was beheaded."[26]

JUNE

2. ✠ Thomas Kurialacherry

Place: Changanacherry, Kerala, India
Fame: Bishop of Changanacherry

In Thomas Kurialacherry's (1873-1925) village of Champakulam, Kerala, the Catholic Church had been established in 417, from Niranom parish, which was one of the seven churches which Saint Thomas the Apostle had founded.[1]

THOMAS KURIALACHERRY

Thomas, the sixth of ten children, early on manifested good faith, intelligence, and sociability. At five, he began serving his priest-uncle's daily Masses. At home, he played "saying Mass." His education, he received at local schools, and the governmental school at Changanacherry, until his father's death which occasioned the boy's return home at Christmas 1885. When Carmelite priests opened Saint Ephrem School at Mannanam, Thomas studied there. Thomas excelled academically, spiritually, and socially.

The Bishop-Vicar Apostolic of Kottayam urged Thomas to consider priesthood. Thomas happily received the invitation. Because of his exceptional qualities, Thomas was sent in January 1890, to Rome to study at Propaganda Fide College. Again, he excelled. Professors and students called him, "*Il Piccolo Santo*" (the little saint). One day after ordination to priesthood on May 27, 1899, Thomas offered Mass at the Gesu Church, where the right arm of Saint Francis Xavier, the evangelizer of India, had been kept for three centuries.

During the next dozen years, Father Thomas served at Champakulam, Chennamkary, Kavalam, and Edathua. Father Thomas always promoted devotion to the Eucharist, the Sacred Heart of Jesus, and the public recitation of the Rosary. He encouraged education for boys and girls by asking governmental authorities to complete construction of schools as promised, by urging parents to send their children to school, by approaching benefactors to provide Catholic schools, and by instituting catechetical instruction for children. Also, he evangelized the Dalits (the untouchables), and received many as converts. To achieve these goals of education and service to the poor, Father Thomas invited religious communities to his parishes, and in 1908, he founded the Congregation of Sisters of the Adoration of the Blessed Sacrament. One delicate issue Thomas confronted was the Kuruvilla-Vedam Schism; "Father Thomas rose to the occasion and fought bravely against this, though he could not achieve much."[2]

The Holy See took note of this young pastor's achievements and attitude. On August 29, 1911, the pope named Thomas the Vicar Apostolic of Changanacherry. He was ordained a bishop on December 3, at Kandy, Ceylon (now Sri Lanka). He chose as his motto, "To renew all things in Christ."

Perceiving that his diocese needed a greater physical presence, Bishop Thomas constructed many churches and chapels. When he had arrived in his diocese in 1911, the region included 101 parishes and 45 chapels, and when he died in 1925, the diocese had grown by 26 parishes and 22 chapels. The bishop promoted the economic self-sufficiency of these churches, and their respective schools. In order for the laity to develop in the spiritual life, and that non-Christians might be converted, the bishop wrote 113 circular letters to instruct and inspire his priests, religious, and laity.

> His pastoral letters deserve a study with great attention and care. They show how he was inspired by the means the church places at our disposal for sanctifying us; the sacraments and the numerous devout exercises centered on them. Adoration of the Blessed Sacrament, devotion to the Most Sacred Heart of Jesus, affection and confidence in the Blessed Mother of God, recognition of the patronage of Saint Joseph were all not mere lip services to him, but they had penetrated marrow of his bones and he unceasingly preached on them and held them up for the unhesi-

> tating acceptance of the faithful. But he was not content with them. He knew the love of neighbour (sic) was the essence of Christian living and that all the pietetical (sic) exercises were aids in promoting the love of brethren. He was keenly alive to the injustices arising from social inequalities.[3]

In preaching, he confronted the contemporary moral ills. "His uncompromising indictment of the evils of alcoholism, prostitution, gambling, litigation, selfishness, scandalous living, family feuds and communal hatred is forthright and absolute."[4]

The bishop traveled to Rome on church business twice. In 1914, he enjoyed a private audience with Pope Pius X, visited Propaganda Fide College, renewed acquaintances among the bishops, and before leaving Rome, attended the funeral of Pius X, and the inaugural ceremonies of Pope Benedict XV. Ten years later, the bishop participated in the Jubilee Year at Rome. He preached in the cathedral before departing, "This is my last Mass. During the thirteen years of my administration, you must have experienced difficulties. Forgive me and pray for me."[5] Along his journey, his rheumatism worsened, and a severe case of the flu struck him. In Rome, after celebrating Mass for the seminarians at the Propaganda Fide College, he fell sick in his room, and died on June 2, 1925.

15. ✠ Clemente Vismara, P.I.M.E.

Place: Burma (now Myanmar)
Fame: "Saint of the Children"

For sixty-five years the Italian priest Clemente Vismara (1897-1988) served in Myanmar.[6] He is one of the few non-martyr foreign missionaries in all of Asia currently included among the official candidates for sainthood.

Born at Agrate Brianza in the Province of Milan, his parents died when he was eight, leaving him an orphan. After having received only an elementary education, he entered at nineteen the Italian army and fought in World War I. He distinguished himself with valor in battle, and

Clemente Vismara, P.I.M.E.

received three medals. At the conclusion of the war, this sergeant major, felt sickened by the sufferings he had witnessed. He entered the seminary of the P.I.M.E. Fathers (Pontifical Institute for Foreign Missions), and was ordained on May 26, 1923. Nine weeks later, he departed for Myanmar. The rest of his life, except for a few months in 1957 when he visited Italy, he remained in Myanmar, whose populace affectionately named him "the Patriarch of Burma."

Father Clemente, an orphan himself, dedicated himself to caring for orphans in Myanmar. Throughout his decades of service, he lived at any given time with about two hundred-fifty orphans. These children had been the victims of war, poverty, and disease which wracked Burma during its years of subjugation to imperial Britain since 1886, and continued during its decades of corruption as a self-governing colony since 1937. During these periods of oppressions and poverty, the priest started parishes and programs to assist especially widows, the sick and poor, and children. He persuaded the Italian community of the *Suore di Maria Bambina* (Sisters of the Holy Child Mary) to implement his vision and plans. In everything he did, he trusted in Divine Providence.

24. ✠ Saint Lucy Wang Cheng and Companions

Place: Hubei Province, China
Fame: Martyrs

On June 24, 1900, soldiers of the xenophobic Boxer Rebellion burned down the Catholic Church in Wangla Village. The soldiers slew outside the church Christians who had sought sanctuary inside the church, but fled during the holocaust.[7] The soldiers set aside, however, four teenage girls for other purposes. The four girls included Lucy Wang Cheng (1882-1900), who had been born in Laochuntan Village in Nangxin County, Mary Fan Kun (1884-1900) and Mary Ji Yu (1885-1900) both of whom originated from Daji Village in Wuqiao County, and Mary Zheng Xu (1889-1900), who came from Kou Village in Dongguang County. All four girls were born and raised in Hubei Province.

The Boxers transported the girls initially to Yingjia, and later to Mazetang. During these forced marches, the leader of the Boxers proposed marriage to Lucy Wang Cheng. Lucy pondered the offer for four days. At the same time, another Boxer leader suggested marriage to Mary Fan Kun. Both girls rejected the proposals. Lucy replied that to marry a persecutor of the Catholic religion would be incompatible with her principles and practices. Mary never had a chance to respond to her suitor because his co-conspirators reminded him that their job was to kill Christians and not to marry them.

The four girls were placed in a cart to be transported back to Wangla Village. Along the way, the soldiers verbally abused the girls, their Christian faith, and God. The three youngest girls felt terrified and wept profusely. Lucy encouraged them, saying, "Don't cry. We are going to heaven soon. God has given us life; He will take it back. We should not be reluctant givers, but offer ourselves cheerfully."[8]

Upon arriving at Wangla Village, the Boxers ordered the girls to step out of the cart, and to renounce their faith. All four refused to budge, physically and spiritually. They proclaimed, "No! We are daughters of God. We will not betray Him."[9] The soldiers immediately put their swords to the girls, and slew them — aged eighteen, sixteen, fifteen, and eleven.

25. ✠ Melchior de Marion Brésillac, S.M.A.

Place: Pondichery and Coimbatore, India
Fame: Proponent of native clergy, opponent of caste system; Vicar Apostolic of Coimbatore

During his twenty years as a priest and bishop, Melchior de Marion Brésillac (1813-1859) spent twelve years in India, where he labored zealously for the Church, especially for native vocations, and against the caste system.[10]

MELCHIOR DE MARION BRÉSILLAC, S.M.A.

Melchior had grown up as the oldest of five children in a family of French nobility. After the French Revolution, the family lost their estate and found refuge in the southern province of Languedoc-Roussillon. The father home-schooled his children because he did not want them exposed to the anti-Catholic teachings of Voltaire.

At eighteen, Melchior entered the seminary. In December 1838, he was ordained a diocesan priest, and was assigned as curate in his home parish. Almost immediately he began writing letters not only to his bishop, but also to the Foreign Missionary Society of Paris (M.E.P.), expressing his desire to minister abroad. In spring 1841, the bishop accepted the young priest's petition to join the M.E.P.

After completing a nine-month orientation program with his new community, Melchior departed Paris on April 12, 1842, and arrived one hundred miles south of Madras (now Chennai) at Pondichery on July 24.

Melchior adapted easily to his new surroundings. The people's music, dance, and vivid colors delighted him. He ate the native foods, and studied diligently the native languages. Ahead of his times, he reasoned that any Indian who would convert to Christianity would intensify his Indian spirit, not lessen appreciation of his native culture.

What shocked the priest, however, was not only the Hindu teaching and practice of the caste system, but also the Catholic Church leaders' acceptance of that status quo. At Nellitop, higher caste parishioners insisted on a wall being constructed in their new church to separate the higher from the lower castes, and that separate ciboria be used to distribute Communion to different castes. The French clergy and hierarchy even opposed the fostering of native vocations. One coadjutor bishop insisted, "Never will I impose hands upon a black man."[11]

In 1844, the Synod of Pondicherry advised Bishop Bonnand to develop native vocations. For this purpose, Bishop Bonnard appointed de Marion Brésillac the superior and rector of the existing seminary at Pondichery. "By the end of 1845, Father Melchior writes, 'I have the happiness of having under my care eight or ten clerics, all aged about twenty, highly intelligent and of good will."[12] When Rome heard about the priest's successes, the Sacred Congregation for the Propagation of the Faith rejoiced with him and his efforts. On October 4, 1846, Melchior was ordained the Pro-Vicar Apostolic of Coimbatore, and four years later, the Vicar Apostolic of Coimbatore. Throughout this ministry, the new bishop lamented the continuous opposition and obstruction of his fellow French priests and bishops. The majority closed their minds to the possibility of changing the caste system or developing a native clergy.

Frustrated, Bishop de Marion Brésillac considered resigning the episcopacy. At the same time, Bishop Bonnand was frustrated with de Brésillac and his progressive ideas. Bonnand convened another synod at Pondichery to deal with clerical formation, implications of the caste system, and strict enforcement of Pope Benedict XIV's publication, "*Ex quo Singulari*," which required missionaries to promise on oath not to employ certain Indian practices. De Marion Brésillac perceived that his fellow M.E.P. bishops and priests were impervious to change on account of their racial and caste prejudices. He wrote to the Paris Mission headquarters his first letter of resignation in October 1849. He wrote repeatedly over the next few years. Finally, in October 1853, he was invited to Rome to present in person his reasons for resignation. After having appointed two priests as Pro-Vicars for the diocese, Bishop de Brésillac left for the Eternal City. In March 1855, his letter of resignation was accepted.

Still desiring to foster native vocations, and being a bishop without a diocese, de Marion Brésillac offered to Rome that he might form a new community, called the Society of African Missionaries. This foundation took place on December 8, 1856.

Tragedy awaited the community. In late 1858 to early 1859, de Marion Brésillac and five other missionaries landed at Freetown. Within six months of arrival, smallpox killed many of the Africans, and yellow fever felled all six Europeans. Many generations later, countless native priests owe in part their vocation to this saintly priest and bishop who did all he could to promote native vocations.

30. ✠ Blessed Mariam Thresia Chiramel Mankidiyan, C.H.F.

***Places:** Puthenchira, Kerala, India*
***Fame:** Foundress of the Holy Family Congregation for Women*

Thresia (1876-1926) was the third child in a family which traced its roots to the original Saint Thomas Christians.[13] The family lived four miles east of Cranganore, where the apostle had landed.

Her mother died when Mariam was twelve. "At fifteen," she writes in her *Autobiography*, "a thought of going to the forest haunted my mind. Thinking that it would be difficult to practice virtues at home, I decided to go to the woods for leading an austere life."[14] One night, however, she awoke, apparently paralyzed in bed. This temporary disability, she interpreted as God's will that she not run away. She writes, "I continued to stay home peacefully, spending the time in prayer and doing everything according to the personal guidance of my spiritual director, I used to go to the church everyday, and I make my confession and receive Holy Communion twice a month."[15]

In 1910, Thresia was admitted into the Third Order of the Carmelite Sisters. Having discerned that her vocation was not in the Carmelite lifestyle, with three other women, she set out to assist the dying and destitute. Although rebuked and ridiculed, Thresia didn't hesitate to do her good works. She writes, "During my meditation, I used to be rapt in ecstasy and see visions."[16] She persisted in her desire for solitude. Her spiritual director approached the bishop and requested permission to build a separate house for Mariam and her three companions. The bishop refused, recommending instead that she enter the Carmelite Order, which she did in 1913. She remained at the house at Ollur for two months. After she left, the people at Puthenchira petitioned for her to return. The bishop approved the construction of the house for Mariam and her three companions. On May 14, 1914, the bishop recognized the women as a religious community. Mariam Thresia was named superior, and the other sisters called her Mother.

Many young women joined the community. In 1915, Mother Mariam Thresia opened a girls' school at Puthenchira. In 1922, she opened a convent at Kuzhikkattussery; and in 1926, another convent at Thumpoor. During the blessing of the chapel in the newest house, she injured her leg, which became gangrenous. Mother's health worsened, and within weeks, she lay on her deathbed. Death became imminent. The day before she died, she wrote the following letter to her sisters in community.

> My children, why should you let your hearts be troubled like people of little faith? You know that I will not be relieved of this illness. If it be the will of the heavenly groom that I leave you so soon in order to accept His invitation, let it be fulfilled! Our Congregation is still an infant. You should not forget that it is your duty as members of this Congregation to protect and help it grow up. Deal with the superiors sincerely and lovingly. Love one another. Help one another.[17]

The next day, June 8, 1926, Mother passed into eternal life. Colleagues observed about Mother Mariam Thresia, "her whole life has been a beautiful and powerful utterance of her passion for the Lord and compassion for His people."[18]

JULY

4. ✠ Peter Kibe Kasui, S.J.

Place: Kibe and Tokyo, Japan
Fame: Martyr

Peter Kibe Kasui (1587-1639) descended from Japanese Catholic nobility.[1] Upon completing his initial education at his native Kibe, in Oita prefecture, he entered the seminary at Arima, followed by the novitiate at Lisbon, Portugal. The name Kasui, he seems to have taken at this time in a manner similar to the Buddhist bonzes, as well as Christian catechists and religious.

PETER KIBE KASUI, S.J.

While serving as a catechist *dojuku* in the Jesuit missions, he suffered the general expulsion of Christians from Japan, according to the edict of the shogun Tokogawa Ieyasu. Like others, he found refuge at Macao. In 1618, in fulfillment of a private vow, he sailed from the China Sea to the Indian Ocean, where he walked across India, Persia, the Arabian Desert, and Palestine, until he arrived at Venice, and eventually Rome, where he was ordained a priest, and attended the canonization of Francis Xavier in 1622.

Father Peter, while in Rome, received permission from the Superior General of the Jesuits to work with the persecuted Christians back in Japan. The young priest traveled to Lisbon, where he completed the novitiate, and took his final vows in the Society of Jesus. In 1623, Father Peter sailed via India, Manila, and Macao in the hopes of entering his native land. Frustrated in his plan, he remained at Macao.

In 1627, Peter sailed to Ayuthaya in Siam (now Thailand). All along the Mekong River, he ministered among the refugee Japanese Christians and native Thai. After two years, having been unable to enter Japan, he made his way to Manila.

In 1630, he and a fellow Jesuit succeeded in entering Japan. There, Father Peter ministered surreptitiously among the Japanese Catholics for nine years. He concentrated his efforts in the northern part of the country near Sendai in Miyagi Prefecture, which is located about 180 miles north of Tokyo.

In July 1639, he was captured, tried, and convicted. He was sentenced, like many other Christians, to be hanged at ancient Edo (now Tokyo). The torture consisted of being hanged on a pole extended over fume-filled sulphur pits, until he approached death. After enduring the customary torture three times, he was released from the pole, and was beheaded.

5. ✠ Saint Andrew Kim Tae-gŏn and Companions

Place: Seoul, Korea (now South Korea)
***Fame:** Korea's first native priest, and first priest-martyr*

Like Saint Paul of Tarsus (2 Cor. 11:22-33), Andrew Kim Tae-gŏn (1821-1846) experienced beatings, stormy seas, dangers from robbers, hunger, thirst, and anxiety for the Church, and was martyred for the sake of the gospel.[2]

Having been born at Solmoi, in the province of Ch'ungch'ong, this son of nobles enjoyed a great Catholic heritage. Kim's great-grandfather had suffered martyrdom in 1814, and Kim's father, in 1839. When Kim was fifteen, a French priest baptized the youth with the Christian name Andrew. On December 9, 1836, the lad and two other Korean seminarians left Seoul, crossed into China, and traveled across Manchuria and Mongolia to Macao, arriving there on June 6, 1837.

A priest-teacher describes our protagonist in the following fashion: "Kim Tae-gŏn Andrew is active but precise, obedient but daring, and has strong will power. He is very promising. He is eloquent and his judgment is good, enabling him to solve problems quickly and easily."[3]

While waiting in Inner Mongolia for propitious circumstances to return to the Hermit Kingdom, Andrew received the deaconate on December 15, 1844. Two weeks later, he met a group of traders who agreed to smuggle him into Korea. By this time, more than two hundred Korean Catholics had been killed for their faith. On January 15, Andrew crossed at P'yongyang into his native country. The next month, Andrew and other Korean Catholics sailed for Shanghai to meet Bishop Verreol to bring him into Korea. At Shanghai, Bishop Verreol ordained Andrew a priest on August 17, 1845. At the end of the month, Andrew, the bishop, and the Catholic crew departed Shanghai, and five weeks later, arrived at Hwansanpo in Ch'ungch'ong Province.

The bishop remained in the village, and sent Andrew to Hanyang to prepare a house, chapel, and a program of ministry for the bishop. Having completed that task, Andrew visited his mother and conducted a nocturnal ministry among the Catholics. In January 1846, the bishop met Andrew at the provincial capital. From Hanyang, the young priest again visited his mother for a few days.

Andrew and seven companions departed from Hanyang on May 14, and spent two weeks talking with fishermen on the Yellow Sea to ascertain the status of the Church in China. Considering their trip a success, they delayed their embarkation for a few hours to allow a crew member to sell the fish he had caught. While the Catholics were waiting for the crew member at Yonp'yong, governmental officials came aboard the vessel. A series of questions led to the arrest of Andrew on the grounds of being "a believer in the Western Religion."[4] Andrew writes from prison to the bishop: "After they brought me ashore, they stripped me, beat me, humiliated me, then took me to the public office, where a great crowd gathered."[5]

During the next ten weeks, the priest-prisoner endured fourteen tortuous interrogations.[6] When the king sent orders for the prisoner to apostatize, Andrew responded:

> "God is above the king and has ordered that He be honored. So betraying Him is a great sin, and no matter how much the king orders me, it could never be right." When they demanded that I hand over the Catholics to them, I told them I could not do that. We Catholics have obligations in charity to love one another. Next, they asked me about the Catholic Church, I explained at length

about the Catholic catechism, the existence of one God who created all things, the immortality of the soul, heaven and hell, the obligation to worship the Creator and the falseness of other religions."[7]

On September 15, 1846, Andrew was sentenced to death by decapitation on the charges of having been the ringleader of an heretical school and betrayer of his country. The sentence was executed the next day at the Han River on the outskirts of Seoul.

7. ✠ Blessed Peter ToRot

Place: *East New Britain (now a province of Papua New Guinea)*
Fame: *Lay catechist and martyr*

Methodist missionaries brought the Christian faith to the Melanesian archipelago in 1878. Four years later, on September 29, priests of the Missionaries of the Sacred Heart arrived at these islands.[8] Thousands of the islanders converted to Christianity and to Catholicism. During World War II, the Japanese military commanders who occupied the islands urged the inhabitants to return to their pre-Christian pagan ways, especially by reverting to polygamy and rejecting monogamy.

In 1898, in the village of Rakunai on the eastern part of the island of New Britain, the Tolai tribal chief Angelo ToPuia and his wife Maria IaTumul converted to Catholicism. They became the first generation of Catholics on the island. The neophytes invited missionaries to settle in the village, and to baptize the large numbers of people who wished to become Catholic. The couple had their new-born son Peter (1912-1945) similarly baptized. Contrary to the tribal custom, Peter's father chose to keep his son directly under the father's care rather than entrust his son to the care of the boy's maternal uncle. Again, contrary to custom, Peter's father encouraged the boy to attend school and daily Mass. When the parish priest suggested that Peter might begin studies for the priesthood, Peter's father objected because he thought this generation was too new to the faith. The father suggested instead that his son might become a catechist.

In 1930, at eighteen, Peter entered St. Paul's Catechists' School to study the Catholic faith, and to learn methods of leadership. Peter conducted himself in an amiable manner and won many friends. After three years, he received a diploma and was named the chief catechist for his village. Peter led prayer groups and religion classes. Walking around the village with his Bible in hand, and learning of people's specific needs, Peter became perceived as the assistant to the parish priest. On November 11, 1936, he married Paula laVarpit. The couple gave birth to three children, two of whom two died in early childhood.[9]

In 1942, the Japanese invaded the islands. The soldiers imprisoned the Christian missionaries and detained them in concentration camps. During the absence of the parish priest, Peter performed baptisms, prepared couples for and served as official witness at Catholic marriages, brought the Eucharist to the sick, cared for orphans and widows, provided food and clothing for the needy, buried the dead and comforted the families. The Japanese authorities detained Peter many times, and warned him to stop his ministry as a catechist. He replied, "I will do the work of God."[10]

In hope of winning popular support from the natives, the Japanese legalized polygamy.

Peter objected to the un-Christian policy. Informants reported him to the Japanese police, who arrested Peter. Many people including the two most important chiefs intervened to seek the release of Peter ToRot. Daily, Peter's mother and wife visited him, bringing him food, chatting with him, and praying with him. His sentence called for two months in jail.

About one month before VJ (Victory in Japan) Day, which occurred on August 15, 1945, the Japanese killed Peter ToRot by lethal injection; the date is identified only as "a certain Friday" in July 1945.

9. ✝ Martyrs of China

Place: Eastern China
Fame: 120 Martyrs of China

Christianity was brought to China in 635, through the missionary efforts of Nestorian monks from either Syria or Palestine.[11] The famous marble monument of Sianfu, which is dated to 781 and measures approximately eight feet by three feet, lists the names and titles of seventy early Christian missionaries. These monks translated Christian texts into Chinese, and constructed monasteries over a wide geographical expanse. The spread of Christianity came to a screeching halt in 845, when the emperor ordered the elimination of all foreign influences, including Buddhism and Christianity.

A second wave of Nestorian successes took place between the eleventh and fourteenth centuries among the non-Chinese tribes of the Mongolian Dynasty. In 1269, Kublai Khan requested that the pope might send one hundred missionaries to the empire. Catholicism was flourishing in the Khan's capital city: churches were being constructed, thousands of Chinese were being baptized, and scriptural and liturgical texts were being translated into the native language. Fifty Franciscans came to China in 1325 to minister there, and soon, more were requested. The Black Death of Europe, however, which occurred between 1348 and 1350, killed approximately one-third of the Western clergy, and prohibited the pope from fulfilling the Khan's request for additional missionaries.

When the Ming Dynasty overthrew the foreign Mongols in 1368, the Mings cast out from China the foreigners and their religion. The Mings successfully halted the expansion of Christianity in China.

In the modern era, of the 120 canonized Martyrs of China killed between 1648 and 1930, 87 were native Chinese and 33 were foreign missionaries. The Chinese came from the provinces of Hebei (56), Shanxi (27), Guizhou (16), Sichuan (7), Fujian (6), Hubei (4), Tibet autonomous region (2), Anhui (1), and Jiangxi (1). The foreigners came from France (13), Italy (12), Spain (6), Belgium (1) and Holland (1). They represented the male religious communities of Franciscans (8), Dominicans (6), Jesuits (4), Society of Foreign Missionaries of Paris (3), Vincentians (2), Salesians (2), P.I.M.E. Fathers (1), and the women's community of the Franciscan Missionaries of Mary (7). The native and foreign clergy and religious included six bishops, twenty-three priests, one brother, seven sisters, and seven seminarians. The laity numbered seventy-six. These heroes and heroines ranged in age from 7 to 79 years old. While eighty-five of these martyrs died during the Boxer Rebellion of 1900, also one died in 1648, five between 1747-1748, twenty-seven between 1814-1862, and two in 1930.

Besides these official martyrs, thousands of other Chinese Catholics suffered for their faith. In the twelfth century, Mongol leaders oppressed Christians, so by the time of that dynasty's demise, Christianity had been obliterated from China. Persecutions during the Yuan Dynasty (1281-1367) focused especially on the ministry of Bishop John of Montecorvino. Towards the end of the Ming Dynasty (1368-1644), Matteo Ricci and his priest-companions suffered either expulsion or execution. The Manchu Dynasty (1368-1644) continued the anti-Christian persecution, until Emperor Yung Cheng introduced religious toleration in 1692. From the beginning of the Chang Dynasty (1648-1907), China celebrates the country's first official martyr: Francisco de Capillas, O.P., who suffered decapitation at Fukien in 1648. Throughout the mid-eighteenth century, a handful of foreign Catholic clergy suffered death for the faith. The nineteenth century proved particularly bloody for Catholics in China. From 1814 to 1842, a dozen clergy died for the faith. By the Treaty of Nanking in 1842 and the Treaty of Tientsin in 1858, Western European powers demanded the end of anti-Christian persecution in China. The worst of times of religious hatred, however, erupted during the two-year Boxer Rebellion, when, in a two-month period in 1900, approximately thirty thousand Catholics were killed by government officials or random robbers who perceived all Catholics as representatives of Western religion. When the Chinese Communists rose to power in 1949, another wave of oppression, imprisonment, and murder took place.

Early in the twenty-first century, bishops, priests, and laity continue to be arrested, imprisoned, and tortured on the grounds of practicing the Christian faith.

Representative stories of these martyrs are presented in this book's brief biographies for the following martyrs: Agatha Lin (February 18), Augustine Zhao Rong (July 9), Francis Regis Clet (February 17), John Gabriel Perboyre (September 11), Joseph Zhang Wenlan (July 29), Lucy Wang Chen (June 24), Marie Hermine and Companions (July 9), and Mary Zhu Wu and Companions (July 20).

9. ☩ Saint Augustine Zhao Rong

Place: Guizhou and Sichuan Provinces, China
Fame: Martyr

Zhao Rong (1746-1815) was born at Wuchan in Guizhou Province.[12] Biographers describe him as having spent his youth in a dissolute lifestyle. At twenty, he found employment as a bailiff in a local jail.

In 1772, in consequence of the anti-Catholic persecution led by Emperor Kia-Kin, Zhao Rong was assigned to lead Catholic prisoners from the jail at Chengdu, the capital city of Sichuan Province, to their imprisonment at Beijing (now Peking), the national capital. During this fifteen hundred mile journey, Zhao was inspired to consider becoming a Christian.

The procession of inmates included the priest Martinus Moye, popularly called Father Mei. The priest encouraged the Catholic and non-Catholic prisoners, and spoke kindly and clearly to all about Jesus and the Church. Zhao overheard many of the conversations, and became interested in what the priest had said.

After a few months, when many of the religious prisoners were released, Zhao sought out Father Mei, and requested religious instruction. The priest accepted his former prison guard as his new catechumen. Four years later, in 1776, Zhao asked for and received baptism, taking the name Augustine. The neophyte began evangelizing other inquirers. When a famine and subsequent plague broke out in 1779, Augustine readily assisted Father Mei and Father Matthew Luo. After closely observing his convert, Father Mei asked Augustine if he might want to become a priest. Augustine responded affirmatively.

Father Mei instructed his seminarian. On May 10, 1781, Augustine was ordained a diocesan priest, and began his ministry as a circuit rider. "His custom was, when he visited a Christian community, to preach three days in succession, emphasizing the Ten Commandments, the seven cardinal sins, the sacrament of penance, the Holy Eucharist, and the Passion of Christ. After that he would hear confessions."[13]

The itinerant preacher continued this ministry for many years. When Father Luo was transferred to neighboring Yunan Province, Father Augustine was assigned to minister to the Christians in western Sichuan.

In 1815, a new anti-Catholic persecution was unleashed. Father Augustine was arrested, imprisoned, and tortured. At the end of that year, on December 18, he died in jail as a result of injuries he had suffered at the hands of his former prison guard colleagues.

9. ✠ Saint Marie Hermine, F.M.M., and Companions

Place: Shanxi, China
Fame: Martyrs

Seven Sisters of the Franciscan Missionaries of Mary (F.M.M.) suffered brutal martyrdom at the hands of the Boxers on July 9, 1900 in Shanxi Province, China.[14] The Sister-Superior of the martyrs was Sister Marie Hermine (1866-1900).

SAINT MARIE HERMINE, F.M.M.

Sister Marie Hermine had grown up as Irma Gravot in the Burgundian village of Beaune, two hundred miles southeast of Paris. "Young Irma had rather delicate health, but was intelligent and studious, completing her primary education in 1883. She was a simple and straightforward child, lively and affectionate, sensitive to the wonders of nature as well as to the call of God."[15]

From her youth, Irma felt called to religious life. At twenty-eight, she entered the Sisters of the Franciscan Missionaries of Mary. She received as her religious name Sister Marie Hermine de Jesus. Authorities soon discovered, however, that "her fragile appearance hid an iron will determined to overcome all difficulties."[16]

Sister Marie Hermine possessed skills of organization, administration, and decision-making. She acquired skills and was appointed nurse, treasurer, and religious superior. "Hermine knew how to relate to everyone: bishops, priests, dedicated lay women, children, and the sick. To her own Sisters she was a mother, a support and an animator until the very end."[17]

The Franciscan Missionaries of Mary, which had been founded in 1877, opened houses in three provinces in China between 1886 and 1898. On March 19, 1899, Hermine and six other Sisters embarked from Marseilles and disembarked on May 4 at Taiyuan-fu, in Shanxi Province.

SAINT MARIE HERMINE, F.M.M., AND COMPANIONS

The mission provided many challenges to the Sisters: language, culture, food and drink, a mountainous climate of much cold and little rain. The motive was "for the love of Christ and by the love of Christ." Their means to express Christ's love was to found an orphanage for girls, a dispensary, and a hospital.

Just after the Sisters celebrated the first anniversary of their arrival, the political climate changed. The leaders of the Boxer Rebellion transformed their verbal threats into bloody violence against foreigners and Chinese affected by foreign influences. In spring 1900, Sister Marie Hermine wrote:

> The rebels from Shantung are invading the neighboring provinces.... Our Sisters in Ichang have to sleep with one eye open. They must prepare themselves to die: they have already seen death close to them so often!... Here everything is very calm, first of all because the Chinese of Shanxi are a peaceful people, and then because the idea of martyrdom does not frighten us.[18]

The Boxer Rebellion broke out in Shantung Province in 1899, soon spread to the northern provinces, and made its way to Shanxi Province by June 1900. On June 27, the bishop warned the Sisters to put aside their Western dress and to don Chinese garb. Sister Hermine replied, "We came here to exercise charity and to shed our blood for the love of Jesus Christ if that needs be."[19] On June 29, civil authorities came to the Sisters' orphanage, and removed all 250 girls.

On July 5, all clergy and sisters were brought by civil authorities to a mandarin's house. Perceiving that death was near, the group prayed intently. Eucharist sustained the captives. On July 9, the governor and Chinese soldiers stormed the mandarin's house. The governor himself raced for the bishop, slew him with the sword, and yelled the command: "Kill! Kill!"[20]

Bishops, priests, seminarians, and laity fell dead — nineteen in all. The seven sisters were still singing the *Te Deum* when the soldiers turned to these women, massacring them.

The seven F.M.M. Sisters represented four countries: Belgium, France, Italy, and the Netherlands. They ranged in age from 25 to 36. The Boxer Rebellion resulted in the deaths of 30,000 Christians who died for their faith in Jesus Christ.

10. ✠ Blessed Emmanuel Ruiz, O.F.M., and Companions

Place: Damascus, Syria
Fame: Martyrs of Damascus

In June 1860, every Christian village in central and southern Lebanon was attacked violently at the hand of the majority Druzes.[21] Six thousand Christians were murdered, mutilated, or assaulted.

When news reached Damascus that the Druzes of Lebanon had attacked many Christian localities and perpetrated massacres with the complicity of the Ottoman authorities [which at that time had extended its Turkish rule as far as present-day Syria] the populace, roused by government agents and leading citizens, attacked, burned, and pillaged the wealthy Christian quarter, killing about four thousand.[22]

This act of religious hatred contradicted the promise which the Sultan of Turkey had made four years earlier, in the Treaty of Paris of 1856, which ended the Crimean War. According to the treaty, the Ottoman

Turks guaranteed religious freedom and equality among all religions in the Muslim-dominated country.

Among the four thousand Christians killed on that night of July 9-10, 1860, the causes of eleven people were advanced for beatification. These eleven consisted of eight Franciscans (seven Spaniards and one Austrian) and three native Syrian businessmen, the Massabki brothers. All the Franciscans were priests except for two lay brothers. The Franciscans' ages spanned between thirty and fifty-eight. The three brothers were just over or under seventy.

The guardian in charge of the community, Emmanuel Ruiz (1804-1860), a native of Santander Province in Spain, heard the mob break into the priests' residence. He ran to the chapel, consumed the Blessed Sacrament, and knelt in front the altar, praying until his attackers arrived. They commanded him, "'Affirm! Affirm!' viz. that there is no god but God, and Mohammed is the prophet of God. 'I am a Christian, and I will die a Christian!', he replied, and laid his head on the altar, where it was split open with axes."[23]

The other friars suffered similar martyrdoms. One Franciscan ran to the roof, but mob members ran after him and dragged him to the ground-level courtyard. The attackers ordered him to give up his Christian faith. He refused. They slew him with swords. Another friar suffered a blow to the head, and lay half-dead for an hour on the floor of the monastery. Two Muslim friends approached, and offered him the safety and comfort of their homes on the condition that he apostatize; he refused. They finished him off on the spot. The two Franciscan lay brothers escaped to the bell tower of the church, but members of the mob discovered and defenestrated the pair.

The three Maronite-Rite laymen had been assisting the friars by their lay labors in the parish school, the church sacristy, and in fund-raising. The brothers had just received Holy Communion, and were accosted in the chapel. A prominent Muslim assured the eldest brother that one of the Muslim men present would pay the large sum of money owed to the eldest brother, if only the brother would deny his faith. That brother told the Muslim debtor that he could keep his money, "but that the Christian would give his soul to no one."[24] With that, the mob slew the three brothers.

20. ☩ Saint Mary Zhu Wu and Companions

Place: Zhujiahe, Hebei Province, China
Fame: Lay leaders, martyrs

One of the Boxer Rebellion's most nefarious massacres of Catholics took place in the walled village of Zhujiahe.[25] During May 1900, as the Boxer persecution of Catholics intensified, the hamlet of Zhujiahe swelled in population beyond its normal three hundred citizens to about three thousand refugees.

In spring 1900, the xenophobic Boxers increased their threats against Catholics in general, and foreign priests in particular. By mid-July, the Boxer rebels and ten thousand professional soldiers of the regular military of the emperor happened to converge at Zhujiahe. The imperial army was hastening from south of the Yangtze River northwards to Beijing to defend the capital from the Eight Western Powers. Since the soldiers' route passed near Zhujiahe, the Boxers requested the army's assistance in attacking the Catholics.

For three days, beginning on July 18, the army attacked the village. For two days, the Catholics held their own. On the third day, the siege overwhelmed the exhausted defenders. Soldiers poured in through the four gates of the city, slaughtering everyone in their path. Some soldiers began abducting young women.

Inside the church, many hundreds of women and children had gathered. At nine o'clock in the morning, soldiers burst into the church. Seeing two foreign-born priests, but unable to capture them because of the believers protecting them, the soldiers opened fire on the crowd, and set fire to the reed-roofed church. Screams shrieked through the church. The priests knelt down and invited all those nearby to pray the Act of Contrition in preparation for death. Mary Zhu (1850-1900), wife of the mayor, who had died on the first day of fighting, stood up and stretched out her arms in the form of a cross to protect the pastor. The soldiers shot her dead. Father Leon Ignace Mangin fell dead beside her. Father

Paul Denn was wounded and crawled behind the altar, where he died as the roof collapsed on him and many others.

Because the soldiers were guarding the doors of the church, the Catholics leapt out the windows. Outside the windows, however, were positioned soldiers and Boxers, who knifed to death the Catholics as soon as they fled the burning building. "These men got tired killing and finally left fifty-one still alive."[26] These were bound and executed later. Some Catholics fled successfully from the church, and jumped into a nearby well, but as successive waves of people jumped in, the persons on the bottom either drowned or suffocated. For many days, moans emanated from the cylindrical grave.

Mary Zhu Wu had been born at Zhujiahe. Months before the siege, when the Boxers initially made their anti-Catholic threats, Mary continued attending Mass, and serving the sick and poor. "She remained quiet and undisturbed, advising everyone to trust God and to pray to our Heavenly Mother for protection. . . . She was an exemplary woman in the village, much revered by her neighbors."[27]

Two priests died with Mary. The Jesuit superior Leon Ignace Mangin (1857-1900) had grown up near the Moselle River in eastern France. He had achieved well at every level of education. Early in religious life, Leon had volunteered for the foreign missions, but his Jesuit superiors always assigned him to teach. When the provincial asked him in 1882 to go to China, Leon responded, "I was granted what I asked for. Now I only wait for the gift of martyrdom."[28] He studied theology and Chinese for four years, and was ordained a priest on July 31, 1886 at Changjiazhuang in the Province of Hebei. In 1890, this capable priest was appointed the pastoral dean of Hejenfu, an area encompassing 240 parishes in which nine priests served twenty thousand Catholics. After seven years of service in that capacity, he was transferred to Jinzhou, Hebei, in which jurisdiction lay Zhujiahe, where he suffered martyrdom.

The second priest was another Jesuit, Paul Denn (1847-1900). He had grown up in Lille, France. Paul received the customary education at home, and participated actively in his parish as altar boy, member of the youth group, member of the St. Vincent de Paul Society, and participant in weekly nocturnal Eucharistic Adoration. On July 6, 1872, he entered the Jesuits. Eight years later, he was ordained a priest. For his first three years of ministry, he served in two parishes and as rector of Changjiazhuang College. "No matter what position he held, he was full of life, filled with zeal for the salvation of souls, and very self-disciplined."[29] When the threats of the Boxers intensified, the Jesuit superior ordered Fr. Paul to take refuge in the walled city of Zhujiahe, where the Jesuits had located their central mission house.

Young Peter Zhu Rixin (1881-1900) was among the fifty-one escapees from the church, who had been bound, only to be killed later. Earilier that day, the soldiers had become exhausted in killing the interminable waves of Christians who kept pouring through the windows of the burning church. Later in the day, "when General Chen came to Peter Zhu, he [the officer] was impressed by this handsome and promising young man and did his best to dissuade him from following God. He failed, so finally he handed him [Peter] over to the executioners."[30]

Because of the chaos brought on by the war, the army's loss to the Eight Western Powers, and the political complexity of dealing with the dead and their religious rites, the corpses lay for up to three months, untouched except by robbers. Beginning in October 1901, a Chinese priest gathered the victims' remains. After he placed sixty corpses into coffins, he and Catholic colleagues placed the other three thousand dead in three mass graves: in the church, just north of the church, and in the well at the orphanage. On March 15, 1902, a public civil and religious burial ceremony was conducted.

24. ✠ Saint Sharbel Makhloof

Place: Annaya, Lebanon
Fame: Hermit

Youssef Antoun Makhloof (1828-1898) was one of five children in a peasant family at Biqa-Kafra in northern Lebanon.[31] From early childhood, he was fascinated by the vocation of two uncles who lived as hermit monks at the nearby monastery of Saint Antonious Kozhaya.

Youssef too wished to become a monk, but his parents and family attempted to discourage him. At twenty-three, he left home to pursue the call he felt from God.

In 1851, Youssef entered the monastery of Our Lady of Mayfouq, north of Byblos. One year later, he began the novitiate at Saint Maron Monastery in Annaya. At the end of the canonical year, he took as his religious name Sharbel, in honor of the second century saintly monk from Antioch. His next six years, he spent in philosophical and theological studies at Saint Cyprian Monastery in Kfifan, Batroun. At the end of his studies, he was ordained a priest in 1859.

For the next thirty-nine years, Sharbel lived in the environs of Saint Maron Monastery: sixteen years as a monk within the monastery, and the next twenty-three years as a hermit living apart from but near the monastery. He spent his days in prayer, work, and study.

> The communal life of a Maronite monk is sufficiently hard, involving perpetual abstinence from flesh meat and tobacco, four periods of fasting in the year, and night office at midnight; but the hermit has to fast all the year round, without meat, fruit or wine; he must join manual labor to his prayer; speech must be kept to a minimum, and he may not go away from the hermitage without express permission. Father Sharbel's bed was a mattress stuffed with leaves, laid on the floor and covered with goatskin, the pillow a block of wood wrapped in a piece of an old habit; and he put himself under obedience to the other hermit with him. In these and other ways he carried on in the nineteenth century the life of the early desert fathers, whose lives he read and re-read.[32]

As a septuagenarian, he became ill while celebrating Mass on December 16, 1898. For eight days, he lay paralyzed and suffering with great pain. On Christmas Eve, he died. He was buried at Annaya.

Within a few months of his death, a dazzling light flickered around his grave site. Passersby began to gather and pray. Miracles began to occur. After three months, the Patriarch requested that the body be exhumed. The body was found floating in watery oil. It was incorrupt and the clothes were intact. The body was reburied in a coffin in the monastery. The miracles continued. Twenty-nine years after his death, the tomb was reopened, and the body had remained incorrupt.

To this day, the unusual oil flows from Charbel's body. Cures continue to occur through a believer's touching Charbel's relics and seeking his intercession.

26. ✠ Blessed Andrew Phú Yên

Place: Phú Yen (now Ran Ran), Vietnam
Fame: First martyr of Vietnam

During the initial evangelization of the Vietnamese people, Father Alexander de Rhodes witnessed the death of that country's first martyr of the Catholic faith: Andrew Phú Yên.[33]

On July 25, 1644, the Mandarin Doctor Ong Nghe Bo had planned to arrest Father de Rhodes and his catechist Ignatius. Ironically, Father de Rhodes and Ignatius, at that same time, were traveling to the city to try to meet with the mandarin. When the mandarin's soldiers arrived at the compound, they found no one except the layman Andrew Phú Yên (1625-1644), who had stayed in the compound to care for the sick. Not wishing to return empty handed to the mandarin, the soldiers arrested Andrew. They beat him up, destroyed all of his religious goods, and transported him to the governor's palace.

Andrew, whose family name remains unknown, is identified by the town of his origin. This youth had received baptism in 1641, and two years later, committed himself to membership in de Rhodes' *Maison Dieu*, a group of catechists dedicated to service in the church. .

Meanwhile, Father de Rhodes and the catechist Ignatius appeared before the Mandarin Bo. The mandarin, following orders of the king of Annam (now Vietnam) to prevent the spread of Christianity, excoriated the pair for having introduced this foreign religion, and especially its doctrine which denigrated ancestor worship. Because the priest was a French citizen, the mandarin chose not to punish him. Instead, the mandarin ordered the foreigner to cease evangelizing among the Indochinese and to leave the country. The polyglot missionary protested:

> I went to Vietnam and wanted to stay here for no other reason than to keep God's commandments which everybody, including you and I, have to observe. Up to this moment, I have preached the faith, but I forced no one to follow it. If people recognized the truth and believed [in it], there has been no reason to hinder them

> [from pursuing it]. To do so would be a terrible sin. Besides in preaching and glorifying God, I always kept the rules and your regulations. Nothing on earth could move me to betray God in order to please people. Therefore, I am not afraid of punishment and death. You can kill me but you can not make me change my beliefs. Please don't judge believers but judge me because I am the one who has preached to them and baptized them.[34]

That evening, the governor's soldiers delivered Andrew Phú Yên to Mandarin Bo. The mandarin attempted to persuade the young man to change his beliefs. Andrew refused to yield. Finally, the mandarin ordered the soldiers to bind the young man in chains, and to return him to the prison at the governor's residence.

The next morning, July 26, 1644, the mandarin tried again to persuade Andrew to deny his faith. Andrew refused. The mandarin ordered the youth to be returned to the governor who imposed the death sentence. Soldiers led Andrew to a field outside the city. There, Father de Rhodes, and many Portuguese and Vietnamese Catholics pleaded with the mandarin to release the youth. The mandarin refused. Andrew spoke to those around him:

> Brothers and sisters, dear Jesus wants us to use love to do what love requires. God suffered and died for us, so let us be ready to give our lives for the sake of life. I was arrested and would not die for any crime except for belief in God our creator and savior. Everything we have comes from God, so I am not afraid of any punishment except hell that awaits those who refuse to believe in God. Be careful not to deny God, and not to go to hell.[35]

De Rhodes embraced Andrew. Andrew wondered aloud why the soldiers were delaying in bringing him to death. He commented, "I was feeling that the heavens were opening for my reception. I saw Jesus at the gates of heaven, and waiting for me with all the martyrs. O heaven. O happiness. Bring me quickly to heaven." People brought food and drink to him. He ate briefly, then said, "That is enough. I will wait to eat my spiritual feast in heaven."[36]

Soldiers stepped forward, took Andrew, and forced him to kneel on the ground. Father de Rhodes spoke encouraging words to Andrew.

Andrew gestured to the people, saying, "Brothers and sisters, be faithful to God until your last breath."[37]

Two executioners stood near Andrew: one, in front; and the other, behind. The soldier behind Andrew raised his arms, and whispered, "O God, if I am guilty of killing this man, forgive me because I have been ordered to do this."[38] This soldier stabbed Andrew three times in the back. The soldier in front of Andrew decapitated him. De Rhodes and others wiped the blood from Andrew, and carried his body back to Hoi An.

27. ✠ Blessed Rudolph Aquaviva, S.J., and Companions

Place: Fatchpur Sikri, India
Fame: Martyrs

In the Kingdom of Naples, Rudolph Aquaviva (1550-1583) was born of noble lineage.[39] The youth possessed a spiritual maturity far beyond his age. He fasted voluntarily every Saturday to prepare for Communion on Sunday. Sensitive to the needs of the poor, he generously distributed his possessions. With playmates, he introduced religious topics into ordinary conversation. He shared with the household's servants that he felt called to die for the Catholic faith in foreign lands.

After his uncle joined the Jesuits, sixteen year old Rudolph took a private vow to do the same. On April 2, 1568, Rudolph entered the Society. Because the Neapolitan had received little education, the Jesuits assigned the newcomer to menial tasks in the kitchen and infirmary. His superiors sent Rudolph, upon completing the novitiate, to study the humanities at Macerata, and later, philosophy and theology at Rome.

In 1577, Rudolph and other Jesuits were missioned to India. In late November, Rudolph and his colleagues left Rome, and traveled through Tuscany to Leghorn, where they embarked for Genoa. From Genoa, they sailed for Lisbon, where they arrived in mid-February. At Lisbon, Rudolph was ordained a priest on March 12, and wrote his last will and testament, in which he renounced all his wealth. Soon, Rudolph and thirteen fellow Jesuit missionaries left for India. Their ship arrived at Goa in mid-September.

His superiors assigned him to teach at Saint Paul's College. After one year, the same superiors missioned Rudolph to the court of the Muslim Emperor Akbar at Fatepur, Sikri, near Agra (about one hundred twenty-five miles south of Delhi). Akbar had descended from Genghis Khan and Tamerlane, and Akbar's grandfather Babur had invaded India in 1526. Akbar requested that Jesuits be assigned to the court to instruct him and his courtiers.

Akbar's request arrived at Goa in September 1579. Two months later, three Jesuits with Rudolph as their superior journeyed to the emperor's court. The trio arrived at Surat (about two hundred miles north of Mumbai) on January 15, 1580. From Surat, the entourage traveled inland six hundred fifty miles, and arrived at Sikri in late February.

Akbar happily greeted the Jesuits. Upon their arrival, the emperor attempted to bestow upon them eight hundred silver pieces. The Jesuits explained that their vow of poverty prohibited them from accepting this extraordinary gift. Akbar arranged a series of meetings whereby the Jesuits would converse with Muslim scholars about the doctrines, moral teachings, and traditional practices of the two religions. The emperor frequently sent gifts to the priests. He granted the priests full freedom to baptize the king's subjects into the Christian religion. At Christmas, the emperor and his sons visited the home of the Jesuits to admire the Christmas crib, and to hear the Christmas story. Akbar thoroughly enjoyed his conversations with Rudolph and his companions. The emperor accepted humbly from Rudolph the priest's reprimands for the emperor's immoral lifestyle.

Akbar received verbal threats and military attacks from his younger brother, who claimed that Akbar's interactions with the Christians indicated Akbar's lack of fidelity to Islam. Akbar went to war against his brother. Along the route, Akbar worshiped at the shrines of Hindus and Muslims, and sought the advice of astrologers. Despite Akbar's openness to talk about Christianity, it became clear to the Jesuits that the Muslim emperor had no interest in converting to Christianity. The Jesuit superiors at Lisbon recalled their three-man mission from the court of Akbar. The threesome left Kabul in February 1583.

The Jesuit Provincial assigned Rudolph to Salsette Island, off the coast of Mumbai. Salsette, beginning about 1560, had experienced much tension between Hindus and Christian converts. A decade before, Jesuit missionaries had destroyed many Hindu temples and shrines. Rudolph, as the new superior, visited the local villages, and met personally with the congregations. Word of his impending visit leaked out, and Hindus at Cuncolim lay in wait for him. On July 25, 1583, Rudolph and fellow priests Alphonsus Pacheco (1551-1583), Anthony Francisco (c. 1550-1583) and Peter Berno (c. 1550-1583), the Jesuit lay brother Francis Aranha (1551-1583), and some local Christians entered the village. The Hindu priest Pondu danced wildly in front of the visitors, shouting, "War, war, this is a good chance, a number of heads will fall."[40] A mob of about two dozen people gathered. They shouted for the great Father to identify himself. Rudolph stepped forward. A sword knocked him to the ground, and subsequent blows nearly severed his left arm, and completely severed several fingers. The priest cried out, "Forgive them, O Lord. Saint Francis, pray for me. Lord Jesus, receive my soul."[41] An arrow to his heart ended his life. Four other Jesuits died during the melee, plus one Portuguese and four Indian Christians. Validating Tertullian's dictum that "the blood of martyrs is the seed of Christians," within the next dozen years, over 35,000 villagers converted to Christianity, and by the end of the century, "there were only a few non-Christians left of the entire population."[42]

As for Akbar, the Jesuits sent subsequent missions to the emperor in 1591 and 1595. Neither mission lasted more than a year, and these missions ended like the first: Akbar showed much interest in learning about Christianity, but showed no interest in converting.

28. ✠ Blessed Alphonsa Muttathupadathu, F.C.C.

Place: Bharananganam, Kerala, India
Fame: Mystic, called "The Passion Flower of India"

Sister Alphonsa Muttathupadathu (1910-1946) suffered excruciating pain physically, emotionally, and spiritually from infancy until her death in early adulthood.[43] She gained the reputation of exemplary response to suffering.

Born at Kudamalloor, Kerala, the child received the name Anna in the Syro-Malabar baptismal rite, and the nickname Annakutty from her family. Within three months of her birth, the young girl's mother died. At three, Anna developed a year-long case of infected eczema. Anna's

BLESSED ALPHONSA MUTTATHUPADATHU, F.C.C.

aunt, who had become the child's foster-mother, proved to be well intentioned but excessively demanding. Anna reports, "For even for the slightest shortcomings my mother used to chide me severely. I was not allowed even to justify myself. . . . My mother never let me enjoy any freedom whatever. I had to talk always in very low tones. . . . I was not allowed but for one or two exceptions to talk to anybody in school, or to look around me on my way there."[44]

Although Anna repeatedly expressed the desire to enter religious life, her foster-mother kept investigating possible suitors for marriage. At thirteen, Anna thought, "I must cause some indisposition to my body to stop my going to church for betrothal. I must disfigure myself and destroy my beauty."[45] The young girl intentionally stepped into an active fire pit behind her home. As she edged one foot into the steeply descending pit, she fell in head over heels. Her clothing and hair caught fire. By the time she was rescued by family and neighbors, she had suffered severe burns over much of her body. Every day for the next three months, the doctor applied ointments and bandages. Most of the wounds healed, although her legs and feet remained permanently scarred and disabled.

Anna joined the Poor Clare Sisters at Bharananganam in May 1927, and received in August 1928, the religious name Alphonsa of the Immaculate Conception. She began formal studies at Changanacherry, but poor health prohibited her from completing studies. She received the religious habit in May 1930.

In late 1930, Sister Alphonsa began teaching elementary school at Vakakad. Her frail health and frequent absences, however, required her to forego a teaching career. In August 1935, she entered the novitiate, but poor health again limited her participation in community activities. During the novitiate, in December 1936, Alphonsa received an instantaneous cure of her continual bleeding. This miracle was attributed to an apparition of her fellow Keralite, Blessed Kuriakose Elias Chavara.

In June 1939, a prolonged case of pneumonia struck Sister Alphonsa. The fever disappeared after an apparent apparition by Saint Thérèse of

Lisieux. Alphonsa reports the following communication occurred during the vision: "You are cured of your fever. You will never suffer from any contagious disease, but you will be tried unto death itself by other sickness."[46]

On October 18, 1940, a thief broke into her room. The shock resulted in Sister Alphonsa's loss of memory, and further weakening of her overall health. She prayed, "My lord of Love, have you not promised a reward to those who renounce everything for your sake? Have I not despised my own will in all things?"[47]

Before long, she developed a swelling in both legs which developed into leg ulcers. She lost too the facility to read. In September of the following year, she received the last rites of the Church because she was expected to die. Gradually, however, her health improved, and she enjoyed three years of relatively good health. In July 1945, she developed stomach convulsions and vomiting that led to her death the next year.

Community life had been difficult for Alphonsa throughout her religious vocation. Her biographer describes the situation, "Community life, in which men and women of diverse temperaments have to submit their wills to the discipline of obedience, poverty and chastity, is not easy at any time, and is described by theologians as a form of martyrdom."[48] Sister Alphonsa writes, "Earlier in life it was very difficult for me to love those who occasioned me grief and who accused me falsely. I could not even have looked at them. But, by persistent prayer and practice, it has become quite easy for me."[49]

Although few people attended Sister Alphonsa's funeral, her tomb soon became a place of pilgrimage. Hundreds of people, especially those suffering from disabilities of the feet and legs, experienced miraculous healings by praying to Sister Alphonsa.

29. ✠ Saint Joseph Zhang Wenlan and Companions

Place: Yaojiaguan, Sichuan, China
Fame: Martyrs

Two seminarians, Joseph Zhang Wenlan (1831-1861) and Paul Chen Changping (1838-1861) were returning from a trip to nearby Yaojiaguan when soldiers arrested them for being Christians.[50] The captors had been searching the seminary, where they arrested the worker John Baptist Luo Tingyin (1825-1861). The arrests having been made, the soldiers marched the trio to an abandoned, dirty, and damp temple, where they confined the prisoners. On July 29, when the day arrived for their execution, Martha Wang-Luo Mande (1802-1861), the seminary's cook and cleaning lady, walked with the prisoners en route to execution. Because she continued to offer support to the three men, despite the soldiers' threats, they arrested her too. Along the way, "all four showed on their faces the peace and joy that rose from the courage to die for their faith, as they prayed up to the last minute before entering the glory of martyrdom."[51] All four died by decapitation. An imperial decree of pardon had arrived a few days before the planned execution but the local magistrate ignored it, and pursued his desire to kill the Christians.

Joseph had been born into a Catholic family at Ba County in Sichuan. As a youth, he studied in the seminary but was expelled because he had violated regulations. His parish priest enlisted Joseph's services as a catechist, and later successfully urged the seminary administrators to re-admit Joseph. When a local persecution arose in 1861, soldiers captured him near the seminary property.

Chen Changping had been born in Xingren County, Guizhou. After his parents divorced, the father asked the local priest to raise Chen. The priest instructed him in studies and in the faith. At sixteen, Chen became baptized, took the name Paul, received confirmation, and entered the seminary. In 1857, the father returned and demanded that Paul leave the seminary. The son won out. In 1861, Paul Chen Changping was arrested while walking with Joseph Zhang Wenlan near the seminary.

John Baptist Luo Tingyin had been born into a wealthy family at Qingyian in Guizhou. He was well educated in the arts and medicine. He operated a medical clinic. While visiting in Shitouzhai, he listened to a street-preaching Catholic, and investigated the faith on his own. He converted and took the name John the Baptist. His passionate attachment to the faith inspired his wife, their two children, and his parents to convert. After a while, he retired from his medical career, and purchased a large farm at Yaojiaguan near the seminary. The rector leased seminary land to John to farm, and entrusted him oversight of the financial matters of the seminary.

Martha Wang Luo Mande (1802-1861), from the town of Zunyi in Guizhou, lived with her husband in Qingyian, where they owned a small vegetable farm. Childless, they adopted two nephews. After her husband died, and her two sons left home to live dissolute lives, she moved to the edge of town where she operated a small inn. When a Catholic from Yaojiaguan came to catechize the people of Qingyian, Wang Luo became intrigued. On Christmas 1852, she converted. Desiring greater accessibility to Mass and Christian community, she moved to Guiyang, where she worked as a cook in a Catholic hostel for young women. When Bishop Hu in 1857 opened a seminary at Yaojiaguan, he hired Martha as a cook. Four years later, she was martyred for the faith. At the moment of execution, the soldiers teased the woman about her being able to endure decapitation. Wang Luo looked at her colleagues about to die for the faith, and replied confidently to the soldiers, "If they can die, so can I."[52]

AUGUST

8. ☩ Blessed Mary MacKillop, R.M.

Place: Melbourne and Sydney, Australia
Fame: Australia's first native-born saint candidate; foundress

Few saints have suffered as much at the hands of the local episcopacy as did Mary MacKillop (1842-1909).[1] Three years after Bishop Laurence Bonaventure Sheil of Adelaide approved Mary's congregation of the Sisters of Saint Joseph, he excommunicated her in 1871 for maintaining the community's independent status and not becoming a diocesan community under his authority. Mary laments to her mother about the situation:

> All I can say and the best I can say is that I have done my duty and that our poor dear old Bishop has made a terrible mistake. Even the very ones who care most about the Bishop remain silent when the sisters ask them if what has been done is right. Let us pray that God may be glorified in all this. His ways are not our ways, and He can and will bring good out of all this, but it is terribly trying at present on account of the scandal.[2]

The bishop reconsidered his extraordinary penalty because he had erred in both canon law and good judgment. Five months later, on his deathbed, the bishop apologized to Sister Mary and reversed the excommunication.

Vatican authorities in 1874 accepted the congregation's Constitutions which included the statement of independent authority. Nonetheless, Bishop Matthew Quinn of Bathurst in the following year demanded that the sisters become diocesan. Again, Mother Mary led the sisters in refusing to act contrary to their canonical rights. Instead, they chose to leave his diocese.

In 1883, Bishop Sheil's successor as Bishop of Adelaide, Bishop Reynolds, uncanonically removed Sister Mary as Superior General when she refused to allow her community to become a diocesan institute. When each of the Sisters refused to acquiesce to his desire, the bishop denied the community the permission to minister in his diocese, even though in the process he was denying them their canonical rights.

In 1885 the bishops of Australia met in Plenary Council and voted fourteen to three that the Sisters of Saint Joseph must become a diocesan community. Rome accepted most of the Council's decisions, but separated from the decisions the legislation which attempted to change the sisters' status. The following year, Rome approved the Constitution of the Sisters of St. Joseph of the Sacred Heart as a community whose central authority transcended diocesan boundaries.

Sister Mary spent long hours praying in front of the Blessed Sacrament and to the Blessed Mother. Despite the unfair treatment directed at her, Mary remained kind to all those who attacked her.

> She [Mary] judged nobody, she blamed nobody, she was never heard to utter a word of criticism or bitterness, and her reverence for the sacred character of priests and bishops was never diminished. She always tried to excuse those who had wronged her, called attention to their good qualities, and reminded the sisters of favours [sic] received from them in the past.[3]

Neither life as a religious sister, nor life at home as a young girl, had been easy for Mary. Fewer then fifty years after the first Europeans had arrived in Australia, Mary's parents arrived from Scotland. The couple met in June 1840, married one month later, and moved from Sydney to Melbourne. The father, a former seminarian, was educated and eloquent. Unfortunately, he experienced repeated failures in extravagant business ventures. The family moved frequently, usually receiving lodging with their mother's relatives. Mary, the first of her parents' eight children, baptized Maria Ellen, describes her childhood in this way: "My life as a child was one of sorrow; my home, when I had it, a most unhappy one."[4]

Mary left school at fourteen in order to support the family. She worked as a clerk and a teacher. By fifteen, she wanted to become a religious sister. At nineteen, to support the family, Mary left home and traveled to Penola, South Australia, where she worked as a governess-nanny for her maternal relatives. Until age twenty-five, Mary supported her family.

At Penola, Mary met Father Julian Tenison Woods. He assisted her in founding the Sisters of Saint Joseph. The community proposed to educate poor children. Because the visionary priest lacked prudence and tact, however, many clergy liked neither him nor the his women's community. Within seven years, the bishop ordered Father Woods to remove himself from association with the sisters.

Mother Mary's congregation grew rapidly. After its founding in 1867, the community expanded to Queensland (1875), New South Wales (1880), New Zealand (1883), and Victoria (1889). Mary was elected superior general of the congregation from 1875 to 1888, and again from 1898 until 1909. At the time of Mary's death, the community had grown to over 750 sisters who were teaching over twelve thousand students.

9. ✠ Blessed Marianne Cope, O.S.F.

Place: Molokai, Hawaii
Fame: Medical missionary to patients with Hansen's Disease

A priest-emissary of the Vicar Apostolic of Hawaii, at the request of the Hawaiian government, sent letters to over fifty women's religious communities.[5] The emissary's letter specified that the sisters "would take charge of our hospitals, and even of our schools, if it were possible."[6]

BLESSED MARIANNE COPE, O.S.F.

The emissary received only one promising response — from Mother Marianne Cope (1838-1918), provincial of the Sisters of the Third Order of St. Francis in Syracuse, New York. Mother Marianne replied in June 1883: "Shall I regard your kind invitation to join you in your missionary labors as coming from God? . . . My interest is awakened and I feel an irresistible force drawing me to follow this call."[7]

The priest traveled to Syracuse to speak with Mother. He had not yet revealed that the hospitals were leprosaria. As Mother Marianne and other sisters whom she had invited to a meeting listened to the emissary's description of the needs of those afflicted with leprosy, the Sisters became intrigued.

Seven sisters arrived at Honolulu in November 1883. Mother intended to establish the new ministry and then return to her responsibilities at Syracuse. In Hawaii, however, Mother Marianne's intellectual and interpersonal gifts were needed to lay a firm foundation for this new work. One year later, when doctors diagnosed Father Damien with terminal leprosy, any likelihood of Mother's returning to Syracuse evaporated.

Within two months of their arrival in Honolulu, the sisters began working at Kakaako Branch Hospital. "No task was too menial for the small group of sisters, and with their scrubbing, cleaning, and just plain caring, they gave the patients an uplift in morale beyond measuring."[8] Mother insisted on strict sanitary procedures, consequently no sister contracted the highly contagious disease. By 1888, Mother had opened three medical facilities: Malulani's first General Hospital at Maui, the Kapiolani Home on Oahu Island for healthy female children of leprous parents, and the C.R. Bishop Home at Molokai for homeless women and girls with leprosy.

In 1888, new political leaders and the Board of Health mandated that leprosy patients be transferred to Molokai. "The desolate island [peninsula] was surrounded on all sides by imposing rock cliffs and rough seas. It was considered the last stop, from which no one returned."[9] Annually, about 700 patients would reside there.

Mother agreed to move her sisters from Oahu to Molokai, on the condition that the bishop would assign a priest and build a chapel there. She writes to the bishop, "Our spiritual wants are of the greatest importance. . . . I cannot accept the mission until I have assurance from Your Lordship that you will kindly supply this want, as you alone can."[10]

Mother had promised to the dying Father Damien that she and her sisters would care for his boys. She took charge of the boys' home at Kalawao, just two miles from the C.R. Bishop Home. At the same time, Mother kept Sisters at Oahu at the Kapiolani Home and the Receiving Station.

In the first days of the Sisters' presence at Molokai, Mother insisted that female patients be protected from drunken men who would come in groups at night to attack the women. She created rules to protect the incoming girls and boys from predators who awaited their arrival at the settlement.

The ministry at Molokai began taking its toll physically on the aging Mother Marianne. In 1902, at sixty-four, she writes to her nephew in Chicago:

> I am wondering how many more [years] our dear Sweet Lord will allow me to spend for Him. I do not think of reward, I am working for God, and do so cheerfully. How many graces did He not shower down on me, from my birth till now. Should I live a thousand years, I could not in ever so small a degree thank Him for His gifts and blessings. I do not expect a high place in heaven. I shall be thankful for a little corner where I may love God for all eternity.[11]

After thirty-five years of service to the victims of Hansen's Disease in the Hawaiian Islands, Mother died at Kalaupapa.

Marianne Cope had been born at Heppenheim, Germany, the fifth child of her father's second marriage. As an infant, she sailed with her family to New York City, whence the family settled in upstate Utica. Marianne delayed until twenty-four her entrance into religious life because her factory salary was needed at home. In religious life, she served for eight years as teacher and principal in Catholic elementary schools. In 1870, she was appointed chief administrator of Saint Joseph's Hospital. Seven years later, she was elected the provincial of her community. During her second term as provincial, she received the letter inviting her to serve the sick poor of Hawaii.

12. ✠ Blessed Maurice Tornay, M.E.P.

Place: Tibet (now an autonomous region of China)
Fame: Martyr

At La Rosiere, in the canton of Valais, Switzerland, a fervently Catholic couple gave birth to the fifth of their seven children: Maurice Tornay (1910-1949).[12] The young boy demonstrated in personality and piety the traits found in someone called to religious vocation: faith-filled, friendly, and helpful. Upon completing secondary education at nearby Saint Maurice's Abbey, he entered the seminary.

The lad joined the Canons Regular of Grand Saint Bernard on August 25,1931. After professing solemn vows in 1935, Maurice volunteered for China. He was assigned to Weixi in western Yunnan Province along the shores of the Mekong River. There he completed his theological studies, and began Chinese language studies. After ordination to priesthood at Hanoi in 1938, the young man was missioned as student director at the high school seminary at Hua-lo-pa.

In 1945, Father Maurice requested a new assignment. He asked to be sent to Yerkalo, Tibet. The mission territory of Yerkalo, which was the only Catholic parish in Tibet, encompassed an area the size of France, in which lived a few thousand faithful Catholics. Since the sixteenth century, when Catholicism had been introduced into Tibet, Catholic clergy and laity had suffered intermittent persecutions and martyrdoms.

Father Maurice did all that he could to adapt to Tibetan culture. The local Buddhist monks, however, viewed unkindly the priest's invitation to the populace to investigate Catholicism. Within a few months of his arrival, Buddhist priests broke into Father Maurice's home, threatening his person and robbing his property. Over the next four years, these unwelcomed visits were repeated. On January 26, 1946, the Buddhist attackers chased the missionary from his residence into exile. The priest found refuge thirty miles away at Pame, China. Regularly his parishioners on business trips passed through this town, and visited their pastor. The parishioners informed the pastor that the Buddhist monks, locally called lamas, prohibited the Catholics from gathering for prayer, and urged them to abandon the Catholic faith.

Desiring to encourage and to aid his Catholic flock, Father Maurice contacted the Apostolic Nuncio and Tibetan governmental authorities, begging them to intercede for the safety and religious freedom of his people. Wanting to take every possible step, he decided to visit in person the political authorities and the Dali Lama at the capital city of Lhasa. From these national leaders Father Maurice hoped to elicit an edict of religious toleration for the minority Catholics.

The local lamas at Yerkalo wanted to stop Father Maurice from appealing to the national authorities. The lamas' network of priests, henchmen, and informers enabled them to keep abreast of the missionary's movements. On July 10, 1949, the Catholic priest left Atuntze with his faithful Catholic servant Dossy on their month-long mountainous journey to Lhasa. Informers continuously updated the lamas about the priest's itinerary. On July 27, at To Thong, just beyond the Chula Pass, a band of robbers attacked the caravan which the priest had joined. The robbers hurt no one and took nothing, except the priest and his servant. They headed for the town of Tchrayul. Near that town, two more bandits approached the robbers and explained that they had orders from the lamas at Yerkalo to bring the priest to his former mission area. For days, the bandits walked with the two captives towards Yerkalo. As the group neared Yerkalo, four lamas with rifles stepped out of the forest. Father Maurice spoke to the gunmen: "Don't shoot. Let's talk."[13] The lamas ignored the priest's invitation, raised their weapons and shot and killed, first, the servant, and next, the priest. The date of the attack and the death of the missionary Father Maurice Tornay was August 11, 1949.

24. ✠ Francisca del Espiritu Santo, O.P.

Place: Manila, Philippines
Fame: *Foundress of Beatorio de Santa Catalina de Siena de Manila, now known as the Congregation of Dominican Sisters of Saint Catherine of Siena, Philippines*

After a brief marriage and early widowhood, Francisca de Fuentes (1647-1711) felt God's call to dedicate the remainder of her life to God through contemplation.[14] Like other women at Manila, she sought and received permission to become a Third Order Dominican. These pious women devoted themselves to prayer and penance in their individual homes, attended Mass daily and received Communion frequently at the monastery of the Dominican Fathers in the Intramuros District. The women wore in their homes and on the streets the distinguishing garb of the Third Order.

Four years after having become a Third Order Dominican in 1682, Francisca led a group of three other women in forming not just an association of individuals but a community of women living the Third Order Dominican life. These pious women were called *beatas*, and their community was called a *beatorio*. In 1690, the women elected Francisca the prioress of the community.

From the earliest days, these *beatas* experienced many difficulties. Because they had no money, they depended on the First Order Dominican friars to provide the nascent community with shelter and board. Within a few months, the original four *beatas* burgeoned to fifteen, but the increase in membership occasioned a decrease in the community's dedication to prayer, penance, and the Rule of Saint Dominic. While many sisters abided by the community's external structures, they failed to maintain contemplation whether inside or outside the convent. The young community became beset by lawsuits; in the colonies no *beatorio* could be built without the explicit approval of the King of Spain through his appointed governor. Also, right after his arrival at Manila in 1697, the Archbishop of Manila disputed with the friars over jurisdiction of the Third Order. In December 1703, the archbishop excommunicated the foundress, and exiled the sisters from their *Beatorio*. The sisters' exile remained in effect for over two years, after which the archbishop invited the sisters to return to their original *beatorio*, on the condition that they would subject themselves to him and not to the friars, and that they would follow the requirements of enclosure with gate and grillwork.

Throughout this period of trials, Mother Francisca maintained a prayerful and peaceful demeanor. The community's difficulties, plus her penances and frequent fasting, however, took its toll on Mother's good health. Just before she died on August 24, 1711, Mother asked the Dominican provincial to pardon her for all those whom she had offended. The provincial responded, "Mother, you should also pardon those who offended you."[15] She said, "Nobody offended me."[16] Mother Francisca died at peace with the Lord and her contemporaries.

25. ✢ Blessed Marie Baouardy, O.C.M.

Place: *Ibellin and Bethlehem, Palestine/Israel; and Mangalore, India*
Fame: *"The Little Arab," foundress of the Carmel of Bethlehem*

In the hills of upper Galilee, at Abilene (now Ibellin), halfway between inland Nazareth and the seacoast city of Haifa, was born Mariam

Baouardy (1846-1878).[17] Before Mariam was born, her father and mother had given birth to twelve sons, but none of these survived infancy. This Melkite-Rite Catholic couple made a pilgrimage to Bethlehem, where they prayed to Mary at the Grotto of Bethlehem for the birth of a daughter. Nine months later, Mariam was born. Two years later, Mariam's brother Paul was born.

Within a few weeks of Paul's birth, both parents died. Paul was taken into the home of a maternal aunt from Tarshiba. Mariam was cared for by her paternal uncle at Ibellin. As a child, Mariam cared for a bird in a cage. Sadly, the bird died. A heavenly voice consoled Mariam, saying, "Everything passes."[18] At eight, Mariam's uncle and family moved to Egypt. At thirteen, on the eve of an arranged marriage, Mariam informed the uncle that she desired to remain a virgin, and dedicate her life to God. The uncle became infuriated. With the opportunity for the marriage having passed, he reduced her status to that of his lowest servant, performing the most menial of tasks.

Mariam spoke of her sufferings with a co-worker. This Muslim youth showed much compassion in his responses to her. She thought she had found a friend. He thought he had found a likely convert to Islam. After she refused his demands that she convert, the supposed friend beat her, kicked her, and slashed her throat with a sword, after which he dumped her limp body in a dark alley. The attack occurred on September 8, 1858. That day, Miriam reported later, a nun dressed in blue stitched the wounded girl's throat. Recovering from her wound, Miriam left Ibellin, and never returned there until two decades later, just before she died.

Mariam desired to enter religious life. In 1860, she joined the Sisters of Saint Joseph. After two years of her having experienced repeated supernatural phenomena, the community decided not to accept her. In 1867, she successfully entered the Carmelite convent at Pau, in southwestern France. She took the name Sister Marie of Jesus Crucified. Soon she began exhibiting the stigmata of the passion of Christ, levitations, frequent ecstasies, and facial radiance.

She set about establishing new convents. The community selected Mangalore, India, and Bethlehem, Palestine as two new sites. Mariam traveled to Mangalore in 1871 and to Bethlehem in 1878. After eight months in Bethlehem, Mariam fell while overseeing the workers constructing the new convent. She developed an infection which traveled to her respiratory system. Within days, she suffocated and died.

29. ✠ Blessed Euphrasia Eluvathingal, C.M.C.

Place: Aranattukara, Kerala, India
Fame: "The Rose of Carmel"

BLESSED EUPHRASIA ELUVATHINGAL, C.M.C.

Rosa Eluvathingal (1877-1952) was the first of her parent's nine children.[19] The family enjoyed a comfortable living from their eighteen acres of land and nine acres of rice paddies at Edathuruthy. One great discomfort which the family suffered at their home in Aranattukara was the father's alcoholism.

Rosa spent much of her youth at the home of her maternal uncle, who provided tutors to educate his niece. At nine, Rosa opened her uncle's front door to some religious sisters who were visiting homes in the neighborhood. Rosa became attracted to the life. At twelve, she entered at Koonammavu the boarding school for candidates for religious life. She studied Christian doctrine, domestic skills, mathematics, music, plus three languages: English, Malayalam and Tamil. Rosa's faculty and schoolmates remembered her as determined in her studies and faithful to the Rule in every detail. Because of her poor health, the religious authorities considered sending her home,

Rosa, however, would suffer from poor health throughout her life, even up to her death at seventy-five. At twelve, she suffered an attack of rheumatism so severe that she could neither eat, nor see, nor sleep well; and she received the last rites of the Church. During this period, she experienced a vision of the Holy Family. "Rosa's pale little face beamed with life and beauty. . . . She stretched out her arms as if she was receiving somebody very dear to her."[20] The religious community leaders wrote about her, "It was decided that this girl should be sent home. But her vision of the Holy Family, her piety, modesty and love of discipline made us decide to let her join the Congregation."[21]

In 1896, when the vicariates of India were re-structured, the new bishop opened a convent at Ambazhakad, where Rosa entered and received as her religious name, Sister Euphrasia of the Sacred Heart. She continued living the simple life of service and suffering. The next year, however, she became so ill with rheumatism that she received again the sacramental anointing of the sick. In 1900, she professed her vows in the Congregation of Our Mother of Carmel at the convent at Ollur, before heading back to Ambazhakad because of continued sickness.

Her responsibilities in the community included infirmarian, social worker, assistant novice director for four years, novice mistress for nine years, and provincial superior for three years. She manifested humility and patience in her dealings with other sisters, the novices, and youth. As superior, she entrusted the community to the care of the Sacred Heart, Hour upon hour, daily, she spent in the chapel. Devoted to the Blessed Mother Mary, Sister Euphrasia daily carried and prayed the fifteen-decade rosary.

This humble sister possessed the gift of anticipating future events which would occur in people's lives. She foresaw sickness, death, and the apparitions of Fatima.

Companions perceived this woman as a living saint, but Sister perceived she ought to be doing more. She writes to her spiritual director: "Father, the only feeling in my heart is that I have not practiced big virtues. But I have great consolation in knowing that by the grace of God I have not given myself up to my own will and desires and to the pleasures that I could enjoy if I wanted. Even if these are permitted pleasures I used to say to myself on such occasions: Let us deny this now for eternal joy. Later you can enjoy it."[22]

At seventy-five, she lay paralyzed, unable to speak, fingering her rosary beads. She received the last rites, and three days later she died. Virtually unknown outside the convent and the local community, the sisters, novices and youth who knew her called her the "praying mother." She was buried at Saint Mary's Convent in Ollur, Thrissur, India.

SEPTEMBER

3. ✣ Blessed Bartolomeo Gutierrez Rodriguez, O.S.A.

Place: Manila, Philippines; and Nagasaki, Japan
Fame: Martyr

Bartolomeo Gutierrez Rodriguez (1580-1632) was born and raised in Mexico City.[1] At sixteen, he entered the Hermits of Saint Augustine. In 1606, he was ordained a priest at Puebla, Mexico.

Shortly after ordination, Bartolomeo was missioned to Manila in the Philippines, where he labored for the next six years.

In 1612, the young priest was sent to Osaka, Japan, where he was named the prior of the religious house. He studied the language and customs of the Japanese in order to serve them well. In 1614, when Shogun Ieyasu exiled all foreign missionaries, Bartolomeo reluctantly returned to Manila.

In 1617, Bartolomeo successfully snuck back into Japan. For the next twelve years, he served his congregations of Japanese Catholics. Having put on various disguises, he traveled at night, hid in people's homes, and repeatedly eluded the near-grasp of police.

Bartolomeo's success in evading the police ended abruptly during the persecution by Nagasaki's governor Takenaka Uneme. A Christian who had apostatized under the pressure reported where and when Bartolomeo could be found. On November 10, 1629, soldiers captured the cleric at the village of Kikzu, Arima, near Osaka.

After his arrest, the priest was transferred to the prison at Omura. Before one month ended, four more foreign priests were brought to Omura. For the next two years, the five prisoners were permitted to celebrate Mass daily, to meet with visitors, and to instruct inquirers in the faith.

In preparation for capital punishment, the five priests were transferred to Nagasaki. The five prisoners were housed in cramped quarters, with an adjoining cell holding fifty-four Christians similarly slated for killing. Prison authorities tried to persuade the priests and laity to apostatize. No one succumbed. In December 1631, the priests were sent to the sulphur springs at Unzen on the Shimabara Peninsula, east of Nagasaki.

Repeatedly the clergy were immersed in the sulphurous water until the skin all over their bodies was burned. A doctor applied remedies so that they could be tortured anew. This barbarous treatment was administered six times a day, for thirty-one continuous days. The missionaries were returned to jail where they remained for another eight months.[2]

The authorities decided that nothing would shake these prisoners from their faith. On September 3, 1632, these five foreign priests, including Bartolomeo Gutierrez, and a native Japanese priest were brought to the Hill of Martyrs at Nagasaki. The six priests received the punishment customarily applied to clerical and lay leaders: they were tied to stakes, and were burned alive slowly.

4. ✢ Vincent Robert Capodanno, M.M.

Place: *Que Son Valley, Vietnam; and Miaoli, Taiwan*
Fame: *Military chaplain, "The Grunt Padre"*

The youngest of ten children of an Italian immigrant and his Italian-American wife, Vincent Robert Capodanno (1929-1967) attended public schools at Mariners' Harbor in Staten Island, New York.[3] At school, his classmates were impressed not by his B-average grades but his appearance, and voted him, "best dresser" and "best looking."[4] After graduating from high school, Vincent worked at an insurance company for two years.

Having decided to become a priest, Vincent entered in September 1949, the order of Maryknoll Missionaries. His program of education and formation included stays at Glen Elyn, IL; Lakewood, NJ; Bedford, MA; and Ossining, NY. On June 14, 1958, he was ordained a priest.

His religious superiors assigned him to Taiwan, where he arrived on August 18, 1958. After traveling to Miaoli, seventy miles south of Taipei, he remained there for nine months, studying the Hakka dialect of Chinese. Because the young priest never mastered the aspirate sounds of the language, he suffered frustration in communication. In June 1959, Father Vincent began serving as a parish priest, celebrating the sacraments, providing food and medical assistance, and instructing catechists. His assignment to the mountaineers of Tunglo and Ching An proved difficult for this New York City native: he tried to retain his customary meticulousness in dress, orderliness in living quarters, and systematic approach, none of which typified the carefree, spontaneous image popularly associated with the "missionary mystique."[5] After six years at Taiwan, Father Vincent returned home to New York City for a six-month furlough.

Vincent Robert Capodanno, M.M.

Upon returning to Taiwan in March 1965, he was shocked to learn that he had been transferred to Maryknoll High School in Hong Kong. To leave Taiwan, where he had been learning the culture and language of the people meant almost to start over again by learning the Chinese customs and language at Hong Kong. The obedient priest arrived at Hong Kong on March 25, 1965. Within a week, however, he began writing letters to his superiors requesting a return to Taiwan. After four rejections for a transfer, he volunteered to serve as a Navy Chaplain in the emerging Vietnam War. His religious superiors reluctantly accepted his request.

After arriving at Hawaii in August 1965, Father Vincent began an interim post as parish priest at Kamuela. At the beginning of the new year, he began Navy Chaplaincy School at Newport, RI, followed by training at the Medical Service School at Camp Pendleton, CA. During Holy Week, he arrived at Da Nang, Vietnam. A reporter asked Father Vincent why he had volunteered for Vietnam. The chaplain replied, "Because I think I am needed here as are many more chaplains. I'm glad to help in the way I can."[6] From there he was assigned to the 7th Marine Regiment at Chu Lai, fifty miles south of Da Nang.

The Marines, known popularly as "grunts," experienced their new chaplain as approachable and available. Testimonies abound about Father Vincent's commitment to his Marines. In a thatched roof chapel, he heard confessions, celebrated Mass, and counseled those who sought his advice.

In the field, he regularly walked the perimeter of the camp, greeting soldiers, listening to and encouraging the grunts, sharing his cigarettes and candies with the men, and consequently becoming one with them. During his first year, the Grunt Padre served on six combat missions with his beloved Marines. Repeatedly the chaplain risked his life to save his men's lives and souls. The formerly fastidious missioner had become a "mud Marine."[7]

A first-person witness to the Padre's commitment to God and his grunts comes from Captain David L. Walker, who reports after he had been wounded, and lay in an indefensible rice paddy, "Father Capodanno was the first at my side, even though he had to run about 75 meters [about eighty yards] through heavy enemy small arms fire. After summoning a Corpsman, he [Father Capodanno] then assisted in carrying me to a safe area where I was med-evaced. During this time, he was constantly exposed to enemy fire."[8] Corporal Henry Hernandez adds about the incident:

> Father Capodanno was kneeling beside Captain Walker, exposed to enemy fire, whispering in his ear, as he did to all Marines that were wounded. He would say some words of comfort, that medical help was coming and say a prayer. Those that were killed in action, he would whisper the Act of Contrition in their ear. He told them that God would hear it and would forgive all their sins.[9]

As Father Capodanno's tour of duty was ending in April 1967, he requested and received permission to extend his tour by six months. When a second request for a six-month extension was denied, he asked for a two-month extension so that he could remain with his grunts through Christmas. The latter extension too was denied. After a brief furlough, Chaplain Capodanno was transferred to the Que Son Valley, 25 km [15 miles] northwest of the Tam Key region because of the heavy fighting in the area.

On September 4, 1967, what began for the Marines as a routine predawn "search and destroy" mission in the village of Thang Binh burgeoned into a bloody battle. While the Marines were searching, the North Vietnamese Army happened upon the same village. The fighting turned into "fixed bayonet" combat. Father Capodanno requested permission to enter the battle arena, and was flown in by helicopter. The Marines were outnumbered five to one. In mid-afternoon, Father Vincent heard the radio operator report, "We can't hold out here. We are being wiped out! There are wounded and dying all around."[10] With that report, Father Vincent leapt over the crest, and rushed down the hill to drag the wounded back to safety. He rescued many men, and prayed with many others as they lay dying. In the process, he was wounded twice, once in the right shoulder and hand which rendered his arm immovable so that he then blessed men with his left hand; and in another instant, he suffered shrapnel wounds to his arms and legs. Despite the injuries, he kept racing down the hill and dragging grunts back up the hill. Again having run downhill, Father Vincent placed his body between a wounded Navy Corpsman and a Vietnamese machine gunner, who was positioned just ten yards away. While Father was ministering to the Marine, the enemy's gun blasted bullets through the back of the priest's head.

Posthumously, Vincent Robert Capodanno, M.M. was awarded the nation's highest military honor, the Medal of Honor, in addition to the Purple Heart, and a Bronze Star.

5. ✠ Blessed Mother Teresa of Calcutta, M.C.

Place: Calcutta (now Kolkata), India
Fame: "Saint of the Gutters," foundress of the Missionaries of Charity

In a hidden corner of the world, where the states of Albania, Bosnia-Herzogovenia, Croatia, and Serbia converge, Agnes Gonxha Bojaxhiu (1910-1997) was born.[11] She would become one of history's most beloved people: Mother Teresa of Calcutta.

Agnes Gonxha was the last of her merchant-class parents' three children. Like countless number of saints, her First Communion made a profound impact on her, whereby she experienced an ineffable love of God and a desire to praise God by service to others. At five and a half, she made her First Communion. Nine months later, in November of 1916, she made her Confirmation. When her father died suddenly, perhaps poisoned by political opponents, Gonxha was eight. Her mother continued

Blessed Mother Teresa of Calcutta, M.C.

to raise the children with strong Catholic faith, hope, and love, as well as generosity in caring for the poor, to whose homes the mother regularly took young Gonxha. Gonxha felt drawn to the religious vocation as exemplified by her Jesuit parish priests, and as presented in the magazine *Catholic Missions*.

In 1928, Agnes Gonxha entered the Sisters of Loreto of Ireland. The eighteen-year-old traveled to Rathfarnham, Ireland, where she studied English for three months before traveling to Darjeeling, India. There, beginning in January 1929, she spent two years as postulant and novice. She received the name Sister Teresa, in honor of Saint Thérèse of Lisieux.

In May 1931, Sister Teresa was assigned to teach at the community's Saint Mary's School for mostly middle-class girls at Calcutta. After school, Sister Teresa took her middle-class students to serve the poor in the surrounding neighborhoods. In 1944, the Sisters of Loretto appointed Sister Teresa principal of the school. During these years, Sister Teresa developed, through prayer, a great intimacy with the Lord. When she took her Final Profession of vows in May 1937, she writes that she became the "spouse of Jesus" for "all eternity."[12] For twenty years, Sister Teresa lived with the Sisters of Loretto. During that time, "noted for her charity, unselfishness and courage, her capacity for hard work and natural talent for organization, she lived out her consecration to Jesus, in the midst of her companions, with fidelity and joy."[13]

On September 10, 1946, while traveling from Calcutta to Darjeeling to make her annual retreat, Sister Teresa received the missionary vocation within a religious vocation, namely, "the call within a call." "Jesus' thirst for love and for souls took hold of her heart and the desire to satiate His thirst became the driving force of her life."[14] Having felt the call to serve the poor in the streets of Calcutta, Sister Teresa did not know how, when, or where she might serve. She discussed the inspiration with her spiritual director, religious community leaders, and bishop.

After two years of discernment, Sister Teresa left her religious community. On August 17, 1948, she put on the now-famous blue-bordered white sari. Departing from the Sisters of Loretto on the best of terms, she received hospitality at Patma from the Medical Missionary Sisters and the Little Sisters of the Poor. On December 21, 1948, she began her ministry in the gutters of Calcutta. A few months later, a former student joined Sister Teresa in this ministry. On October 7, 1950, the bishop granted the Missionaries of Charity diocesan recognition as a religious community.

The community and its works grew by leaps and bounds. By the time of Mother Teresa's death on September 5, 1997, she had been joined by almost 4,000 sisters, who were working in 610 foundations in 123 countries. She founded not only the sister Missionaries of Charity, but also the Mission of Charity Brothers (1963), the contemplative female Missionaries of Charity (1967), the Contemplative Brothers (1979), and the Mission of Charity Fathers (1984). For the laity, she instituted the Co-Workers of Mother Teresa, the Sick and Suffering Co-Workers, and the Lay Missionaries of Charity. For priests world-wide, she founded the Corpus Christi Movement for Priests as a "little way of holiness" whereby priests could participate spiritually in the corporal and spiritual works of mercy performed by her orders.

She won numerous awards including the Indian Padmashri Award (1962), the Nobel Peace Prize (1979), and over fifty honorary degrees and diplomas from various universities and colleges world-wide. She received these awards "for the glory of God, and in the name of the poor."[15]

8. ✠ Our Lady of Vailankanni

Place: Vailankanni, Tamil Nadu, India
Fame: "Lourdes of the East"

A series of alleged apparitions and miracles attributed to the Blessed Mother gave foundation to devotion to Our Lady of Good Health, known also as Our Lady of Vailankanni.[16] Each year, millions of people,

Our Lady of Vailankanni

Catholics and non-Catholics, make pilgrimages to this shrine; it has become known as "Lourdes of the East."

The first apparition of the Blessed Mother occurred in the sixteenth century. A shepherd boy milked his goats and proceeded from Vailankanni to his master's home at Nagapattinam, a distance of six miles. Along the way, the boy sat down under a banyan tree, faced a pond, and fell asleep. He was awakened by a vision of Mary, the Mother of Jesus, holding her infant Son in her arms. She asked the boy for some milk for her child. The boy happily complied. The Blessed Mother and her Son smiled. When the young worker arrived at Nagapattinam, his master scolded him for his tardiness. The boy explained what had occurred. The master scoffed at the story. "But to the greater astonishment of all present, the milk began to surge over the pot and flow out."[17]

Another apparition and accompanying miracle occurred at Vailankanni near the end of the sixteenth century. A poor widow and her lame son customarily sat under a banyan tree and sold buttermilk to passersby. One day, the Blessed Virgin appeared with her Son in her arms. She asked for a cup of buttermilk. The lad served her. The Blessed Virgin asked the boy to report to a certain Catholic gentleman at Nagapattinam that the Blessed Virgin desired a chapel to be built in her name on the site of this apparition. The boy stood up and discovered that he was no longer lame. He ran to the home of the man at Nagapattinam and reported the apparition, miracle, and request. The gentleman, having been alerted by the Blessed Virgin, accepted the boy's request . The man led neighbors in building the chapel. Devotees began to call Mary "Our Lady of Good Health." The chapel has since been replaced by the Shrine Basilica of Annai Vailankanni.

The third event occurred early in the seventeenth century when a Portuguese merchant ship was sailing from Macao to Colombo, the capital of Ceylon (now Sri Lanka). Caught in a storm on the Sea of Bengal, the sailors prayed to Our Lady Star of the Sea. They promised to build a church in her name wherever she might deliver the ship to safe haven. The winds blew the ship to Vailankanni. In gratitude, the sailors reconstructed the thatched chapel into a stone chapel. On a subsequent visit, the same sailors decorated the altar with porcelain plates depicting biblical themes.

Today, the basilica lies within the Diocese of Thanjavar. Surrounding the basilica are an outdoor amphitheatre for conducting sacred services and a Saint Vincent de Paul Center, whose members distribute food to the poor of all faiths.

11. ✠ Saint John Gabriel Perboyre, C.M.

Place: Chiang-his, Ho-nan, and Hu-pei, China
Fame: Martyr

John Gabriel Perboyre (1802-1840) grew up the oldest of eight children on the family farm about seventy miles north of Toulouse, France.[18] Based on birth order, his role in life would be to inherit the farm. During the winter months, he accompanied his brother Louis to the seminary. While there, John too felt called to be a priest.

SAINT JOHN GABRIEL PERBOYRE, C.M.

John entered the Vincentian seminary in 1816, and ten years later, was ordained a priest on September 23, 1826. During the next nine years, John spent five years teaching in and administering a high school seminary, one year teaching theology, and three years as assistant director of novices. While serving in formation ministry, John felt the continuing call to serve in China. Perhaps the God-given desire percolated because his brother had been assigned to China, but died en route at sea; or because two seminary classmates ministering in China wrote frequent letters to John about their experience.

Throughout the second half of 1834, John petitioned his superiors to send him to China. Concerns about his frail health, however, caused the superiors to refuse John's request. In February 1835, however, John writes to his priest uncle, "Fourteen years ago, I asked to go to China. I entered the [Vincentian] community for this purpose."[19] John continues:

> "I have great news to tell you. God has granted me a very special favor, of which I am most unworthy. When he deigned to give me a priestly vocation, the principal reason that moved me to respond . . . was the hope of being able to preach the gospel to unbelievers. I have never completely lost sight of this objective; the goal of the missions of China has always made my heart skip a beat. Well, my dear uncle, today my prayers were finally answered."[20]

John sailed from Le Havre in March 1835, and arrived at Macao six months later. Shortly before Christmas, John and other missionaries sailed six-hundred miles north to the coastal city Fuchien. Because of the prohibition of foreigners' entering China, John and the others disguised themselves with pigtails and mustaches. In later February, Catholic laity smuggled the missionaries onto Chinese soil. A few days later, John and a fellow Vincentian and four lay Catholics began the six-hundred mile trek inland to the central mission station located at Ho-nan, where John arrived in mid-August 1836.

For the next three years, John served in the provinces of Ho-nan and Hu-pei. Between September 1838 and Pentecost 1839, he preached seventeen parish missions. In September 1839, he was to begin another round of missions, but poor health prevented him. Although practicing the Catholic faith had been prohibited under penalty of death, the last two decades in China had been rather peaceful ones. A new viceroy in Ho-nan, however, wished to unleash a new persecution. He advised the mandarins to observe their populace in order to identify Catholic clergy and laity.

Suddenly, on the morning of September 8, 1839, while John was preparing to celebrate Mass, lay Catholics rushed to the priest's residence. They warned the priest that soldiers were en route to arrest the missionary. The priest ran for his life, and hid in a bamboo forest. The next day, however, he was discovered. During the next nine months, he was assigned to three successive prisons, where each one heightened mistreatment of the prisoner: at Ho-nan, officials interrogated him twice; at Hsiang-yang, he was interrogated four times, and was forced to kneel on iron chains for hours at a time; at Wu-ch'ang, he suffered more than twenty interrogations, and countless beatings with bamboo sticks across his mouth. The local Viceroy condemned the priest. Four months later, the emperor confirmed the death sentence. On September 11, 1840, soldiers led the missionary up the Red Mountain, where they tied him to an upright stake, with arms outstretched and roped to a crossbeam. The customary triple strangulation was applied; the first two times, the cord was released just before the prisoner asphyxiated, and the third time, the cord was tightened until he expired.

What had inspired and empowered this priest to die in defense of the Catholic faith? The answer lies in an excerpt from one of his conferences.

> "There is but one thing necessary," Our Lord tells us in the Gospel. But what is that one thing necessary? It is the imitation of him. We can only attain salvation through conformity with Jesus Christ. After our death we will not be asked if we have been scholars, if we have held prominent positions, if we have had people speak favorably about us in the world; but we will be asked if we have busied ourselves with the study and the imitation of Jesus Christ....
>
> Let us keep our eyes continuously fixed on Jesus Christ. Let us not content ourselves with catching one or two traits of our model, but let us enter into all his sentiments, let us acquire all his virtues. Let us start again, and let us continue every day without ever getting tired."[21]

20. ☩ Martyrs of Korea

Place: Seoul, Korea (now South Korea)
Fame: 103 Martyrs of Korea

Uniquely, the Catholic faith was brought to and was developed in Korea by lay people.[22] During the Japanese invasion and occupation of 1592 to1599, Japanese Catholic soldiers baptized some Koreans, nine of whom ministered in that island nation, and are included among the Martyrs of Japan.

Almost two centuries later, Korean diplomatic envoys who traveled regularly into China encountered Jesuit Catholic priests. The scholarly Koreans became interested in the teachings of Jesus and the Church, and continued their inquiry back home by reading and discussing various Catholic texts which the Jesuits had provided to them. In 1784, one of the envoys received baptism in China, and, upon his return home, organized the first Catholic community in Korea. Subsequently, laity instructed and baptized other laity. The first home-church was located at Myongdong, on which site stands the current Cathedral of Myongdong.

Korea is the only country in the world throughout the centuries, where the Catholic Church was founded, not by foreign missionaries, but spontaneously by the native people themselves. The Catholic Church is very proud of this fact. The Catholics in those days called one another "believing friends," abolished class distinctions, stopped offering sacrifices to their ancestors, and spread the faith, using books written in the Korean alphabet which is different from the Chinese characters. The Catholic community, which had been so miraculously founded, was detected by the government officials in March of 1785, and the Catholics were dispersed.[23]

The Korean government, which for two hundred years had prohibited foreign influences from entering the country, hence its name the Hermit Kingdom, began to persecute Catholics. In 1787, the first martyr died: Kim Bom-u who had provided his home as a church-house, was arrested, tortured, and exiled. In 1791 and 1794 a few more Catholics among the four thousand baptized practicing Catholics were killed. In 1801, over three-hundred out of ten-thousand total Catholics were killed on account of their faith. In 1839, ten thousand Catholics were killed, of whom seventy-nine are considered martyrs. All these persons were Koreans except for three Frenchmen, namely, one bishop and two priests, which resulted in a complete absence of priests in Korea until 1845. In that year, the first native Korean priest, Andrew Kim Taegon, arrived home from Macao. The next year, however, he was killed during the persecution which took the lives of hundreds of Korean Catholics. In 1849, the second native Korean priest arrived. Giving veracity to Tertullian's dictum that "the blood of martyrs is the seed of Christians," by the time of the 1866-1869 persecution, the Catholic population had grown to twenty-three-thousand, of which over ten-thousand suffered martyrdom, of whom twenty-six have been canonized. Relative calm and religious freedom evolved from Korea's opening to the outside world for commercial and political purposes. Two periods of additional persecution occurred, namely, in 1901, when sorcerers on the island of Cheju slaughtered seven hundred Catholics; and during the Korean Conflict in 1950-1953, when Communists from North Korea killed thousands of Catholics. In 1953, Catholics numbered 166,000 in the nation, and a decade later, numbered 628,000 in the South, with no reliable information available about the number of Catholics in the North.

Among the canonized 103 Martyrs of Korea are included 94 native Koreans and nine French clergymen. The martyrs included 92 laity, eight priests, and three bishops. Seven of the martyrs were sixty or older, and three were seventeen or younger. Because Korean law forbade the decapitation of minors, two of the youths were strangled to death, and the other one died beforehand from mistreatment in prison. Among the remaining hundred martyrs, 87 died by decapitation, and the others by strangulation, beatings, or from mistreatment in prison. Occupations ranged from the royal chamberlain, ladies in waiting at the royal court, a provincial governor, soldier, sailor, merchants, pharmacist, farmers and assistants to priests. These martyrs died between 1838 (1) and 1867 (1). Most of these witnesses died in 1839 (54). Unusual among the Korean martyrs is the large number of female martyrs: 48 out of 103.

Missing among these martyrs are representatives from the founding fathers, that is, those who suffered martyrdom during the persecutions of 1785, 1791, 1801 and 1815. Many of the canonized 103 martyrs had family elders who had died for the faith a generation or two earlier.

Representatives included in this book among the Martyrs of Korea include Andrew Kim Taegon (July 5), Paul Chong Hasang (September 22), Lawrence Imbert (September 20), Lucy Pak Hui-Sun (May 24), Agatha Yi (January 9), and Peter Yu Tae-Chol (October 31).

20. ☩ Saint Lawrence Imbert, M.E.P.

Place: Seoul, South Korea
Fame: Missionary bishop and martyr of Korea

Lawrence Marie Joseph Imbert (1796-1839) was born near Aix-en-Provence, France.[24] Because his parents could not afford to educate him, this eight-year old sought out a teacher for instructions. He entered the local seminary, and earned his keep by making and selling rosary beads.

At the seminary, he studied diligently, and completed theological studies earlier than the canonical age required for ordination. He disciplined his body by denying himself sleep, food, and warmth. Desiring to go to the foreign missions, he applied to the Society of Foreign Mission of Paris (*Societe des Missions Etrangeres de Paris*: MEP) After entering the Society in autumn 1818, he was ordained a priest on December 8, 1819. He left Paris on March 20, 1820, and embarked from Bordeaux on May 1 for Szechuan, China.

For the next fourteen years, Lawrence served effectively in China. He began his ministry by teaching for six months at the College General in Penang, after which he was transferred to Indochina (now Vietnam). Two years later, 1824, he returned to Szechuan Province, where he founded a seminary for native vocations at Moupin.

On April 26, 1836, Imbert was named to succeed Bishop Bruguinere as Vicar Apostolic of Korea. Bruguinere had never entered Korea because he had died en route at Somanja in October 1835. Imbert was ordained bishop in May 1837. The ordaining bishop describes Lawrence: "He is loved by all and is most indispensable. He speaks excellent Chinese and knows Chinese characters. He is good natured and mild, polite and outgoing, and brave too. For twelve years, he has served in Szechuan and has gained much experience. He is only forty-two and he has a talent for learning languages."[25]

In October 1836, Imbert entered Somanja, Inner Mongolia, where he resided with the Vincentian Fathers. A month later, he and his guides departed for Korea. Avoiding population centers, "the journey continued with the constant danger that they might be captured even before they could step foot on Korean land."[26] On December 17, Imbert's party crossed the border into Korea. Two weeks later, they arrived at Hanyang, the capital of Korea. On that day, fifty-four years after its establishment as a diocese, and seven years after its independence from China, Korea received its first residential bishop.

Bishop Imbert enjoyed the assistance of two confreres: Peter Maubant; and Jaques Honore Chastan. These three clergymen worked zealously. When the bishop arrived in Korea, Catholics numbered six thousand. One year later, Catholics had increased by 50%. The bishop writes about his active ministry:

> I am weary and am confronted with great danger from time to time. I wake up at 2:30 a.m. every day, and pray with the people at 3 a.m. At 3:30, I give baptism or the sacrament of confirmation to new believers, and then I celebrate Mass and offer a prayer of thanks. Thus, about fifteen to twenty believers can receive the sacraments before the sun rises.
>
> In the day, I hear the confessions of about the same number of believers. They receive the Eucharist the next morning and then leave. By then I am almost starving. This is because I wake up at 2:30 a.m. and it is not until lunchtime that I can have something to eat and even then the food is often not very nutritious. It is not easy to eat well in Korea, which is extremely cold and dry. After lunch, I take a rest and then I teach the students. When this is over, I hear confessions until it is dark.
>
> Only at 9 p.m. can I lie down to sleep on the ground, covering myself with a quilted blanket made from Mongolian wool. There is no bed or blanket in Korea. Therefore, my body is weak and I am constantly tired. I seem to have reached my limits. I am sure you understand our feelings when we say that we are not in the least afraid of the sword that will cut off our heads and free us from this difficult and exhausting life.[27]

In 1839, the Queen Dowager Kim assumed political power. In June, she initiated a bloody anti-Christian persecution. Bishop Imbert left Hanyang, and found refuge at the seaport town of Sanggol, Suwon. Fathers Maubant and Chastan joined him there. All three decided to remain in Korea.

A woman apostate seized the moment. Claiming that members of the Royal Court wished to learn more about the faith from Bishop Imbert, she inquired of believers until she discovered someone who knew the bishop's hiding place. The naïve believer led the traitor to the bishop's refuge. Meanwhile, the apostate alerted police who followed her. When the believer addressed the bishop, he replied, "You have been deceived by the devil."[28]

The next day, August 11, 1839, the bishop traveled to Hanyang, where the police arrested him. Interrogators asked about the locations of the two priests. Each time that the bishop refused to answer their questions, the police tightened the leg-screws binding his ankles. Soon, Fathers Maubert and Chastan turned in themselves. Day after day, police interrogated and tortured the three priests. None yielded information.

Under the directions of a governmental official, the three prisoners were stripped to the waist. Their hands were bound in front of their chests, and a stick was placed under each armpit. Their ears were pierced with arrows, and water and cement were thrown on their faces. Torturers dragged them by the sticks-under-armpits around the execution grounds, taunting them.[29]

The tortures stopped. The death sentence was proclaimed. A government official ordered the three to kneel on the ground. A sword swiftly separated their heads from their torsos. All three were buried on Noku Mountain.

22. ✢ Saint Paul Chŏng Ha-sang

Place: Seoul, Korea (now South Korea)
Fame: Martyr of Korea; lay leader

Five members of the family of Paul Chŏng Ha-sang (1795-1839) died as martyrs, and in 1984, Pope John Paul II canonized three of them among the 103 Martyrs of Korea: Paul, his mother, and sister.[30] When Chŏng was six, his father and older brother were martyred at Hanyang. Almost four decades later, Paul was beheaded for the faith at Seoul on September 22, 1839. His mother Cecilia Yu So-sa died in prison on November

23, 1839; and his elder sister Elizabeth Chŏng Chŏng-hye suffered decapitation on December 29, 1839.

Chŏng was born at Mahyon, Yanggungun in Kyŏnggi Province, near Seoul. His uncle Chŏng Yak-yong, who is counted among Korea's ancient scholars.

After Chŏng's father wrote and distributed the catechism, *Important Doctrines of Catholicism*, he was arrested during the anti-Catholic persecution which Shin-Yu had ordered, and which eliminated all Catholic clergy from Korea. From then on, Chŏng's family was stripped of ancestral properties and was reduced to poverty.

At twenty, Paul decided to re-invigorate the country's scattered, frightened, and priestless Catholics. He moved to Seoul. He obtained an entry level position in the Korean diplomatic corps, whereby he hoped to travel abroad and bring back priests into Korea. Nine times he traveled into China, and three times, to Manchuria. On visits to Peking (now Beijing) in 1816 and 1817, he communicated with the bishop of Peking, who agreed to send priests to Korea. Bishop Bruguiere was appointed, but he died before reaching Korea. Undaunted, Paul wrote directly and frequently to the pope at Rome. On September 9, 1831, the Vatican established the Vicariate Apostolic of Korea. When the Vatican asked the Paris Foreign Missionary Society to take on this mission, the French missionaries responded wholeheartedly. When the missionaries finally arrived, including Bishop Lawrence Imbert, Paul happily and effectively assisted the clergy. Bishop Imbert encouraged Paul to become a priest, and in early 1839, the bishop began instructing the young man.

A few months later, another persecution erupted. Paul forewent his studies. In hiding. Paul composed an explanation and defense of the Catholic faith. His famous *Sangje-sangso* (*A Letter to the Prime Minister*) was published in Hong Kong in 1887. Paul writes:

> Alas! What are we to make of those who point to gold and precious jewels and call them mud and gravel, or those who possess what is good to eat and claim it is inedible. They seem to regard the truth or falsehood of a doctrine to be quite irrelevant, and so they write off Catholic doctrine for no other reason than that it is foreign. But gold does not receive its value from the place where it is found, if it is truly gold then it is precious. Religion is

> the same. If it is true, whatever its region of origin, how can there be national boundaries in proclaiming it?[31]

On June 1, 1839, Paul was arrested with his mother and sister. Because he was considered a leader among the Catholics, he was singled out for particularly harsh torture. Paul Chŏng Ha-sang is credited with having "rehabilitated the Church, which was in danger of annihilation because of the severe persecutions, and made the establishment of the Vicariate Apostolic of Korea possible."[32]

26. ✠ Blessed John Baptist Mazzucconi, P.I.M.E.

Place: Papua New Guinea
Fame: Priest and martyr

Blessed John Baptist Mazzucconi, P.I.M.E.

In summer 1845, a few seminary classmates visited the Carthusian monastery at Pavia, twenty miles south of Milan, and spoke with the prior who had labored as a missionary in India.[33] This conversation led to a continuing correspondence between the youthful John Baptist Mazzucconi (1826-1855) and the prior. John, wishing to become a missionary, began to study English, French, and German. The seminarian confided to his spiritual director the desire to serve in the missions, to which the director responded, "You're crazy. Your India is here."[34]

In 1847, Pope Pius IX expressed publicly the hope that a seminary might be founded to prepare men for the missionary vocation. Soon, schools were founded at Milan in 1850, and at Rome in 1874. Later, the faculties of these two schools combined to form the *Pontificium Institutum pro Missionibus Exteris*, known popularly as the P.I.M.E. Fathers.

After ordination as a deacon in March 1850, John asked to be admitted to the Seminary for Foreign Missions. Two months later, on the same day he was ordained a priest, John received a letter of admission. He writes from the seminary at Saronno about the nascent community, "We pray, study, and laugh."[35] The members of the community formulated the Constitutions in which they committed themselves: "The Institute, from its very beginning, will attempt to have its own missions among the most neglected and primitive of peoples."[36] At this same time, the Marist Community wished to depart from its mission at Melanesia-Micronesia so the Vatican transferred responsibility for this mission field to the new Institute.

On March 16, 1852, the seven founding members of the Institute, i.e., five priests and two brothers, departed Milan for London, whence they sailed for Sydney. After a one-hundred-day voyage, the missionaries arrived on July 26, 1852 at the southeastern harbor of Australia. The Institute's members lived with the Marist Community for the next two months, learning the language and customs of the Papuans.

In fall 1852, the missionaries set out for the islands of Woodlark (now Muyua) and Rock. The seven saw a paradisiacal setting: forest-laden mountains and hillsides, white-sand beaches, and flowers aplenty. Ashore at Rock Island, Father John Mazzucconi plus two other priests and a lay brother discovered their home: a rain-soaked hut, inhabited by snakes and insects, devoid of food except taro root, and isolated from civilization except for an annual ship-visit which brought mail and foods.

Beginning their pre-evangelization of the peoples at Rock Island, the Italians listened to Papuans, then instructed the Pacific Islanders about rolling wheels, planting seeds, and constructing buildings out of bricks and mortar. The natives, however, proved obstinate. John writes, "It is just as useless to try to teach them how to sew, to purify stagnant water, to apply the basic principles of hygiene. Respect for tradition is absolute, as is the rejection of anything new. The inhabitants despise the missionaries and do not understand their motivation for coming to the island."[37]

Right from the start of John's two-and-a-half years on the island, he suffered from malaria and malnutrition. Consequently, he suffered daily fevers and sores, and diminution of his eye-sight. In January 1855, the P.I.M.E. superior required John to go to Australia to recover his health. The medical treatment received at Sydney helped John immediately. On May 25, 1855, he writes: "This health is a gift from God, which must therefore be used for God. And that is what I will do. I will set out again on the first ship and return to the island, see my 'children' once again, embrace the confreres, and place myself anew in the service of God; then He will take care of the rest."[38]

On August 18, John departed Sydney for Rock Island. A few days later, however, his confreres arrived at Sydney, after having abandoned their mission at Woodlark and Rock Islands. One confrere had become sick and died at Rock Island. The others had yielded to the obstinacy of the natives.

On September 7, when John returned to Rock Island, the natives gathered on the beach to witness his arrival. The captain of the boat became stuck on the coral reef. One canoe containing four natives went out to meet John. A friend named Puerer informed the priest that his confreres had left the islands. The same friend writes the following:

> Meanwhile, onshore, the natives decide to take advantage of the situation and release their pent-up hatred for the missionaries. They push off from the shore in many canoes and surround the ship. . . . One [of the natives], Aviocar, heads directly for the missionaries with his hand extended as if in greeting. But suddenly he pulls out an ax from beneath his loincloth and violently strikes at Father John's head. It is the beginning of the massacre. After John, all of the sailors are dismembered and their bodies are thrown into the sea.[39]

28. ✠ Saint Lorenzo Ruiz and Companions

***Place:** Manila, Philippines; and Nagasaki, Japan*
***Fame:** First martyrs of the Philippines, lay leaders*

Lorenzo Ruiz (c. 1600-1637) grew up at Binondo, on the outskirts of Manila.[40] His Chinese father and Filipina mother raised him in the Catholic faith. In the parish church, young Lorenzo served as an altar-boy, and participated in the Confraternity of the Holy Rosary. As an adult, he worked as the church's sacristan, whose duties included writing in calligraphy in the proper church books the names of recipients of sacraments. Lorenzo married, and fathered two sons and a daughter.

Saint Lorenzo Ruiz

At thirty-six, Lorenzo was accused of murder, but no evidence was presented to sustain the charge. The Dominican Fathers, who administered Lorenzo's parish, aided the defendant in fleeing the country.

The Dominicans hid Lorenzo on a boat. The ship was headed for Japan's "forbidden empire," where the Dominicans hoped to evangelize. On that providential embarkation on June 10, 1636, Lorenzo's companions included three Spanish Dominican priests including the religious superior Antonio Gonzalez, a Japanese Dominican priest, and their leprous lay guide Lazaro of Kyoto. The group departed from Bataan.

After passing three hundred fifty miles and three months, the monsoon-wearied sailors arrived at Okinawa. Although Okinawa was a vassal-state of Japan, less danger surrounded landing there than at Japan. The four priests and two laymen went ashore, hid their religious garb and sacred vessels, and sought out local Catholics. A few days later, soldiers arrested the six men, who remained imprisoned for the next year at the southern tip of Kyushu.

In September 1637, these prisoners were transported to Nagasaki. This provincial capital, which the Jesuits had founded in 1571, claimed a Catholic population of fifty thousand people. Besides ten churches, the city was blessed with a seminary, college, hospital, school for painting, and a printing press. "The Jesuit Fathers had made Nagasaki the glory of the Church in Japan and a stronghold of missionary expansion."[41] Since 1597, however, Catholics at Nagasaki had witnessed hundreds of martyrdoms.

On September 13, all the priests except for the religious superior were brought to the courtroom. Three days of interrogation and torture ensued. The two Spaniards held firm to their faith. The Japanese priest weakened under torture, but after a couple of days, reaffirmed his willingness to die for the faith. These missionaries suffered many tortures. Initially, the priests were forced to lie with their backs on the ground, while soldiers poured five hundred gallons of water through a funnel into each man's mouth. Meanwhile, a flat board was placed over each victim's stomach and soldiers jumped on the board, causing water to shoot from every orifice in the head and torso.[42] Another torture consisted of hanging the prisoner upside down by his feet, and dipping his head into a barrel full of water, causing him to suffocate, and then raising his head and inquiring if he wished to deny his faith. At the bottom of these water-filled barrels were sharpened stakes which would penetrate the prisoner's head. An additional practice consisted of placing embroidery needles under each prisoner's fingernails, and pushing the needles ever deeper into the fingers.[43] A universal practice in Japan included placing images of Jesus and Mary on the ground, upon which soldiers stamped, and on which they ordered prisoners to do the same.

On September 21, Lorenzo, Lazaro, and the priest superior Antonio Gonzalez received their turns at trial by torture. Lazaro, fearing the tortures, immediately gave up his faith. Father Antonio remained resolute in the faith. Lorenzo inquired if he would be exempted from the tortures if he apostatized. An interrogator left the room to place that question before a higher authority. During the few minutes' absence of the interrogator, Lorenzo reconsidered. As soon as the interrogator returned, and before he could say anything, Lorenzo spoke:

> Sir, what I said to you before, I said it like an ignorant, without knowing what I was saying. I am a Christian, and this I profess until the hour of my death; and for God I shall give my life; and although I did not come to Japan to be a martyr but because I could not stay in Manila, however, as a Christian and for God I shall give my life. And so do with me as you please.[44]

Two days later, new tortures were applied. Again, Lorenzo was asked, "If we grant you life, will you renounce your faith?" The layman replied, "That I will never do, because I am a Christian, and I shall die for God, and for Him I will give many thousands of lives if I had them. And so, do with me as you please."[45] That same night, Father Antonio died from mistreatment.

On September 27, graves were dug in front of five gallows. The five prisoners rode on horseback to the site. Their mouths were covered so that they could not preach to on-lookers. All five were hanged upside down, and were lowered halfway into their respective holes. Two semi-circular boards were placed around their waists. The posture created enormous pressure on the body. Knife slashes were made on the men's temples and foreheads to relieve some of the pressure. The deaths were intended to be slow and painful. Two days later, officials, wanting to go on a hunting trip, decided to end the torture. Soldiers discovered that Lazaro and Lorenzo already were dead, but the three priests, the soldiers quickly decapitated. Lest the local Christians gather the martyrs' remains as relics, soldiers burned the corpses, and tossed the ashes into the nearby sea.

OCTOBER

5. ☩ Matthew Kavukatt

Place: Changanacherry, Kerala, India
Fame: The "Good Shepherd" Archbishop

As a seminarian, priest, bishop and archbishop, Matthew Kavukatt (1904-1969) gained the reputation of sainthood.[1]

He grew up as his parents' fifth child in the village of Pravithanam in the diocese of Pala. "According to tradition, of the sixty-four Namboothiri families that had received the faith from Saint Thomas, one was Kuthukallunkal of which Kavukatt was a descendant."[2]

Prior to entering the seminary, Matthew assisted at daily Mass, read the Scriptures, and pondered his spiritual path. He invited local youths to visit the Blessed Sacrament, and instructed them in praying. The money he had earned as a substitute teacher for six months, he gave to the poor. A high school classmate commented about Matthew, "He was calm and serene, disciplined and well-deserving of the unanimous praise of all the teachers."[3]

In June 1928, Matthew entered Saint Thomas Minor Seminary at Kottayam. Two years later, he advanced to Puthenpally Seminary where he undertook the professional studies of philosophy and theology. On December 21, 1935, Matthew was ordained a priest. A seminary classmate writes about the deceased archbishop, "I am not aware of his having got (sic) angry all the five years I was with him in the seminary."[4]

For the first fifteen years of priesthood, he served as headmaster of Poonjar Cambridge School, as spiritual director and vice-rector at Saint Thomas Minor Seminary, headmaster of Saint Dominic's Malayalam School, and assistant parish priest at Kanjirapally. In 1941, he was assigned as instructor of Syriac in Saint Berchman's College at Changanacherry, and director of Saint Thomas Hostel and later, of Saint Joseph Hostel.

MATTHEW KAVUKATT

In August 1950, Father Matthew was named Bishop of Changanacherry. Twice, he had declined to accept the position, but the Holy See prevailed upon him. The new bishop chose as his motto, "*Caritate Servire*" ("to serve with love"). The Vatican increased the jurisdiction of the diocese to include Kottar, Trivandrum, and Cape Comerin, after which, in 1956, Matthew was named Archbishop of Changanacherry. The archbishop played a significant role in having Prime Minister Pandit Nehru dismiss the communist government from Kerala. During his archepiscopacy, he initiated building houses for the poor, which program the government of Kerala soon adopted as its own. In anticipation of Vatican Council II, he served on the Preparatory Commission for Oriental Churches, although poor health prohibited him from attending the Council. In 1964, he participated in the Eucharistic Congress at Bombay (now Mumbai), and the following year, he inaugurated the Diocesan Catechetical Center. In November 1966, he suffered two heart attacks, and from their consequences, he died the following October 5. As bishop and archbishop, he prayed often before the Blessed Sacrament, and practiced great devotion to Mary and Joseph. The rosary, he prayed daily. He urged his flock, "Offer to God all your troubles. He will bring it all to a happy conclusion."[5]

The lay president of the Catholic Congress and Central Council of the Saint Vincent de Paul Society said of the archbishop, "Undoubtedly he was a saint. He excelled in meekness, calmness, spirit of dedication, sympathy, 'becoming all things to all men'."[6]

12. ✠ The Talangpaz Sisters: Dionicia, A.R., and Cecilia Rosa, A.R.

Place: Calumpit, Bulacan, Philippines
Fame: Foundresses of the Beatorio de San Sebastian de Calumpang (now the Congregation of the Augustinian Recollect Sisters)

Perseverance and prayer characterized the lives of the Talangpaz Sisters: Dionicia (1691-1732) and Cecilia Rosa (1693-1731).[7]

Dionicia and Cecilia Rosa were the youngest of their parents' four living children. The two daughters benefited from their parents' noble heritage and wealth. They received instruction at home in reading and writing, in Arabic and Spanish, and public speaking.

At twenty-five, both sisters dedicated themselves to living at home the eremetical life.. They separated themselves from the usual social activities enjoyed by families and friends in order to dedicate themselves to prayer and asceticism. "They left their house only to hear Mass daily and receive the holy sacraments either in the parish church or in the barrio chapel."[8]

They wished to join a Third Order since in that colonial period, native born Filipinos and Filipinas were not allowed to join the first two orders: priesthood and sisterhood. Three times between 1716 and 1718, the Talangpaz sisters requested admission into the Third Order of the Augustinians. Each time, the Augustinian pastor refused their request. After prayer and consultation with their spiritual director and family, the pair decided to leave Calumpit and take the one-day trip to Calumpang, a district of Manila, where they hoped to spend their days in prayer at the Shrine of Our Lady of Mount Carmel.

At the shrine in Calumpang, the sisters' daily schedule consisted of attending Mass at dawn and remaining in the church until ten each morning, returning home for their meal and housework, returning to the church in late afternoon for Vespers and the Angelus, and taking care of the linens and vestments needed for the sanctuary and sacristy. From 1719 to 1725, the two sisters continued their regimen of prayer, penance, and productive labor. On the feast of Our Lady of Mount Carmel in

1725, the pair requested of the Recollect prior of the Convent of San Sebastian if they might form a beatorio associated with the Recollects' house. After meeting with his councilors, the prior agreed to the request. He had a small house built behind the priory for the pious women.

The sisters donned the religious habit and adopted religious names: Dionicia chose to be called Sor Dionisia de Santa Maria; and Cecilia Rosa, Sor Cecilia Rosa de Jesus. Within a few months, four more women joined the beatorio. Other candidates kept arriving. The Recollect Fathers began feeling stressed by the demands on both their finances and their time for screening candidates. The prior precipitously called the half-dozen beatas, and shouted that he was closing the beatorio. He demanded that the women return their religious habits, and leave the property. He personally demolished the house which he had had built for the women. The women fled from the outraged churchman.

After a respite of some days, the Talangpaz sisters returned to the prior, and begged that he re-consider his action. The prior, after some reflection and encouragement from confreres, relented. He welcomed the women warmly, and promised to build a larger house. To defray costs, and to assist the priests, the sisters arranged to incorporate as part of their apostolate the care of the linens and vestments of the Convent of San Sebastian.

In a little while, the other four sisters re-joined the original pair, and two more women came to make a community of eight. The first superior of the beatorio was Mother Dionicia. Three years after co-founding the beatorio, Mother Cecilia Rosa de Jesus became deathly ill. The prior permitted her to profess simple vows. Rosa died four months later, on July 31, 1731. The next year, her elder sister Dionicia neared death, took vows, and died on October 12, 1732.

12. ✠ Walter Ciszek, S.J.

Place: *Siberia, U.S.S.R., (now the Russian Federation)*
Fame: *Spent 22 faith-filled, long-suffering years in prison camps*

Walter Ciszek (1904-1984) was born and raised at Shenandoah, Pennsylvania, about one hundred miles northwest of Philadelphia.[9] His father worked as a coal miner and saloon-owner; his mother cared for the couple's thirteen children, of which Walter was the seventh.

After graduating from Saint Casimir's Elementary School, Walter entered Saints Cyril and Methodius Seminary at Orchard Lake, Michigan. After hearing a Jesuit priest speak about their Society's young saint Stanislaus Kostka, Walter became inspired to enter the Society of Jesus.

WALTER CISZEK, S.J.

A few months after entering Saint Andrew's Novitiate at Poughkeepsie, New York; Walter read Pope Pius XI's letter addressed "To all seminarians, especially our Jesuit sons," seeking volunteers to minister in the Communist-controlled Soviet Union.[10] Walter submitted his name. After completing studies at Wernersville, Pennsylvania, and Woodstock, Maryland, Walter sailed for Rome, where he studied at the Gregorian University and the Collegio Russico. He and another seminarian Nestrov, a Russian Jesuit, devoured everything they could read about Russian geography, history, language, culture, and the Oriental liturgical rite. After ordination to priesthood at Rome on June 24, 1937, Father Walter was assigned to a parish in Albertyn, Poland.

In September 1939, just after Germany and the Soviet Union had signed a mutual non-aggression pact, both countries invaded Poland. Father Walter and his friend Nestrov obtained false working permits for the Ural Mountain region, and in March 1940, fled with other Poles in a railway-boxcar for Russia. At Tepkaya-Gora, due east of Moscow, Father Walter used an alias to obtain work as an unskilled laborer hauling logs from the river. He and Nestrov periodically walked into the woods, where one said Mass while the other stood guard. They used a tree stump for the altar, and spoke the memorized Mass prayers. At night, the two wandered into the woods where they instructed and administered sacraments to sincere laity.

In June 1941, Germany invaded the Soviet Union. Within weeks, the Russian NKVD (which soon would become known as the KGB) arrested hundreds of people, including Father Walter. For the next two months, the KGB beat Father Walter with rubber clubs during interrogations, and locked him in a cell with little ventilation. Having concluded that Father Walter was a German spy, the KGB transferred their prisoner to Lubianka Prison in Moscow. For the next four years, Father Walter's living quarters consisted of a cell measuring six feet by ten feet. The priest-prisoner was allowed out of his cell twenty minutes daily for a walk around the courtyard. He created a routine of praying morning and evening prayers, meditation, Mass Prayers without celebrating Mass, the Rosary, and the Angelus.

At Lubianka, Father Walter's initial nine months consisted of unrelenting questioning. Guards could not comprehend the selfless ministry of the priest. Presuming he was involved in espionage, they asked him to spy for them at the Vatican. After many months of discussion, when the prisoner refused to sign an agreement to spy for the government, the guards removed the incorrigible prisoner.

In July 1942, Father Walter was sentenced to fifteen years of hard labor in Siberia. He remained imprisoned at Lubianka and Butirka for a combined four years, before being sent to slave-labor camps above the Arctic Circle at Dudinka and Norilsk. Besides his manual labor, Father Walter worked also as a priest. At Dudinka, he celebrated Mass for the first time in five years. At Norilsk, he met a dozen priests from the Baltic region and Poland, and these men encouraged each other and the laity who came to them.

Three months before completing his fifteen-year sentence, he was released from prison in April 1955. He was told that he could not leave Siberia. In Norilsk, Father Walter took up residence with two priest friends. The three shared a small apartment. Laity came cautiously to the apartment. The three priests began celebrating Sunday Masses, which oftentimes were followed by baptisms, weddings, and visits to the sick.

At times, officials warned Father Walter not to engage in "missionary work," and "subversive activities."[11] During Easter Week 1958, governmental officials, intending to silence him, gave him ten days to leave Norilsk. He traveled seven-hundred miles south to Krasnoyarsk, where the lack of official communication about him left him fairly free. Eventually, authorities ordered him to live at nearby Abakan.

In September 1963, the KGB called him to their office. Without explanation they transported him to Moscow. On October 11, 1963,

Russian authorities exchanged Father Walter and another American for a Russian couple who had been convicted of spying in the United States. The next day, he arrived at New York City.

Father Walter spent his next twenty-one years in the USA, composing a manuscript which led to two books: *With God in Russia* (1964) and *He Leadeth Me* (1973), and teaching and counseling at Fordham University, where he died.

How did he survive? "Providence," he answers. He continues, "God has a special purpose, a special love, a special providence for all those he has created. God cares for each of us individually, watches over us, provides for us."[12]

16. ✠ Blessed Augustine Thevarparampil

Place: Ramapuram, Kerala, India
Fame: Apostle of the Untouchables

Augustine Thevarparampil (1891-1973), popularly known as Kunjachan, dedicated virtually all the years of his priesthood to serving the "untouchables," or "suppressed people" known officially as the Dalits.[13] Until the Indian Constitution was passed in1949, the "untouchables" had been regarded as outside the Hindu caste system. They had been relegated to the lowest positions of labor.

Kunjachan was born at Ramapuram, just south of Madras (now Chennai). Descendants of the original sixty-four Saint Thomas Christian families had founded his village in 1450. After the original settlement expanded, Kunjachan's parish was established in 1599. Kunjachan, the youngest of five children, attended local schools until he traveled to Mannanam to study at Saint Ephraem High School. In 1913, he entered the minor seminary at Changanacherry, and two years later, graduated to the major seminary at Puthenpally. On December 21, 1921, he was ordained a priest. During these years of education and formation, Kunjachan gained the reputation for possessing an easy-going, likeable disposition. While his classmates observed that he excelled in prayerfulness, the faculty noted that Kunjachan did not excel in academics. Everybody

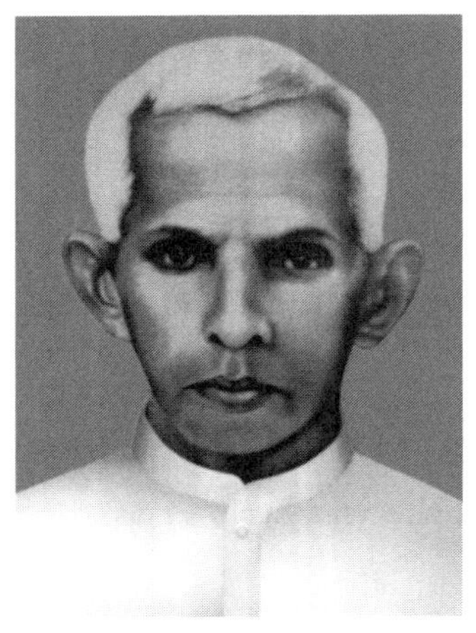

Blessed Augustine Thevarparampil

enjoyed kidding Kunjachan about his height; throughout his school years, he was always the shortest in his class. Even his ordaining bishop joked that Kunjachan might be too small to ordain, since the young man would be too short to reach the tabernacle on most altars.

After ordination, Kunjachan spent the next fifty years always as an assistant pastor, and never as pastor. After serving a total of four years at Ramapuram, Kadanad, and Manathoor, he was assigned back to Ramapuram, where the young priest met with Dalits for the first time. Soon, over two hundred untouchables requested and received baptism. Kunjachan was inspired by this experience to dedicate the remainder of his life to the evangelization and service of the Dalits.

Kunjachan searched out the Dalits. Because of their oppressed social status, it was difficult to locate the Dalits. They often hid themselves from the public view.

> Even as late as the first half of the twentieth century, Pulayas and Pariahs lived in inhuman conditions in small huts in hilly areas and caves. They believed in superstitions and did not enjoy even basic amenities of life. For centuries, they were considered untouchables; none of them owned a piece of land and caste Hindus kept them at a distance. They were illiterate and their children were denied admission in schools. They were not allowed to use public roads, go near temples nor places of Hindu worship nor schools and public places.[14]

As Kunjachan walked, he prayed for his people. As he found them, he spoke to each one-on-one. He came to know and call people by name. He instructed them, forgave men and women for their habitual drunkenness, baptized them, and when they drifted from the faith under the pressure of anti-conversion legislation, recovered them for the faith. Although Dalit women were forbidden by tradition to wear any clothing above the waist, he gathered non-Dalit women to provide blouses for these deprived women. He himself lived a simple lifestyle, in imitation of the Dalits. What few rupees he accumulated, he distributed to Dalit families at times of births and deaths.

Beginning in 1961, he felt the ill-effects of age and sickness. He remained at home more often, praying for his people. Now, the Dalits came to visit him. For his impending death, he purchased the simplest of caskets. Monies that would have been spent on traditional death-anniversary ceremonial meals, he requested to be spent instead on Masses to be said for the repose of his soul. He wrote in his will, "I do not possess anything, either landed property or cash; neither do I owe anybody anything."[15] He asked to be buried among the Dalits.

20. ✠ Saint Magdalene of Nagasaki

Place: Nagasaki, Japan
Fame: Martyr

The devoutly Catholic parents of Magdalene (c. 1600-1634) raised her in the faith.[16] In 1620, when the government killed her parents on account of their being Catholic, young Magdalene deepened her faith.

Around this same time, members of the Augustinian community arrived in Japan. Magdalene served as a catechist for these missionaries, and assisted them in learning the language and customs of the native people. While ministering closely with the Augustinian friars, she became attracted to their spirituality, which balanced interior reflection and community action. In 1625, she requested and received admission into the Augustinian Third Order.

Since the start of the anti-Christian persecution in 1597, the waves of persecutions had grown increasingly severe. The government's plan expanded from expelling foreign missionaries to intimidating native Catholics. After the Great Persecution of 1622, during which thousands of native Catholics suffered martyrdom, Magdalene, like many other Japanese Catholics, fled to the hills.

Beginning in 1632, a series of her successive spiritual directors suffered martyrdom. In 1634, after the fourth spiritual director was arrested and killed, she simply declared publicly to the governmental soldiers that she too was a Christian.

Government authorities imprisoned her. For thirteen days, they tortured her by hanging her from her feet suspended over a garbage pit. When she died, the political leaders took down her body, and burned the corpse to ashes.

31. ✢ Saint Peter Yu Tae-ch'ŏl

Place: *Seoul, Korea (now South Korea)*
Fame: *Youngest martyr of the 103 Korean Martyrs*

Peter Yu Tae-ch'ŏl (1826-1839), the youngest of the 103 Korean Martyrs, grew up in a family of mixed religion: his father was Catholic, whereas his mother and older sister chose not to convert.[17] Peter's father earned his living as a governmental interpreter, but when officials discovered their employee was Catholic, he was arrested and imprisoned for six months, after which time he suffered decapitation. Fearful, Peter's mother and sister urged the boy to renounce his Catholic faith. The young boy, however, remained steadfast.

After the anti-Catholic persecution of 1839 had erupted, Peter, wishing to imitate his father, walked into the offices of the governmental authorities, and identified himself as a Catholic. The local judge urged the youth to renounce his faith. Peter refused. Police imprisoned him. Soon, police brought him before another judge, who similarly urged the youth to deny his faith. Again, Peter refused. The police returned the youth to prison.

In prison, Peter suffered much mistreatment. One time, a prison guard whacked a long tobacco pipe against the boy's leg, which ripped away a lengthy strip of flesh. The guard asked angrily if the boy still believed in his God. Peter replied, "Yes. I certainly do. I am not afraid of being hit."[18] Another guard threatened to stuff a burning coal into Peter's mouth. Peter opened his mouth wide, and challenged the officer to follow through on this threat. The guard chose not to torture the boy in that matter. Another time, soldiers beat Peter so badly that he fainted. When he returned to consciousness, his fellow prisoners tried to soothe his pain. The boy responded, "Don't worry. I will not die because of this pain."[19] The boy seemed fearless.

"Peter was interrogated fourteen times and was tortured on fourteen occasions. He was whipped six hundred times and beaten with a cudgel forty-five times. His whole body was covered with wounds, his bones were broken and his flesh was torn off."[20] Young Peter, however, maintained a smiling face. He radiated a love of God, which seemed to ridicule the adult torturers. One time, Peter took a piece of flesh that had been whipped off his shoulder and threw it at the prison guard. Bystanders were shocked at his bravery. At least ten witnesses testified to Peter's tortures and courage.

No matter how often and how severely this thirteen-year old was beaten, Peter remained alive. Frustrated over the guards' apparent inability to beat the boy to death, government authorities ordered the boy to be strangled to death. The death sentence was executed on September 25, 1839. Father and son were canonized together.

NOVEMBER

7. ✝ Constant Lievens, S.J.

Place: Calcutta (now Kolkata); and Chotanagpur (now includes the States of Bihar, Jharkhand, Madhya Pradesh and Orissa), India
Fame: Defender of the tribals, Apostle of Chotanagpur

Constant Lievens (1856-1893) was born and raised at Moorslede, Belgium.[1] He received his elementary education locally, his secondary education at Roeselare, and his professional studies in philosophy and theology at Brugge.

After entering the Society of Jesus in October 1878, Constant made religious profession two years later, and immediately was missioned to India. After arriving at Calcutta in December 1880, he undertook learning another culture with its new customs, languages, and ways of social interactions. He observed perceptively and listened attentively to the Madurai people. After being ordained a priest at Calcutta on January 14, 1883, he received two successive mission assignments: at Calcutta in 1883, and Chotanagpur in 1885. In August 1888, the Jesuits appointed him director of the mission house located at Ranchi.

Whereas previous missionaries had provided the people with spiritual consolations and material goods, Father Constant Lievens undertook defending the people from unscrupulous landowners and moneylenders. The priest studied British Law as it applied to India, sought out lawyers supportive of his causes, spent countless hours preparing court cases, and defended the lowly tribal members in the courts. The priest was slow to baptize Indians who wanted to become Catholics; instead, he urged them to study the catechism, to refrain from labor on Sunday, and to avoid invoking the millions of Hindu gods. During his seven years of ministry in Madurai, thousands of tribals converted to Catholicism. When he had arrived at Chotanagpur in 1885, only fifty-six tribals identified themselves as Catholics, and when he left seven years later, the number of Catholics had burgeoned to more than seventy thousand.

This seemingly indefatigable priest contracted tuberculosis in mid-1892. A few months later, he departed India for Belgium for temporary rest and recuperation. Father Constant, however, never returned to his adopted country; he died at Louvain, Belgium on November 7, 1893. He died at such a young age, that he had never made his final profession of vows. He had labored a dozen years in India.

15. ✝ Blessed Mary of the Passion, F.M.M.

Place: *Ootacamund (now Udagamandalam), Tamil Nadu, India*
Fame: *Founder of the Institute of the Franciscan Missionaries of Mary*

Helene Marie Philippine de Chappotin de Neuville (1839-1904) was born in Nantes, France.[2] Her parents and their five children lived in rural Le Fort under the same roof as Helene's maternal uncle and aunt with their six children. Helene was blessed with a strong self-will and a deep religious spirit. When the mother punished her daughter by taking away the child's book, Helene countered by writing her own "book." When Helene was playing with dolls, she realized, "I was taking a lot of trouble over this empty shell, this thing of cloth and plaster, which had no love for me. So I cast it aside. I had understood that loving and being loved perfectly was where true happiness lay, and so dolls no longer interested me."[3]

Blessed Mary of the Passion, F.M.M.

At Vannes, to where the family moved, Helene's older sister prepared the younger sibling for First Communion. On the occasion of Helene's First Communion at ten, she writes, "I felt I belonged so completely to God after this First Communion that it seemed to me that I would not be greatly missed here on earth; I begged God to take me before I could commit any sin."[4]

A turning point occurred when Helene was seventeen. While making a spiritual retreat, she experienced "something of what happened to Saint Paul on the road to Damascus. . . . It seemed to me that no barriers existed between God and myself."[5]

She entered the Poor Clares in December 1860. Later, she wrote about her first visit to the Poor Clare Monastery prior to her entrance: "At that moment, my vocation was settled without my being even aware of it. Poverty took possession of my heart. I became a daughter of Saint Francis, and never have I ceased to be."[6] On January 23, 1861, Helene had a profound experience of God, whereby she felt a call to "absolute love".[7] In this experience, she accepted the name: Mary Victim of Jesus and of Jesus Crucified. This name became for Helene the foundation of her identity.[8] This experience so overwhelmed her that she became ill, and her family brought her home to Le Fort.

Sometime later, Helene learned about the recently founded congregation of the Society of Mary Reparatrix. This religious community dedicated itself to Eucharistic adoration in the spirit of Mary at the foot of the cross in reparation for the sins of the world. In May 1864, Helene traveled to Paris, where she entered the Reparatrix. On the feast of the Assumption 1864, she received her religious habit and name: Mary of the Passion. At the beginning of 1865, Mother Mary Jesus, the foundress and Superior General of the Reparatrix came to the novitiate in Toulouse, and said to the young sister, "Passion, I am sending you away."[9] The response was equally terse, "I will go wherever you send me."[10] On March 19, 1865, after pronouncing private vows, Mary of the Passion with two other sisters sailed from Marseilles. Six weeks later, the trio arrived at Trichinopoly in southern India. Mary of the Passion studied the Tamil language, and adjusted well to the challenge of being Christian in an overwhelmingly Hindu country. In May 1866, the Superior General appointed Mary superior of the local house, and six months later, the provincial of all three community houses in the Madurai region.

Challenges abounded for the young provincial. She belonged to a community which had originated in Western Europe, and which asked her to serve in South Central Asia. Her community was contemplative, but the local Church needed active sisters. Mary of the Passion adjusted to the ministries of education, health care and child care.

Difficulties arose regarding how the Reparatrix Sisters might apply the community's charism at Madurai: the place of the missionary Sister in the existing structures of evangelization, and the difficulties of communication between India and Europe. Because of differences in visions of applying the charism, the Superior General in Paris removed Mary of the Passion in Madurai as provincial, and named her superior of the local house at Ootacamund. Mary wrote to the new provincial assuring her of obedience and cooperation. Other sisters from the Madurai region wrote to the Superior General, and requested that she might reconsider her decision. The Superior General sent an assistant to Madurai. The assistant presented the local Reparatrix Sisters with a clear choice: either to accept a list of juridical and pastoral demands, or to leave the Society of Mary Reparatrix. After several days of prayer and discernment, the majority of the sisters in the three Madurai houses decided to leave the Reparatrix Sisters and to join Mother Mary, where she had remained silent at Ootacamund.[11]

The Vicar Apostolic of Coimbatore took the disenfranchised sisters under his protection as a diocesan congregation, and called them the Missionaries of Mary. Necessarily, Mother Mary, a few other sisters, and laity traveled to Rome to submit to the pope and Propaganda Fide the case for establishing a new religious community. The pope accepted the group as an Institute in January 1877. Mother Mary was named the first Superior General, was urged to develop a novitiate in France, and to write a *Constitution*. In April 1877, Mary of the Passion drew up a *Plan of the Institute of the Missionaries of Mary*. Mary of the Passion was the first woman to found a missionary institute for women.

In June 1882, Mary of the Passion met with the definitor general of Orders of Friars Minor. These two took steps towards having the Missionaries of Mary enter the Franciscan Order.[12] The new congregation opened a house in Rome at this time.

On January 23, 1883, however, the cardinal-vicar of Rome reduced the sisters' Roman community to four sisters, and stipulated that their Roman convent was to be only a 'procure." On March 1, the same cardinal deposed Mary as Superior General, and forbade her to write to any of her communities. Mary suffered not only having been removed as Superior

General, but also not having her side of the story listened to. From her writings during this time, Mary reveals that she spent long-suffering hours of prayer before the Eucharist, wherein she contemplated the meaning of the Paschal Mystery, and refined her God-given charism.

One year later, March 28,1884, the Holy Father re-instated Mother Mary as Superior General. One bishop had persevered in re-opening the case, and presenting the truths of the matter. During the summer, the Institute held a General Chapter at Chatelets, France, and its members unanimously re-elected Mary as Superior General.

In 1885, Propaganda Fide approved the community's *Constitution* and its name: Institute of the Franciscan Missionaries of Mary. The community grew by leaps and bounds throughout Africa, South Central and Far East Asia, Europe and North America. After having ministered for a dozen years in India, 1865 to 1877, Mother Mary spent the remaining years of her life at the motherhouse in Italy. In addition to her far-reaching travels, Mary of the Passion authored five books on *Liturgical and Franciscan Meditations*, produced biographies about the saints, and wrote extensively on spiritual, formational and juridical matters. She labored diligently for the growth of the community, and insisted strongly on the importance of communication for the unity of a missionary Institute. At sixty-five, she became ill, and died shortly thereafter on November 15, 1904.

16. ✠ Venerable Aurelian of the Blessed Sacrament, O.C.D.

Place: Puthenpally and Alwaye (now Aluva), in Kerala, India
Fame: Seminary rector, known as "Apostle of the Eucharist"

For fifty-one years in India, Basque-born Father Aurelian of the Blessed Sacrament (1887-1963) devoted his life to the formation and education of seminarians.[13] Two years after his ordination to priesthood in 1910, responding to the Holy See's request for missionaries, Aurelian volunteered to work in India, where he spent the rest of his life as professor, spiritual director, vice-rector and rector. For him, the center of the priest's

Venerable Aurelian of the Blessed Sacrament, O.C.D.

life was the Eucharist, and the promotion of devotion to the Eucharist earned for him the encomium, "Apostle of the Eucharist."

Aurelian, whose secular name was Pedro Landeta y Azcueta, was born and raised in the village of Artunduaga de Basauri on the outskirts of Bilbao in northwestern Spain. On his parents' farm, this eldest of seven siblings grew up plowing fields and pasturing cattle. At ten, precociously serious and spiritual, he sensed the stirrings of vocation after hearing visiting priests preach. Later in life, Father Aurelian reflects, "I decided to become a priest like them."[14]

In 1902, at fifteen, he entered the novitiate of Carmel, where he took the name Aurelian of the Blessed Sacrament. Eight years later, he was ordained a priest.

Shortly after ordination, Father Aurelian volunteered for the mission of Verapoly, India. He and his confrere Brother Zacharias were sent to Rome, where they studied missionary methodology. In September 1912, the pair departed from Rome to Naples, whence they sailed for Bombay (now Mumbai), and reached Cochin in mid-October. Although Aurelian had hoped to serve amongst the poor, his superiors assigned him to minister among the seminarians.

Aurelian ministered to seminarians for a half-century as professor and spiritual director in the Apostolic Seminary at Puthenpally, as rector in the Pontifical Seminary at Aluva, and as vice-rector of the major seminary at Carmelgiri. Overall, he taught Church History for thirty years, served as Spiritual Director for thirty years, worked as Vice-Rector for fourteen years, and served as Rector for fifteen years. During his half-century in the seminary apostolate, Father Aurelian participated in the formation and education of over 1,500 priests.

He served his religious community as local superior, provincial delegate, and provincial. During the decade beginning in 1922, he authored three spiritual theology books: *Cursus Asceticus* on the purgative, illuminative and contemplative way of the mystical life; *Thesaurus Electorum*, which provided meditative readings and prayers; and the *Mirror of Priests*, a collection of his meditations on the priesthood. In the seminary, Father Aurelian emphasized the centrality of the Eucharist in the life of the priest, writing: "A priest who does not have a personal love for the Eucharist and true devotion does not deserve to be a priest."[15]

Devotion to the Eucharist characterized Father Aurelian's life. In 1928, he became the national director of the Priests' Eucharistic League. During his seventeen year tenure, he tripled the membership of the League from its original one thousand priests. In 1931, he organized the National Eucharistic Congress at Goa, and six years later, he repeated the same feat at Madras (now Chennai). For the laity, he promoted initially daily adoration, and eventually nocturnal adoration. From an original few thousand devotees of Eucharistic adoration, he oversaw the growth of this devotion to 180,000 persons.

Father Aurelian's final days were spent in praying his usual devotions: the Passion of Jesus, the Stations of the Cross, plus devotions to the Sacred Heart of Jesus, the Blessed Mother, and Saint Joseph. Rheumatism, which had afflicted him for the last three decades, worsened his already weakened condition, and led to death by pneumonia at seventy-seven.

On having been appointed rector in 1944, he left his pastoral position of spiritual director to take up the primarily administrative role of rector. In the transition, he assured the students,

> I am with you more than before. I am completely at your service. The measure of my service to God will be the measure of my service to you. . . . I have only one policy, to help you to attain your noble ideal, that is, to become learned and holy priests. From now on, to live for you alone is a personal duty. I will offer God with complete willingness the sacrifice He expects from me.[16]

16. ✠ Blessed Veronica of the Passion, A.C.

Place: Mangalore, India
Fame: Foundress of Apostolic Carmel

Sophie Leeves (1823-1906) was born at Constantinople, the first of five children of a distinguished English couple.[17] Sophie's father Henry Daniel

Blessed Veronica of the Passion, A.C.

Leeves was serving as Anglican chaplain to the British Ambassador at Constantinople. The father was an Oxford scholar, and a descendant of a family famous for its heritage of Protestant ministers. Sophie's mother, Marina Haultain, was the daughter of an English colonel, whose family boasted of many soldiers and sailors. The parents provided an exemplary Christian upbringing. "Sophie inherited from her parents a largeness of heart, fiery ardour, indomitable courage, perseverance in the face of difficulties, love for the poor, and, above all, deep faith in God and love for the Scriptures."[18]

Sophie and her siblings received a marvelous education. She learned French, Italian, and ancient Greek, which enabled her to read the New Testament in the original. She studied vocal and instrumental music. Because her parents envisioned travel as part of education, Sophie visited nearly all the countries of Europe, and "lived in London, Paris, Rome, Athens, Bethlehem, Geneva, Naples and Malta."[19]

Sophie developed a deep faith and spirituality. Raised in the Anglican religion, she received First Communion and Confirmation at seventeen. While living in England, she imbibed the contemporary fascination with the Oxford Movement, which John Newman had originated; his conversion from Protestantism to Catholicism in 1845, after years of scholarly study of Church History, impressed her.

Returning to Athens, she received a marriage proposal from an English marine. Her mother accepted on the daughter's behalf. The marriage was planned for two years later. In the interim, Sophie enjoyed a spiritual experience while lying in bed: "She was awakened by a sweet and clear interior voice which said, 'Peace I leave you. My peace I give to you, not as the world gives.'"[20] She decided to forego marriage, and to enter religious life in the Anglican Church. She writes, "Jesus has taken possession of my heart and he has driven out all other affections and all other desires except to become a nun somehow or other." [21] As was her custom while in Malta, she went to pray at the Catholic Cathedral, where she, believing in the Real

Presence, knelt before the Blessed Sacrament. Some weeks later, she made a private vow of perpetual virginity. A couple of years later, after much instruction and prayer, Sophie and her sister converted to the Catholic faith on February 3, 1850. Her mother was heartbroken.

In September 1851, Sophie entered the Congregation of Saint Joseph of the Apparition. She took the name Sister Mary Veronica of the Passion, revealing her devotion to the Stations of the Cross and the Passion of the Lord. She taught school and worked with the poor at Syros and Piraeus in Greece, and in Brittany, France. In 1862, the religious congregation sent her to Calicut on the Malabar Coast of India. During a retreat in preparation for this mission, she enjoyed numerous mystical experiences. On mission, she learned the Malayalam language, and won many converts to Catholicism, and assisted many Hindus and Parsees in praying.

In India, she felt called to found a Third Order Regular of Active Carmelites for the Missions. Her superior general opposed her transfer. With great pain, in May 1867, she left the Sisters of Saint Joseph and joined the community of Carmel at Pau, France. After completing novitiate, and professing vows, she founded the Apostolic Carmel at Bayonne, France in July 1868. Two years later, the Apostolic Carmel was founded at Mangalore, India. Sadly, the bishop claimed complete authority over the religious community, ultimately displacing Mother Mary Veronica. Meanwhile, the French bishop in the sending diocese of Bayonne refused to cooperate with the high-handed Indian bishop at Mangalore, and forbade any sisters in his diocese to go the missions in India. The community closed in France; it had lost its lifeline of vocations.

Wearied by the controversies, Sophie chose to re-enter the Cloistered Carmel of Pau, where she made her final profession in 1874, and took the name Sister Marie Therese of Jesus. Meanwhile, Indian vocations flourished in the congregation which Mother Veronica had founded. In 1878, some of Mother Veronica's original sisters left the diocese of Mangalore in order to work with the Carmelite bishop at Verapoly vicariate. This group called themselves the Third Order Apostolic of Our Lady of Mount Carmel of Trivandrum. In 1971, the name was changed to the Congregation of Carmelite Religious.

In 1875, Mother Veronica and nine other sisters went to Bethlehem to establish a community. Mother remained in that mission for a dozen years. After that she returned to Pau, where she remained for the last nineteen years of her life, performing mundane tasks and enjoying mystical prayer. Much of her life was filled with courage in the face of rejection. Her greatest joy was her faith in the Real Presence which sustained her during the key turning points in her life: her religious vocation, conversion to Catholicism, entering religious life, transferring from one congregation to found another, returning to the cloister after conflicts with the bishop at Mangalore, rejoicing over the two flourishing communities which she had founded, and returning from Bethlehem to Pau, where she spent her final years in hidden service and mystical prayer.

20. ✢ Venerable Agnelo Gustavo Adolfo de Souza, S.F.X.

***Place:** Goa and Karnataka states, India*
***Fame:** Preacher and pastor*

This spiritually-gifted and brilliant student became a spiritual director and inspiring preacher in the Society of Pilar.[22]

Agnelo Gustavo Adolfo de Souza (1869-1927) was born at Anjuna, Goa, the sixth of nine children. His parents, members of the landed gentry, owned paddy fields and fruit groves. Agnelo's father generously provided for his employees. His mother, educated in religion, piano and violin, regularly gathered children of the neighborhood to instruct in the faith by word and music. Various Hindus converted to Catholicism. Agnelo learned from his parents' good example. He respected every person regardless of class or creed. He communicated easily with all companions the teachings which he had learned at church and at home.

At a young age, Agnelo lost his parents: his father, when Agnelo was eleven, and his mother, two years later. At first a paternal uncle, and later, Agnelo's oldest brother raised the orphaned children.

Agnelo received his primary and secondary education locally at the government school, and at a private academy. Upon graduating, he entered the minor seminary at Mapusa, followed by the major seminary at Rachol, both in his native Goa. At every level, he attained the highest marks among his peers.

After receiving minor orders and sub-deaconate in preparation for ordination as a diocesan priest, Agnelo felt called by God to join a religious community. He chose the Society of Pilar, known officially as the Society of Saint Francis Xavier of Pilar, which community had been founded ten years previously in 1887. Agnelo made his first profession of vows in 1898, and was ordained to priesthood the following year.

For ten years, he ministered at the monastery, and rarely ventured beyond the walls. Priests with whom he resided, and priests and laity who visited the monastery perceived in him a high degree of sanctity. From 1909 until 1927, he held the double responsibility of Spiritual Director for the seminary students, and parish priest at Siroda and Kumta in the state of Karnataka, and at Sanvorden in the neighboring state of Goa. In 1920, he accepted the additional responsibility of national Director for the Apostleship of Prayer.

AGNELO GUSTAVO ADOLPHO DE SOUZA

The seminarians, he urged to reach for sanctity. He would say, "We ought to be saints in order to attain our goal."[23] The preacher gave the students an option: "We have to burn ourselves somewhere: either in this world with love of the Sacred Heart of Jesus or in the next life in hell."[24] The holy priest urged the seminarians, "Let us put our trust in God, and remain like a dog sleeping at the feet of his master."[25]

People oftentimes referred to Agnelo as a Martyr to Preaching because he gave so much time, prayer, effort, and travel to preaching. Just before he died, he had committed to preaching the Novena to the Sacred Heart at the major seminary at Rachol. He struggled physically all week in the assignment, and at the end of the last evening's preaching, he collapsed in the pulpit. He had suffered a stroke while preaching to his beloved seminarians. The next morning he expired.

22. ☩ Our Lady of La Vang

Place: Quang Tri City, Vietnam
Fame: Apparitions of Our Lady

Almost 270 years after Catholicism was introduced to Vietnam, and throughout almost a century of continued persecution, the Blessed Mother appeared many times to Catholics hiding in the forest (now near Quang Tri City) in central Vietnam, approximately thirty-five miles north of the coastal city of Hue. "A great number of these people suffered from the bitter cold weather, lurking wild beasts, jungle sickness and starvation. At night, the people often gathered in small groups to say the rosary and to pray."[26]

The apparitions of the Blessed Mother began in 1798, and continued until the persecution ended in 1883. Our Lady identified herself as the Mother of God. She appeared with the child Jesus in her arms and an angel on either side of her. She assured the believers of her care for them and advised them to use as medicines the abundant forest fern called "la vang." She told them that she heard their prayers and would respond generously.

In 1802, when one period of persecution ended, Christians left the forest and returned to their villages. The story of the apparitions circulated widely. Believers built a chapel at the jungle site in 1820. Beginning in 1830, two more periods of intense anti-Catholic persecutions erupted and lasted more than a half-century. In 1885, a rabid opponent destroyed the chapel in the forest. The next year, a new chapel replaced the destroyed one. The chapel was consecrated fifteen years later with a congregation of twelve thousand in attendance. As pilgrims increased in number, a church was built in 1923 to replace the small chapel. Five years later, that church was consecrated with twenty thousand people in attendance. In 1959, the church of Our Lady of La Vang was declared the National Sacred Marian Center. Three years later, Pope John XXIII designated the church a minor basilica. In 1972, this church was destroyed during the Vietnam War. Pope John Paul II visited the shell of the basilica in 1988, when he canonized the 117 Vietnamese Martyrs.

22. ✠ Blessed Salvator Lilli, O.F.M., and Companions

Place: Marasco, and Mujuk-Deresi, Armenia
Fame: Martyrs of Armenia

Islamic Turks killed Salvator Lilli (1853-1895) and seven other Franciscan priests at Mujuk-Deresi, in Armenia (now in Turkey) on November 22, 1895.[27] The Muslim captors killed the Christian clergy specifically after the priests refused to deny their belief in Jesus Christ, and in the Church which Jesus had founded.

Salvator Lilli, his parents' sixth and final child, had grown up in the Abruzzi region of Italy. Salvator's father, a successful businessman, provided for his son an excellent education. At eighteen, Salvator entered the Order of Friars Minor, and a year later took his vows on August 6, 1871. Because of the political turmoil in Italy in 1870, and because of King Victor Emmanuel's suppression of religious orders in 1873, Salvator left his homeland in order to study for the priesthood.

The student traveled to Palestine, where he studied philosophy at Bethlehem, and theology at Jerusalem. After being ordained a priest at Bethlehem on April 6, 1878, he was assigned as custodian of the Franciscans at Saint Savior Church and the Basilica of the Holy Sepulcher in Jerusalem.

In 1880, Salvator was assigned to Marasco, Armenia, where he served as parish priest and religious superior. He learned well the three main languages of the area: Arabic, Turkish, and Armenian. His pastoral duties he performed in exemplary manner: opening schools, clinics, and shelters; and introducing practices of good hygiene and good labor skills. With the parish's money, he purchased farmland and farm equipment to be used by and for the benefit of the parishioners. When a cholera epidemic besieged the region for six weeks beginning in November 1891, he heroically served the sick without regard for his own exposure to the life-threatening disease.

Beginning as early as 1885, Muslims began a systematic, brutal, and bloody persecution of Christians. Having been in his new assignment at Mujuk-Deresi, in Armenia for only sixteen months, he was confronted by an authorized band of Muslims who insisted he convert to Islam. He refused, so they wounded him in the leg. Soon, he was arrested, along with ten parishioners. The officials used alternating compliments and threats to have the Catholics become Muslims. Salvator urged his flock, "Brothers and sisters, keep the faith; do not become Muslims. The world is passing away. In heaven, Jesus and all his saints wait for us. Be strong! After suffering, we will enjoy the glory of Paradise."[28] On November 22, 1895, Salvator, his Franciscan confreres, and lay companions were bayoneted to death. The Muslim militia later burned the corpses of the Christian martyrs.

24. ☩ Martyrs of Vietnam

***Place:** Hanoi, Vietnam*
***Fame:** 17 Martyrs*

The Catholic religion received a peaceful reception in 1533, enjoyed a stable development beginning in 1615, and blossomed under the guidance of "the Apostle of Vietnam," Alexander de Rhodes, from his arrival in 1624 to his death in 1660.[29] Many hundreds of thousands of Vietnamese accepted baptism. The first seminary was founded in 1666, and two years later, the first native vocations were ordained priests. In 1670, the women's famous religious community of Lovers of the Holy Cross was founded.

Persecutions had occurred sporadically from 1625 to 1698, when the first severe persecution took place, followed by similar widespread persecutions, especially in 1712, 1723, and 1750. "As many as 100,000 may have suffered [death] up to this point."[30] The Treaty of Versailles of 1787 brought French troops and relative peace to the Church in Vietnam.

Terrible persecutions occurred again between 1833 and 1883, during the reigns of Emperor Minh Mang (r. 1820-1840), Emperor Thieu-Tri (1840-1847), and Emperor Tu Duc (1847-1883). During this half-century, "between 100,000 and 300,000 Christians had been put to death or made to suffer for their religion."[31]

Almost all of the canonized 117 Martyrs of Vietnam died for the faith between 1833 and 1862. Although two of these martyrs died each year in 1745, 1773, and 1798, fifty-eight of the martyrs died between 1833 and 1840, three during 1840-1847, and another fifty between 1847 and 1862. Royal decrees placed at the grave site of each martyr indicate the manner of death: seventy-five suffered decapitation, twenty-two died by strangulation, six were burned to death, five died in exile, and nine succumbed to tortures received in prison.

Of the 117 total, ninety-six were native Vietnamese, and the remaining martyrs consisted of Spanish (eleven) and French (ten). Among the Vietnamese, thirty-seven were priests and fifty-nine were laity, including one seminarian, sixteen catechists, ten Third Order Dominicans, one woman, and one boy. Many of the martyrs were Dominicans: all eleven Spanish priests, eleven of the Vietnamese priests, and the ten Third Order members. The other religious community represented was the Paris Foreign Missionary Society (MEP), to which all ten Frenchmen belonged. Among the foreign clergy, six Dominicans and two MEP's were bishops.

Representative vignettes of these martyrs are presented in the brief biographies of Agnes Le Thi Thanh (February 18), Andrew Dung Lac an Tran (December 21), Andrew Phu Yen (July 26), Michael Hồ Đình Hy (November 22), Paul Lê-Báo Tịnh (April 6), and Theophane Venard (November 24).

24. ✢ Saint Théophane Vénard, M.E.P.

Place: *Hanoi, Vietnam*
Fame: *Martyr*

Outside of Poitiers in western France, Jean-Théophane Vénard (1829-1861) was born and raised.[32] The boy's love of study and reflection revealed itself in a serious demeanor. At eight, after having read about the missionary martyrs of Tonkin, he became inspired to follow their example. Théophane's schoolmaster-father oversaw the son's elementary education until 1841, when the youth began studies in the college at Doue-la-Fontaine. Six years later, the boy entered the seminary at Montmorillon, and continued at Poitiers, which institution the Society of Foreign Missionaries of Paris administered. After one year in the Society's seminary, Theophane joined that community. The following year, on June 5, 1852, he was ordained a priest.

A few months after ordination, Théophane was sent to Hong Kong, where he studied the Vietnamese language and customs. Fifteen months later, in February 1854, he was missioned to West Tonkin (now northern Vietnam). Because of the virulent anti-Catholic persecution which Emperor Ming Meng had initiated in 1848, Théophane entered secretly into Tonkin in February 1854. For the next seven years, young Father Théophane ministered heroically: traveling at night, hiding in caves, sleeping in sampans, and celebrating sacraments in the homes of trusted Catholic faithful. For a priest friend, Théophane describes his concealment:

> I write to you from Tonkin, from a dark little hole where the only light comes through the crack of a partially opened door, which just makes it possible for me to trace these lines, and now and then to read a few pages of a book. One has to be ever watchful. If the dog barks, or any stranger passes, the door is instantly closed, and I prepare to hide myself in a still lower hole, which has been excavated in my temporary retreat. This is how I have lived for three months, sometimes alone, sometimes together with my dear friend Monsignor Theural. The convent which sheltered us before has been destroyed by the pagans. . . . We took our refuge in a smoky dung-heap belonging to a pious old Christian widow, where we were joined by another missionary.
>
> What do you think of our position? Three missionaries, one of whom is a bishop, lying side by side, day and night, in a space about a yard and a half square, our only light and means of breathing being three holes, the size of a little finger, made in the mud wall, which our poor old woman is obliged to conceal by some faggots thrown down outside. Under our feet is a brick cellar, constructed in the dead of night with great skill by one of our catechists. In this cellar there are three bamboo tubes which are cleverly contrived to open on to the borders of the neighboring lake with its fresh air.
>
> You might well ask: "Why don't you go mad? Always shut up in the thickness of two walls, with a roof one can touch with one's

hand, our companions spiders, rats and toads, always obliged to speak in a low voice, "like the wind," as the Annamites [Vietnamese] say, receiving every day the most terrible news of the torture and death of our fellow-missionaries, and worse still, of their occasional apostasy under torture. It requires, I must admit, a special grace not to be utterly discouraged and dejected.[33]

After four years of secretive and successful ministry, Théophane was betrayed to the authorities by a member of his congregation. He was arrested at Kimbang on November 30, 1860. Because Théophane refused to abandon his faith, the local mandarin sentenced the priest to beheading. Soldiers locked the prisoner into a bamboo cage. On January 20, 1861, the young priest writes to his father,

> A light blow of the sword will sever my head, like a spring flower which the Master of the garden picks for his pleasure. We are all flowers planted on this earth. God picks these flowers, some a little earlier, others a bit later. One is a purple rose; another, the virgin lily; another, the humble violet. Let us all try to please the sovereign Lord and Master according to the perfume or radiance which God has given us."[34]

In early December, soldiers transported the prisoner in a cage to Hanoi. Along the journey, Théophane chanted psalms and sang hymns. An onlooker described the priest's attitude in this way: "He is as jolly and cheerful as someone traveling to a feast. He doesn't seem at all afraid."[35]

The authorities at Hanoi interrogated Father Théophane. They urged him to save his life by giving up his faith. To demonstrate apostasy, the authorities required him to trample on the crucifix. Theophane responded to the officials as he had written to his father the day before, "What! Have I preached the religion of the cross all my life until now, and you expect me to desert it? I do not treasure the things of this world so highly that I wish to buy them by apostasy."[36]

On February 2, 1861, Father Théophane Vénard died by decapitation. That morning, the mandarins ordered soldiers to bring the prisoner to the court for final questioning. After the priest reaffirmed his faith, the mandarins ordered the soldiers to take him to the place of execution. When the half-hour's march ended, the prisoner extended his neck over the executioner's block. The experienced executioner raised his sword, slashed at Father Venard's neck. The prisoner's neck broke, but was not severed from the head. A second time, the executioner crashed the sword against the neck, this time almost completely slicing the head from the body. Three more chops were required until the head fell from the neck. As the mandarins had decreed, the head was displayed for three days as a warning to other Christians. After this period, the head was retrieved from its bamboo pole, and was tossed unceremoniously into the Red River. Father Venard's torso had been retrieved immediately after the execution, and the head was recovered from the river on February 15. Over the course of the next four years, the combined remains of the martyr were brought to Paris, where the parts have been interred.

DECEMBER

3. ✠ Saint Francis Xavier, S.J.

Place: *Cape Comorin, India; Kagoshima, Japan*
Fame: *"Apostle of India" and "Apostle of Japan," Patron of Foreign Missions*

SAINT FRANCIS XAVIER, S.J.

Born at the family's castle near Saguesa, Navarre, in northern Spain, Francis Xavier (1506-1552) studied locally until 1525, when he traveled to Paris and entered the College of Sainte-Barbe.[1] There he developed a friendship with his new roommate, Pierre Favre. Francis earned the Master of Arts degree in 1530 and began a four-year teaching stint at Beauvais.

Attending the same school, beginning in 1529, was Ignatius of Loyola. Ignatius envisioned forming a band of Catholic men dedicated to the service of the Church. Ignatius' plan attracted Pierre Favre, who joined Ignatius' band in 1533. Francis followed a few months later. Soon, four more men joined. The group of seven made a spiritual retreat at Montmartre. At the conclusion of the retreat on August 15, 1534, the seven took religious vows, thereby founding the Society of Jesus. For the next two years, Francis studied theology, wishing to teach and preach accurately the truths of the Catholic faith. In mid-November 1536, Francis left Paris and traveled to Venice, where he was ordained on June 24, 1537. Like the other early Jesuits, Francis wished to go to Palestine but the war being waged between the Venetians and the Turks prohibited safe travel. Francis passed time at Bologna, until April 1538, when he and the other six Jesuits went to Rome to offer their services to the pope. The next year, the pope gave his verbal approval of the Society.

When one of the original seven, Nicholas Bobadilla, became ill and could not fulfill the King of Portugal's request to minister to the Christians in Portuguese-controlled Goa in India, Francis volunteered to substitute for the ill Bobadilla. On April 7, 1541, the king appointed Francis Xavier apostolic nuncio in the East.

Thirteen months after having departed from Lisbon, Francis landed at Goa, on the west coast of India, on May 6, 1542. His voyage had been interrupted by tempestuous seas which forced him to winter at Mozambique. At the African island, Francis studied the native language and, using it, wrote a catechism for the instruction of the people.

Beginning in September 1542, Francis sailed from Goa to Cape Comorin, opposite Ceylon (now Sri Lanka), where he settled at Mannar. Christianity had been introduced there about a half dozen years earlier. Francis labored there for the next two years among the low-caste Paravas. He enjoyed much success among the Paravas, but not among the Brahmans, only one of whom converted. Evangelizing and baptizing the Paravas simultaneously exhausted him and energized him. He writes:

> There is such a great multitude of those who are being converted to the faith of Christ in this land where I am that it frequently happens that my arms become exhausted from baptizing, and I can no longer speak from having recited so often the Creed and the Commandments in their language, and the other prayers, along with an exhortation which I know in their language, in which I explain to them what it is to be a Christian, what paradise is, and what hell is, telling them what kind of people they are who go to the former and what kind to the latter. I recite the Creed and the Commandments more frequently than the other prayers. There are days when I baptize an entire village, and on the coast where I now am here are thirty Christian villages [between Manapar and Tuticorin].[2]

When the ruler of Jaffna on the northern coast of Ceylon physically attacked the Paravas, Francis remained with his flock. He assisted them as best he could in their escape to safety, although six hundred new Christians died at the hands of the attackers.

In August 1545, Francis sailed from Mylapore (now Mailapuram) to Malacca in the Malay Peninsula. There, Francis catechized and baptized for the next four months.

On April 7, 1549, Francis set out for Japan. Two other Jesuits and a young Japanese convert from Goa named Anjiro assisted Francis in the mission. The group landed at Kagoshima on Kyushu in southern Japan.

Francis studied the native language, and, with Anjiro's expertise, produced in Japanese a small catechism, and an explanation of the Catholic creed. Although the daimyo welcomed Francis, the Buddhist monks and religious leaders resisted him. The Spanish missionary put on the clothes of a Japanese scholar, and shared the truths of Christianity with the bonzes. Overall, Francis won about two thousand coverts during his twenty-seven months of ministry among the Japanese.

Francis was returning to Malacca, when in December 1551, he was elected provincial of the newly established Province of India. By February of the next year, he arrived at Goa, where he appointed a vice-provincial to take care of administrative responsibilities.

Half-a-year later, he sailed for China, where he hoped to preach the faith. By August 1552, his ship reached Sancian (near Canton), which lies a half dozen miles from the coast, and a hundred miles southwest of Hong Kong. He was waiting for a propitious moment for entering the mainland. In late November, he caught a fever. On December 3, 1552, he died. Two months later, his incorrupt body was exhumed, and was transported first to Malacca and, at the end of the year, to Goa, where Francis' body remains.

14. ✠ Saint Nimattullah Youssef Kassab al-Hardini

Place: Hardine, Lebanon
Fame: Profoundly prayerful monk

Youssef Kassab (1810-1858) grew up in a faith-filled family who followed the Maronite Rite.[3] Of his parents' seven children, three sons became priests, and one daughter entered religious life. Youssef was the third child and third son.

The family lived in the Taurus Mountains at Hardine, above Batroun, in north-central Lebanon. Youssef attended the local school before being sent to Tannourine to live with his maternal grandfather who was a priest. Daily, the boy served his grandfather's Mass, before going to school at the Monastery of Saint Anthony Haoub. At thirteen, Youssef returned to Hardine. Besides the usual recitation of prayers and attendance at daily Mass, "from an early age, Al-Hardini acquired devotion to God and isolated himself from the world in his desire to serve Him."[4] Unlike most young boys, Youssef enjoyed being alone; "rather than playing with children, he preferred to stay alone praying"[5]

Youssef entered the novitiate of the Maronite Order in 1828, at St. Anthony's Monastery in Kozhaya. He took Nimattullah as his religious name. Two years later, he advanced to study philosophy and theology at the Monastery of Saints Cyprian and Justina in Kfifan, where he professed solemn vows. Because this seminarian scrupulously kept every rule and regulation, and seemed obsessive about details of the religious life, his religious superiors "feared he might begin to hallucinate, stopped his theological studies and sent him to rest at the monastery of Saint Moussa Al-Habashe at Dawar."[6] After a brief hiatus, the superiors sent Nimattullah back to Kfifan to complete his studies. He was ordained a priest on Christmas Day 1833.

In ministry, Nimattullah worked as a teacher and administrator. In 1834, his superiors assigned him to the theologate at Kfifan, where he taught moral theology for five years, and served as director of theological students for another seven years. Beginning in 1845, he served three terms (1845-1847, 1850-1853, and 1856-1858) as assistant to the superior general of the Maronite Order. He refused to submit his name as a candidate for the position of superior general. Between terms as general assistant of the Maronite Order, he again taught moral theology in Bharsouf and Kfifan. While teaching at Kfifan 1853-1856, he influenced one of his students, Charbel Makhlouf, who in 1977, was canonized a saint. Besides his professional duties, Nimattullah devoted himself to the manual tasks of binding books and sewing vestments.

Nimattullah is credited with having started a new model of monastic life in Lebanon. Rather than hold as the apogee of monastic life, the hermit who leaves community life and encounters God in isolation in the wilderness, Nimattullah "remained living in the monastery instead, where he carried the cross of community life."[7] Regarding personal conduct in community life, he writes, "The monk must be careful about his reputation and conduct, lest he cause others to doubt him and become suspicious."[8] Regarding interaction in community life, the monk advises, "If you have something to say to your brother, go and confront him in the spirit of Christ. Don't allow your tongue the opportunity to blame and accuse."[9]

Nimattullah's spirituality focused on prayer, the Eucharist, and the Blessed Virgin Mary. Regularly, he passed long hours in front of the Blessed Sacrament. He prayed kneeling on the chapel floor, with his extended in the shape of a cross, and eyes focused on the tabernacle. In honor of the Blessed Mother, and especially of the Immaculate Conception, he prayed the rosary and other Marian devotions daily, and fasted not only for the three days surrounding Marian feasts but also for the entire month of May.

In early December 1858, Nimattullah became ill at Kfifan. The sickness deteriorated quickly into pneumonia. On December 14, he died in the monastery, placing on his chest an icon of the Blessed Mother, while surrounded by community members who kept praying for the saintly monk.

16. ✠ Blessed Philip Siphong Onphithah, Agnes Phila, and Companions

Place: Songkhon, Siam (now Thailand)
Fame: Martyrs

Early in the sixteenth century, Portuguese merchants introduced Christianity to Siam (now Thailand).[10] Half a century later, and for the next four hundred years, missionaries arrived in small numbers. Conversions remained very few. Brief anti-Christian persecutions took place in 1688 and 1765. In the twentieth century, Christians represented less than one percent of the population in this overwhelmingly Buddhist country.

In December 1940, the Siamese government in the far northern village of Songkhon ordered Catholics, under the penalty of death, to deny their Christian faith, and to declare their belief in Buddhism. Seven Catholics refused to abandon their faith; these six women and one man were put to death.

Philip Siphong Onphithah (1907-1940) became the first native martyr of Thailand. After the Catholic clergy had been expelled in November 1940, Philip assumed leadership of the church. This school teacher doubled as the chief catechist in the village. When government officials summoned him to the sheriff's office in the neighboring town of Mukdahan, Philip's wife, their five children, and neighbors urged Philip not to go. Nonetheless, Philip went, but he never returned. He was shot dead by government officials in a nearby forest on December 15, 1940.

Sister Agnes Phila (1909-1940) and Sister Lucy Khambang (1917-1940) picked up the torch of teaching the local children their Catholic faith. The two religious sisters belonged to the Congregation of the Lovers of the Holy Cross, which congregation is different from the three-hundred-year-old congregation of Vietnamese sisters of the same name. On Christmas Day, 1939, the police chief of Songkhon visited the convent of the Congregation of the Lovers of the Holy Cross, and furiously threatened the sisters and the catechumens and children in the convent, "I've told you many times not to speak about Jesus. You must not mention God in Thailand, otherwise I'll kill you all."[11] Sister Agnes challenged the police officer, and assured him that she and the others would not relinquish their faith, even under the threat of death.

That night, Sister Agnes wrote a letter to the police chief. The signatures at the end of the letter included those of Sister Agnes, Sister Lucy, their housekeeper Agatha Phutta (1881-1940), and three young catechists: Cecilia Butsi (1924-1940), Bibiana Hampai (1925-1940), and Mary Phon (1926-1940). The letter reads in part:

> We profess that the religion of Christ is the only true religion.... We are ready to give back our lives to God, Who has given them to us. We do not wish to be the prey of the devil. Please carry out your order. Please open the door of heaven to us. . . . We are well prepared. When we will be gone, we will remember you.[12]

On the day after Christmas, the police returned to the convent. The police ordered the women to walk to the Mekong River so that the police might shoot them there. Sister Agnes rebutted that the women preferred to die on the holy ground in the parish cemetery. The police chief accepted this accommodation. The women left the convent, singing hymns, and praying psalms. They waved to passersby, and encouraged the Catholic on-lookers, "Good bye. We are going to heaven. We are going to become martyrs for Christ."[13] At the cemetery, the half-dozen women knelt and prayed. Sister Agnes declared to the policemen, "You may kill us but you cannot kill the Church, and you cannot kill God. One day the Church will return to Thailand and will flourish more than ever."[14]

The police shot the six women. Four died instantly. Sister Agnes and Mary Phon lay wounded but not dead. At Sister Agnes' request, the villagers reported to the police that two victims still lay alive, and wished to be killed so that they may be freed to enter heaven. The police returned, and completed their work. The villagers buried the six women martyrs.

21. ✠ Saint Andrew Dũng Lạc an Trần

Place: Hanoi, Vietnam
Fame: Martyr

An Trần (c. 1795-1839) was born to pagan parents at Bac Ninh in northern Vietnam.[15] Because of their poverty, his parents let this twelve-year old boy make his own way at Hanoi. In that northern capital, a catechist discovered the youth, and provided him with food and shelter.

For three years, the catechist instructed the boy in the Catholic faith. The youth then asked for and received at Vinh Tri the sacrament of baptism and the Christian name Andrew. The young man studied Latin and Chinese, and, after maturing in formation and education, he became a catechist.

Desiring to become a priest, Andrew studied theology, and was ordained for his diocese on March 15, 1823. This young parish priest at Ke-Dam, by his preaching, teaching, austerities, and kindnesses, won many converts to Christianity.

At this same time, Emperor Minh Mang was conducting a cruel persecution against the Catholic Church. The emperor ordered the destruction of churches, and the capture of priests. Lay Catholics were forbidden to practice their religion, and to use their homes to shelter priests or religious sisters, or to host religious gatherings, on the penalty of their homes being liable to confiscation. Transgressors of the emperor's anti-Catholic edict were threatened with jail, exile or the death penalty.

Father Andrew was arrested and imprisoned twice: in 1835, and 1839. Both times, parishioners gained his release by bribing the guards. After his first release, Father Andrew changed his name to Lạc, and moved to another prefecture where he continued his church service. After his second arrest, imprisonment, and release in 1839, Andrew urged his parishioners no longer to interfere if he would be re-arrested. He explained, "Those who die for their faith in Jesus go straight to heaven. Why do we need to hide ourselves from the authorities or to pay bribes to get out of jail?"[16]

Within a few days of his second release, he was re-arrested. Governmental authorities sent him to Hanoi, where soldiers inflicted great tortures. When the soldiers ordered him to trample on the cross, which demand was applied customarily to Catholic prisoners, Father Andrew refused. In response, the soldiers dragged his body across the crucifix. The priest, however, lifted his legs high enough to avoid touching the crucifix.

On December 21, 1839, Father Andrew was sentenced to death by decapitation. Immediately, he was led to the prison yard. Calmly, he knelt in front of the block on which he stretched out his neck. While Father Andrew was praying and praising God, executioners beheaded him.

Among the 117 martyrs of Vietnam, Pope John Paul II chose Andrew Dũng Lạc an Trần as the representative of the group.

ENDNOTES

Introduction

[1] The territorial boundary for Asia applied by the author is the following: on the west, from the Ural Mountains, down the Ural River, past the Caspian and Black Seas, to the Dardanelles; on the north, the Arctic Ocean above the Russian Federation; on the south, the Red Sea and the Indian Ocean; and on the east, the Pacific Ocean. In this book, Oceania is included, although this territory is geographically distinct from Asia; Oceania has just a handful of saints and candidates, and the author desires to publicize their names and stories in this text.

[2] Pope John Paul II, "*Ecclesia in Asia: Apostolic Exhortation of the Holy Father John Paul II on Jesus Christ the Savior and His Mission of Love and Service in Asia*" (Pasay City, Philippines: Paulines Publishing House, 2000), ch. 1, para. 9, p. 25.

[3] Pope John Paul II, *Ecclesia*, p. 26.

[4] Pope John Paul II, *Ecclesia*, pp. 26-27.

[5] "Asia is the largest and most populous continent, and although it is the birthplace of the Church, it is also the least Catholic continent. . . . Yet while it contains one-third of the global population, it has just one in ten of all Catholics worldwide. . . . Only three countries have majority Catholic populations, and in most countries Catholics make up less than 4 percent of the population. The religions with the greatest number of adherents in Asia are Islam, Hinduism, and Buddhism." Bryan T. Froehle and Mary L. Gautier, *Global Catholicism: Portrait of a World Church*. Center for Applied Research in the Apostolate. (Maryknoll, NY: Orbis Books, 2002), p. 85.

[6] Froehle and Gautier, p. 86.

[7] United States Conference of Catholic Bishops, *Asian and Pacific Presence: Harmony in Faith* (Washington, D.C.: USCCB, Inc.; 2002), p. 6.

[8] USCCB, p. 9.

[9] The six regions consist of the Near East (aka the Middle East), Northern Asia, Central Asia, Southern Asia, Southeast Asia, and Far East Asia. The Middle East consists of fifteen countries located from the eastern shore of the Mediterranean Sea as far west as Iran. The remaining regions consist of thirty-three nations. Asia includes over one-third of the world's land mass, and almost two-thirds of the world's population. Oceania consists of fourteen countries, and twenty-two dependencies and territories. [Gordon Cheers, gen. ed., and others,

Geographica: The Complete Illustrated Atlas of the World. (New York, NY: Barnes & Noble, 2001), pp. 109, 145, and 147.]

[10] Pope John Paul II, *Ecclesia*, para. 50; p. 153.

January

[11] Kuriakose Elias Chavara, C.M.I., was beatified on February 8, 1996. The author thanks Father James Madathikkardam, C.M.I., vice postulator, for providing information, and for reviewing the draft of this biography.

[12] Private correspondence with Father James Madathikkardam, C.M.I., vice postulator.

[13] Zacharias M. Moozhoor, C.M.I., *Blessed Chavara: The Star of the East*, tr. by Sheila Kannath, C.M.C. (Kottayam, Kerala, India: D.C. Offset Printers, 1993), p. 115.

[14] Agatha Yi was canonized on May 6, 1984, along with the 103 Korean Martyrs. The author thanks Father Gregory Kim Yong Ki, C.M., parish priest at Seoul, for providing information, and for reviewing the draft of this biography. Father, mother, and daughter were canonized together on May 6, 1984.

[15] Kim Chang-seok Thaddeus, *Lives of 103 Martyr Saints Of Korea*. (Seoul, South Korea: Catholic Publishing House, second edition, 1984), p. 103.

[16] Hugh MacMahon, *The Korean Martyr Saints: Founders of a Church*, (Seoul, South Korea: St. Hwang Sok Tu Luke Publishing House, 1995), p. 160.

[17] Diego Luis de San Vitores was beatified on October 6, 1985.

[18] Las Islas de los Ladrones (Islands of the Robbers) received its name from Ferdinand Magellan in March 1521, as he watched the natives row out to his ships and help themselves to everything that they could get their hands on.

[19] Ildebrando Jesus Alino Leyson, *Pedro Calungsod Vissaya: Prospects of a Teenage Filipino* (Cebu, Philippines: Claretian Publications, 1999), p. 41.

[20] www.Bisitaguam.com/Episodes/14/body.html; p. 2.

[21] Nicholas Bunkerd Kitbamrung was beatified on March 5, 2000. The author thanks Father Daniel Abogado, C.M., parish priest, for providing information.

[22] James M. Fitzpatrick, O.M.I., *Priest and Martyr: Blessed Nicholas Bunkerd Kitbamrung: A.D. 1895-1944*, (Bangkok, Thailand: Assumption Printing Press, 2003), p. 15.

[23] Fitzpatrick, p. 16.

[24] Fitzpatrick, p. 25-26.

[25] Joseph Vaz was beatified on January 21, 1995.

[26] Joseph Anthony Wahl, C.Or., "Vaz, Joseph," *New Catholic Encyclopedia*, vol. 14, p. 580.

[27] Fernanda Riva was named a Servant of God on August 13, 1994.

[28] Teresa Mathias, F.D.C.C., *Fernanda, Fragrance of Humble Love*. (Mumbai, India: Canossian Daughters of Charity, 1996), p. 24.

[29] Mathias, p. 35.
[30] Mathias, p. 89.
[31] Mathias, p. 91.
[32] Mathias, p. 119.

February

[1] Takayama Ukon was named a Servant of God on July 9, 1976. The author thanks Rev. Paolo Molinari, S.J., postulator for the cause, for providing information, and for reviewing the draft of this biography.

[2] Paolo Molinari, S.J., "Takayama Ukon," *Bibliotheca Sanctorum*, Prima Appendice, col. 1350.

[3] Molinari, col. 1354.

[4] Joseph N. Tylenda, S.J., "Blessed Francis Pacheco and Eight Companions," in *Jesuit Saints & Martyrs: Short Biographies of the Saints, Blesseds, Venerables, and Servants of God of the Society of Jesus* (Chicago, IL: Loyola Press, second edition, 1998), p. 184.

[5] Tylenda. p. 184.

[6] John de Brittó, S.J., was canonized on June 22, 1947.

[7] Felix Raj, S.J., www.goethals.org/life.htm, p. 1.

[8] Puthenkalam, Joseph, S.D.B., and Mampra, Anthony, S.D.B. *Sanctity in India*. (Chennai, Tamil Nadu: Salesian Institute of Graphic Arts, 2000), p. 82.

[9] Gonzalo García, O.F.M., was canonized on June 10, 1862.

[10] Puthenkalam and Mampra, p. 57.

[11] Puthenkalam and Mampra, p. 66.

[12] Puthenkalam and Mampra, p. 66.

[13] Paul Miki, S.J., and Companions were canonized on June 8, 1862. The author thanks Father Renzo de Luca, S.J., assistant director of 26 Martyrs Museum, for providing information, and for reviewing the draft of this biography.

[14] *The Liturgy of the Hours*, vol. III, (New York, N.Y.: Catholic Book Publishing Co.; 1976), p. 1368.

[15] *The Liturgy of the Hours*. p. 1368.

[16] *The Liturgy of the Hours*. p. 1369.

[17] *The Liturgy of the Hours*. p. 1369.

[18] Puthenkalam and Mampra, p. 425.

[19] Puthenkalam and Mampra, p. 426.

[20] Puthenkalam and Mampra, p. 427.

[21] Puthenkalam and Mampra. p. 430.

[22] Puthenkalam and Mampra, p. 434.

[23] Francis Régis Clet, C.M. was canonized on October 1, 2000. The author thanks Father John Carven, C.M, archivist, for providing information, and for reviewing the draft of the biography.

[24] Agatha Lin Zhao was canonized on October 1, 2000. The author thanks the confreres of the Vincentian China Province for providing information, and for reviewing the draft of this biography.

[25] Agnes Lê Thị Thành was canonized on June 19, 1988. The author thanks Rev. Francis Xavier Nhi Nguyen, parish priest serving in the Archdiocese of Baltimore, for providing information and for reviewing the draft of the biography.

[26] Adrien Launay, *Les Trente-Cinq Venerables Serviteurs de Dieu: Francais, Anamies, Chinois Mis A Mort Pour La Foi En Extreme Orient, De 1815 a 1862.* (Paris, France: P. Lethielleux, Libraire-Editeur, troisieme edition, 1907), p. 274.

[27] Adrien Launay., p. 277.

[28] Adrien Launay, p. 277.

[29] Adrien Launay., p. 278.

[30] Sister Rani Maria Kunju Vattalil, F.C.C. was named a Servant of God on February 25, 2003. .

[31] Giuseppe Segalla, *Martyr Of Charity — Sister Rani Maria.* Schor Series, # 9 (Tellicherry, Kerala, India: Institute For Research In Social Sciences And Humanities; 2003), p. 19.

[32] Segalla., p. 21

[33] Segalla, pp. 74-75.

[34] Segalla, p. 12.

[35] Segalla, p. 13.

March

[1] Aloysius Schwartz was declared Servant of God on December 10, 2003. The author thanks Mrs. Dolores Vita, sister of Msgr. Aloysius Schwartz, for providing information, and for reviewing the draft of this biography.

[2] Aloysius Schwartz, *Killing Me Softly: The Inspiring Story of a Champion of the Poor.* (New York, N.Y.: Alba House, 1993), p. 105.

[3] Felice Tantardini, P.I.M.E. was declared Servant of God on January 28, 2005. The author thanks Father Sergio Fossati, P.I.M.E. Mission Center Director, for providing information, and for reviewing the draft of this biography.

[4] Piero Gheddo, Il Santo Col Martello, Felice Tantardini, *70 Anni Di Birmania.* (Bologna, Italy: Editrice Missionaria Italiana, 2000), pp. 205-06.

[5] Gheddo, p. 33.

[6] Gheddo, p. 136.

[7] Gheddo, p. 177.

[8] Rafqa de Hamlaya was canonized on June 10, 2001.

[9] www.maronite.org.au/stcharbel/rafka.html., p. 2.

[10] www.maronite.org.au/stcharbel/rafka.html., p. 2.

[11] www.maronite.org.au/stcharbel/rafka.html., p. 2.

April

[1] Everything we know definitively about Pedro Calungsod (c. 1655-1672) comes through documents pertinent to Blessed Diego Luis de San Vitores. Pedro Calungsod was beatified March 5, 2005.

[2] Ildebrando Jesus Alino Leyson, Pedro *Calungsod Vissaya: Prospects of a Teenage Filipino* (Cebu City, Philippines: Claretian Publications, 1999), p. 14.

[3] Paul Lê-Báo Tịnh was canonized June 19, 1988. The author thanks Father Francis Xavier Nhi Nguyen, parish priest serving in the Archdiocese of Baltimore, for providing information, and for reviewing the draft of this biography.

[4] Adrien Launay, *Les Trente-Cinq Venerables Serviteurs De Dieu, Francais, Annamites, Chinois Mis A Mort Pour La Foi En Extreme Orient, De 1815 A 1862.* (Paris: P. Lethielleux, Libraire-Editeur, troisieme edition, 1907), pp. 236-38.

[5] Private correspondence with Father Francis Nguyen.

[6] Adrien Launay, Les Teste-Cinq, p. 250.

[7] Marioi Borzaga and Thoj Xyooj Paolo were named Servants of God on October 15, 2006. The author thanks James Allen, O.M.I., associate director of Oblate Communications Services at the Oblate General House in Rome, Italy, for providing information and for reviewing the draft of this biography.

[8] Mario Borzaga, "To be a Happy Man," Ed. Lucia Borzaga. (Rome, Italy: Oblate General Postulation, 1992) p. 7.

[9] Borzaga, p. 9.

[10] Borzaga, p. 10.

[11] Borzaga, p. 12.

[12] Borzaga, p. 15.

[13] Borzaga, p. 17.

[14] Borzaga, p. 19.

[15] Borzaga, p. 19.

[16] Anastasius Hartmann, O.F.M., Cap. was declared venerable on December 21, 1998. The author thanks Father Mark D'Souza, O.F.M., Cap., of the Capuchin Generalate; and Father FlorioTelleri, O.F.M. Cap., for providing information, and for reviewing the draft of this biography.

[17] Puthenkalam and Mampra, p. 195.

[18] Puthenkalam and Mampra, p. 198.

[19] Puthenkalam and Mampra, p. 199.

[20] Fulgentius Vannini, O.F.M. Cap., Bishop Hartmann. (Allahabad, India: St. Paul's Press Training School, 1966), p. 296.

[21] Puthenkalam and Mampra, p. 211.

[22] Peter Chanel was canonized on June 12, 1954. The author thanks Mr. Gayle Peters, archivist, for providing information, and for reviewing the draft of the biography.

May

[1] Damien de Veuster, SS.CC. was beatified on June 4, 1995. The author thanks Father David P. Reid, SS.CC., provincial, for providing information, and for reviewing the draft of this biography.

[2] No author, pamphlet, *Blessed Damien of Molokai, Servant of God, Servant of Humanity*. (Honolulu, HI: Knights of Columbus Kamiano Council #11743, 1997), p. 2)

[3] Joseph N. Tylenda, S.J., "A Greater Love, Damien de Veuster, SS.CC. (1840-1889)" in *Portraits in American Sanctity* (Chicago, IL: Franciscan Herald Press, 1982), p. 68.

[4] Tylenda, Portraits, p. 71.

[5] Vital Jourdain, *The Heart of Father Damien*, tr. by Francis Larkin and Charles Davenport, (Milwaukee, WI: The Bruce Publishing Company, 1955), p. 253.

[6] Matteo Ricci, S.J. was declared Servant of God on April 9, 1984. The author thanks Father Paolo Molinari, S.J., for providing information and for reviewing the draft of this biography.

[7] Francis Albert Rouleau, "Ricci, Matteo," *New Catholic Encyclopedia*, vol. 12, p. 471.

[8] Rouleau, p. 471.

[9] Rouleau, p. 471.

[10] Rouleau, p. 471.

[11] Rouleau, p. 472.

[12] Michael Hồ Đình Hy was canonized on June 19, 1988. The author thanks Father Francis Xavier Nhi Nguyen, parish priest serving in the Archdiocese of Baltimore, for providing information, and for reviewing the draft of this biography.

[13] Adrien Launay, *Les Trente-Cinq Vénérables Serviteurs De Dieu: Francais, Anamies, Chinois Mis A Mort Pour La Foi En Extreme Orient, De 1815 A 1862*. Paris, France: P. Lethielleux, Libraire-Editeur, troisieme edition, 1907), p. 130.

[14] Adrien Launay, Les Trente-Cinq, p. 132.

[15] Adrien Launay, Les Trente-Cinq, p. 136.

[16] Matthew Kadalikkattil was declared Servant of God on April 12, 1989.

[17] Puthenkalam and Mampra, p. 336.

[18] Final papal approbation was received in 1976, and the community's constitutions were approved in 1986.

[19] Puthenkalam and Mampra, p. 337.

[20] Zacharias Salterinte, O.C.D. was declared Servant of God on January 14, 1984. The author thanks Rev. Dr. Antony Pinheiro, O.C.D., vice postulator, for providing information, and for reviewing the draft of this biography.

[21] Puthenkalam and Mampra, p. 384.

[22] Lucy Pak Hŏi-sun was canonized on May 6, 1984. The author thanks Father Gregory Kim Yong Ki, C.M., parish priest at Seoul, for providing information, and for reviewing the draft of this biography.

[23] Kim Chang-seok Thaddeus, *Lives of 103 Martyr Saints of Korea* (Seoul, South Korea: Catholic Publishing House, second edition, 1984), p. 39.

[24] Kim Chang-seok, p. 39.

[25] Kim Chang-seok, p. 40.

[26] Kim Chang-seok, p. 40.

June

[1] Thomas Kurialacherry was declared Servant of God on March 18, 1996. The author thanks Mar Thomas Kurialacherry Vikas, vice postulator, for providing information, and for reviewing the draft of this biography.

[2] Chavalier K. C. Chacko, *The Vigilant Shepherd: Bishop Mar Thomas Kurialacherry*. (Alwaye, Kerala, India: The Cenacle, 1986), p. 11.

[3] Chacko, *The Vigilant Shepherd: Bishop Mar Thomas Kurialacherry*, pp. 10-11.

[4] Chacko, *The Vigilant Shepherd: Bishop Mar Thomas Kurialacherry*, p. 22.

[5] Puthenkalam and Mampra, p. 354.

[6] Clemente Vismara, P.I.M.E. was named Servant of God on April 11, 2005. The author thanks Father Sergio Fossati, P.I.M.E. Mission Center Director, for providing information, and for reviewing the draft of this biography.

[7] Saint Lucy Wang Cheng and three female teenage companions were canonized on October 1, 2000 as part of the 120 Martyrs of China. The author thanks the confreres of the Vincentian China Province for providing information, and for reviewing the draft of this biography.

[8] Episcopal Commission for Canonization of Saints and Martyrs of China, *The Newly Canonized Martyr-Saints of China*. (Taiwan: CRBC, 2000), p. 69.

[9] Episcopal Commission for Canonization of Saints and Martyrs of China, p. 69.

[10] Melchior de Marion Brésillac, S.M.A. was named Servant of God on May 24, 2000. The author thanks Father Michael O'Shea, S.M.A., for providing information, and for reviewing the draft of this biography.

[11] Puthenkalam and Mampra, p. 283.

[12] Puthenkalam and Mampra, p. 284.

[13] Mariam Thresia, C.H.F. was beatified on April 9, 2000.

[14] Mathias Mundadan, C.M.I., ed., *The Writings of Mother Mariam Thresia* (Mannuthy, Kerala, India: Holy Family Generalate, 1991), p. 377.

[15] Mundadan, Writings, p. 378.

[16] Mundadan, Writings, p. 382.

[17] Mundadan, Writings, p. 484.

[18] Pamphlet, *Bl. Mariam Thresia* (Mannuthy, Kerala, India: Holy Family Generalate, 2000), p. 3.

July

[1] Petrer Kibe Kasui, S.J. was named a Servant of God on September 2, 1994. The author thanks Paolo Molinar,S.J., postulator, for providing information, and for reviewing the draft of this biography.

[2] Andrew Kim Tae-gŏn was canonized on May 6, 1984. The author thanks Father Gregory Kim Yong Ki, C.M., parish priest at Seoul, for providing information, and for reviewing the draft of this biography.

[3] MacMahon, p. 59.

[4] MacMahon, p. 74.

[5] MacMahon, p. 74.

[6] Kim Chang-seok, p. 23.

[7] MacMahon, p. 80.

[8] Peter ToRot was beatified on January 17, 1995. The author thanks Most Rev. Rochus Josef Tatami, M.S.C., Auxiliary Bishop of Kerema, for providing information, and for reviewing the draft of this biography.

[9] The surviving daughter Rufina IaMama was present at the beatification ceremony of her father in 1995.

[10] Private correspondence with Bishop Rochus Josef Tatamai, M.S.C.; November 18, 2005.

[11] The 120 Martyrs of China were canonized on October 1, 2000.

[12] Augustine Zhao Rong was canonized, October 1, 2000. The author thanks the confreres of the Vincentian China Province for providing information, and for reviewing the draft of the biography.

[13] Episcopal Commission for Canonization of Saints and Martyrs of China, pp. 3-4.

[14] Marie Hermine, F.M.M., and Companions were canonized on October 1, 2000. The author thanks Sister Rosemarie Higgins, F.M.M., Director of Communications, for providing information, and for reviewing the draft of the biography. For more information on the Martyrs, please see www.fmm.org.

[15] Justina Fanego, F.M.M., tr. by Sheila Patenaude, F.M.M., *In Order To Give Life! A Community That Delivered Itself Up To Death.* (France: Nouvelle Imprimerie Laballery, 2000), p. 63.

[16] Fanego, p. 63.

[17] Fanego p. 64.

[18] Fanego, p. 30.

[19] Fanego., p. 33.

[20] Fanego., p. 35.

[21] Emmanuel Ruiz and Companions were beatified on October 10, 1926. The author thanks Paolo Molinar, S.J., postulator, for providing information, and for reviewing the draft of this biography.

[22] Henri Jalabert, S.J., "Damascus, Martyrs of," *New Catholic Encyclopedia*, vol. 4, p. 624.

[23] Jalabert, p. 624.

[24] Jalabert, p. 624.

[25] Mary Zhu Wu and Companions were canonized on October 1, 2000. The author thanks the confreres of the Vincentian China Province for providing information, and for reviewing the draft of this biography.

[26] Episcopal Commission for Canonization of Saints and Martyrs of China, p. 58.

[27] Episcopal Commission for Canonization of Saints and Martyrs of China, p. 53.

[28] Episcopal Commission for Canonization of Saints and Martyrs of China, p. 94.

[29] Episcopal Commission for Canonization of Saints and Martyrs of China, p. 95.

[30] Episcopal Commission for Canonization of Saints and Martyrs of China, p. 95.

[31] Sharbel Makhloof was canonized on October 9, 1977.

[32] Donald Attwater, *Saints Of The East.* (London, England: The Catholic Book Club, 1962), p. 185.

[33] Andrew Phú Yên was beatified on March 5, 2000. The author thanks Father Francis Xavier Nhi Nguyen, parish priest serving in the Archdiocese of Baltimore, for providing information, and for reviewing the draft of this biography.

[34] Dung Lac Tan Cao Tuong, Duong Song cac Thanh Tu Dao Viet Nam; www: Vietcatholic.net; no pagination.

[35] Dung Lac Tan Cao Tuong, Duong Song cac Thanh Tu Dao Viet Nam.

[36] Dung Lac Tan Cao Tuong, Duong Song cac Thanh Tu Dao Viet Nam.

[37] Dung Lac Tan Cao Tuong, Duong Song cac Thanh Tu Dao Viet Nam.

[38] Dung Lac Tan Cao Tuong, Duong Song cac Thanh Tu Dao Viet Nam.

[39] Rudolph Aquaviva, S.J., and Companions were beatified on April 16, 1893.

[40] Puthenkalam and Mampra, p. 105.

[41] Puthenkalam and Mampra, p. 107.

[42] Puthenkalam and Mampra, p. 108.

[43] Alphonsa Muttathupadathu, F.C.C. was beatified on February 8, 1986.

[44] Chevalier K.C. Chacko, *Sister Alphonsa* (Bharananganam, Kerala, India: Vice Postulator for the Cause of Sister Alphonsa, 2000), p. 31.

[45] Chacko, Sister Alphonsa., p. 34.

[46] Chacko, Sister Alphonsa., p. 42.

[47] Chacko, Sister Alphonsa, p. 46.

[48] Chacko, Sister Alphonsa., p. 44.

[49] Chacko, Sister Alphonsa, p. 49.

[50] Joseph Zhang Wenlan and Companions were canonized on October 1, 2000. The author thanks the confreres of the Vincentian China Province for providing information, and for reviewing the draft of the biography.

[51] Episcopal Commission for Canonization of Saints and Martyrs of China, p. 19.

[52] Episcopal Commission for Canonization of Saints and Martyrs of China, p. 18.

August

[1] Mary MacKillop, R.M. was beatified on January 19, 1995.

[2] Osmund Thorpe, O.P., *Mary MacKillop*, second edition. (Rydalmere, Australia: The Petty Publishing Company Limited, 1980), p. 109.

[3] www.xavier.sa.au/subjects/religed /mackillop/mackillop2.htm; p. 2.

[4] www.achievers-odds.com.au/topac.mmackillopfull.htm; p. 1.

[5] Marianne Cope, O.S.F. was beatified on May 14, 2005. The author thanks Sister Mary Laurence Hanley, O.S.F., director for the cause of Mother Marianne, for providing information, and for reviewing the draft of the biography.

[6] Private correspondence with Hanley, p. 14.

[7] Private correspondence with Hanley, p. 14.

[8] Hanley, p. 246.

[9] *The Catholic Sun*, diocese of Syracuse, NY; July 12-25, 2001; vol. 120, no. 26; pp. 1, 4.

[10] Private correspondence with Mary Laurence Hanley, O.S.F., *Representative Writings* (Syracuse, N.Y.: Sisters of the Third Franciscan Order, n.d.), letter to Bishop K., 9/15/1888; p. 11.

[11] Hanley, *Representative Writings*, letter to Paul Cope, p. 17.

[12] Maurice Tornay, M.E.P., was beatified on May 16, 1993.

[13] Robert Loup, Martyr in Tibet. *The Heroic Life and Death of Father Maurice Tornay, St. Bernard Missionary to Tibet*, tr. by Charles Davenport (New York, N.Y.: David McKay Company, Inc.; 1956), p. 211.

[14] Francisca del Espiritu Santo was declared Servant of God on July 8, 2003.

[15] Juan de Santo Domingo, O.P., *The Beatorio De Santa Catalina. The Cradle Years of the Dominican Sisters In The Philippines*, second edition (Quezon City, Philippines: GPV Printing Ventures Co., 2000), p. 94.

[16] De Santo Domingo, p. 94.

[17] Marie Baouardy was beatified on November 13, 1983. The author thanks Sister Lea Hargis, O.C.M., librarian; and Brother Bryan Paquette, promotion director, for providing information, and for reviewing the draft of this biography.

[18] Doris C. Neger, "The Little Arab — Mariam Bouardy, Blessed Mary of Christ Crucified," *Sophia*, vol. 31, no. 1, Jan.-Feb. 2002, reprinted in http://www.melkite.org/sa33.htm; p. 2.

[19] Euphrasia Eluvathingal, C.M.C., was beatified on December 3, 2006.

[20] J. Ephrem C.R., *The Praying Mother: Servant of God Mother Euphrasia*, ed. by Sister Cleopatra, C.M.C., tr. by C. A. Regina. (Thrissur, Kerala, India: Holy Trinity Convent, 1999), p. 7.

[21] Puthenkalam and Mampra, p. 361.

[22] Ephrem, p. 32.

September

[1] Bartolomeo Gutierrez Rodriguez, O.S.A., was beatified on July 7, 1867.

[2] Marion A. Habig, *Saints Of The Americas*, (Huntington, IN: Our Sunday, Visitor, 1974), p. 178.

[3] Vincent Robert Capodanno was named Servant of God on May 21, 2006. The author thanks Father Daniel Mode, priest of the Diocese of Arlington and postulator for the cause of Vincent Capodanno; and Mary Preece, the Coordinator for the Cause of Canonization of Vincent Capodanno, for providing information and reviewing the draft of this biography. The author thanks too June Loguirato for alerting him to include this cause in this book.

[4] Daniel L. Mode, *The Grunt Padre. The Service & Sacrifice Of Father Vincent Robert Capodanno*, Vietnam 1966-1967. (Oak Lawn, IL: CMJ Marian Books, 2000), p. 11.

[5] Mode, p. 46.

[6] Mode, p. 56.

[7] Mode, p. 97.

[8] Mode, p. 96.

[9] Mode, p. 96.

[10] Mode, p. 129.

[11] Mother Teresa, M.C., was beatified on October 19, 2003. The author thanks Sister M. Ozana, M.C., for providing information, and for reviewing the draft of this biography.

[12] Habig, p. 2.

[13] Habig, p. 3.

[14] Habig, p. 2.

[15] Habig., p. 3.

[16] The village of Vailankanni is located on the Bay of Bengal approximately 220 miles south of Madras (now Chennai).

[17] *Novena to Our Lady of Vailankanni*, p. 5.

[18] John Gabriel Perboyre, C.M. was canonized on June 2, 1996. The author thanks Father John Carven, C.M, provincial archivist, for providing information, and for reviewing the draft of this biography.

[19] Andre Sylvestre, CM, *Jean Gabriel Perboyre, Pretre De La Congregation De La Mission Saint-Lazare, Martrise En Chine Le 11 Septembre 1840* (Peuch-Montgesty, Catus: Association Jean Gabriel Perboyre, n.d.), p. 14.

[20] Thomas Davitt, C.M., "The Cause for the Canonization of John Gabriel Perboyre, C.M.", *Vincentian Heritage*, vol. XVI, no. 2, 1995, p. 210.

[21] *The Liturgy of the Hours*, Proper of the Congregation of the Mission, New York, N.Y.: Catholic Book Publishing Co., 1978; pp. 51-52.

[22] The Martyrs of Korea were canonized on May 6, 1984. The author thanks Father Gregory Kim Yong Ki, C.M., parish priest at Seoul, for providing information, and for reviewing the draft of this biography.

[23] Kim Chang-seok, p. 7.

[24] Lawrence Imbert, M.E.P. was canonized May 6, 1984.

[25] MacMahon, pp. 551-552.

[26] MacMahon, p. 553.

[27] MacMahon p. 554.

[28] MacMahon, p. 558.

[29] MacMahon, p. 563.

[30] Saint Paul Chŏng Ha-sang was canonized on May 6, 1984. The author thanks Father Gregory Kim Yong Ki, C.M., parish priest at Seoul, for providing information, and for reviewing the draft of this biography.

[31] MacMahon, p. 120.

[32] Kim Chang-seok, p. 27.

[33] John Baptist Mazzucconi, P.I.M.E., was beatified on February 19, 1984. The author thanks Father Sergio Fossati, P.I.M.E. Mission Center Director, for providing information, and for reviewing the draft of this biography.

[34] Mariagrazia Zambon, *Crimson Seeds: Eighteen P.I.M.E. Martyrs*. (Detroit, MI: P.I.M.E. World Press, 1997), p. 21.

[35] Zambon, p. 23.

[36] Zambon, p. 23.

[37] Zambon, p. 27.

[38] Zambon, p. 29.

[39] Zambon, pp. 29-30.

[40] Saint Lorenzo Ruiz and Companions were canonized on October 18, 1987. The author thanks Father Erno Diaz, director of the Chapel of San

Lorenzo Ruiz in New York City, for providing information, and for reviewing the draft of this biography.

[41] Fidel Villaroel, O.P., *Lorenzo De Manila: The Protomartyr of the Philippines, and His Companions.* (Manila, Philippines: UST Press, 1988), p. 74.

[42] Villarroel, p. 89.

[43] Villarroel, p. 91.

[44] Villarroel, pp. 104-105.

[45] Villarroel, p. 108.

October

[1] Matthew Kavukatt was declared Servant of God on October 25,1996. The author thanks Father Jacob Kattoor and Sister Jane Kottaram, C.M.C., vice postulators, for providing information, and for reviewing the draft of this biography.

[2] Puthenkalam, and Mampra, p. 445.

[3] Puthenkalam, and Mampra, p. 450.

[4] Puthenkalam, and Mampra, p. 450..

[5] Puthenkalam, and Mampra, p. 451.

[6] Puthenkalam, and Mampra, p. 457.

[7] The Talangpaz Sisters were declared Servants of God on November 24, 1999.

[8] Luciano P. R. Santiago, *Stars of Peace: The Talangpaz Sisters* (Manila, Philippines: Congregation of the Augustinian Recollect Sisters, 2001), p. 68.

[9] Walter Ciszek, S.J., was declared Servant of God on October 11, 1990. The author thanks Sister Albertine, O.S.F., archivist, and secretary for the Board of the Walter Ciszek Prayer League for providing information, and for reviewing the draft of this biography.

[10] Walter Ciszek, S.J, with Daniel L. Flaherty, S.J., *With God in Russia.* (New York, N.Y.: The America Press, 1964), pp. 6-7.

[11] Edmund Murphy, S.J., *The Walter Ciszek Story* (Scranton, PA: The Association of Jesuit University Presses, n.d.), pp. 24-25.

[12] Murphy, p. 201.

[13] Augustine Thevarparampil was beatified on January 1, 2006.

[14] Puthenkalam and Mampra, p. 396.

[15] Puthenkalam and Mampra, p. 398.

[16] Magdalene of Nagasaki was canonized on October 18, 1987.

[17] Saint Yu Tae-ch'ŏl Peter was canonized on May 6, 1984. The author thanks Father Gregory Kim Yong Ki, CM, parish priest at Seoul, for providing information, and for reviewing the draft of this biography.

[18] Kim Chang-seok, p. 91.

[19] Kim Chang-seok, p. 91.

[20] Kim Chang-seok, p. 91.

November

[1] Constant Lievens, S.J. was declared Servant of God on March 15, 2000.

[2] Blessed Mary of the Passion, F.M.M. was beatified on October 20, 2002. The author thanks Sister Rosemarie Higgins, F.M.M., director of F.M.M communications, for providing information and for reviewing the draft of this biography.

[3] Marie Therese de Maleissye, F.M.M., *A Short Life of Mary of the Passion* (Mumbai, Maharashtra, India: St. Paul Training School Press, 2002), p. 12.

[4] De Maleissye, p. 17.

[5] De Maleissye, p. 21-22.

[6] De Maleissye, pp. 30-31.

[7] Marcel Launay, *Helene de Chappotin and the Missionaries of Mary* (Paris, France: Editions du Cerf, 2001), p. 67.

[8] De Maleissye, pp. 33-34.

[9] De Maleissye, p. 44.

[10] De Maleissye, p. 44.

[11] De Maleissye, pp. 70-71.

[12] De Maleissye., pp. 92-102.

[13] Aurelian of the Blessed Sacrament, O.C.D. was declared Venerable on March 26, 1999. The author thanks Rev. Dr. Antony Pinheiro, O.C.D., for providing information, and for reviewing the draft of this biography.

[14] Puthenkalam and Mampra, p. 252.

[15] Puthenkalam and Mampra,, p. 267.

[16] Puthenkalam and Mampra, p. 264.

[17] Veronica of the Passion, A.C. was beatified on April 23, 2002. The author thanks Sister M. Liceria, A.C., vice postulator, for providing information, and for reviewing the draft of this biography.

[18] Monograph, no author, *A Biographical Sketch of the Servant of God, Mother Mary Veronica of the Passion, Nee Sophie Leeves, 1823-1906* (n.d.), p. 1.

[19] Puthenkalam and Mampra, p. 300.

[20] Puthenkalam and Mampra, p. 302.

[21] Puthenkalam and Mampra, p. 302.

[22] Agnelo Gustavo Adolfo de Souza, S.F.X. was declared Venerable on November 10, 1986. The author thanks Father Tony Fernandes, S.F.X., vice postulator, for providing information, and for reviewing the draft of this biography.

[23] Agnelo Noronha, S.F.X., *Venerable Father Agnelo De Souza — A Saint For India*. (Pilar, Goa, India: Cause of Fr. Agnelo, 1988), p. 11.

[24] Noronha, p. 8.

[25] Noronha, p. 13.

[26] http://members.iglou.com/jvianney/ollavang.html; p. 2.

[27] Blessed Salvator Lilli, O.F.M., and Companions were beatified on October 3, 1982. The author thanks Father Lucas De Rosa, O.F.M., postulator, for providing information, and for reviewing the draft of this biography.

[28] www.vidasejemplares.org/BeatoSalvador.pdf; p. 3.

[29] The Martyrs of Vietnam, know also as Martyrs of Indo-China, or Tonkin, or Annam, were canonized on June 19, 1988. The author thanks Father Francis Xavier Nhi Nguyen, parish priest serving in the Archdiocese of Baltimore, for providing information, and for reviewing the draft of this biography.

[30] Andre Gelinas, "Vietnam," *New Catholic Encyclopedia*, 1967 edition, vol. 14, p. 661.

[31] Gelinas, p. 662.

[32] Théophane Vénard, M.E.P., was canonized on June 19, 1988.

[33] John Cumming, *Letters From Saints To Sinners*. (New York, N.Y.: The Crossroad Publishing Company, 1996), pp. 239-240.

[34] Adrien Launay, p. 221.

[35] Cumming, p. 243.

[36] Cumming, p. 243.

December

[1] Francis Xavier, S.J. was canonized on March 12, 1622.

[2] Martin Joseph Costelloe, tr., *The Letters and Instructions of Francis Xavier* (St. Louis, MO: The Institute of Jesuit Sources, 1992), pp. 68-69; letter of 1/15/1544.

[3] Nimattullah Youssef Kassab al-Hardini was canonized on May 16, 2004.

[4] Paul Sfeir, *Blessed Nimattullah Kassab Al-Hardini: His Life, Words and Spiritualities*, tr. by Kozhayà S. Akiki. (Kaslik, Lebanon: Holy Spirit University, 2001), p. 23.

[5] Sfeir, p. 22.

[6] Sfeir, p. 27.

[7] Sfeir, p. 101.

[8] Sfeir, p. 81.

[9] Sfeir, p. 81.

[10] Philip Siphong Onphithah and Companions were beatified on October 22, 1989. The author thanks Father Daniel Abogado, C.M., professor at St. Vincent Seminary, Samphran, Thailand, for providing information.

[11] www.sspxasia.com/Seven Blessed Martyrs of Thailand, p.2.

[12] www.sspxasia.com/Seven, p. 3.

[13] www.sspxasia.com/Seven, p. 3.

[14] www.sspxasia.com/Seven, p. 4.

[15] Andrew Dũng Lạc an Trần was canonized on June 19, 1988. The author thanks Father Francis Xavier Nhi Nguyen, parish priest serving in the Archdio-

cese of Baltimore, for providing information, and for reviewing the draft of the biography.

[16] Dung Lac Tan Cao Tuong, Duong Song cac Thanh Tu Dao Viet Nam; www.Vietcatholic.net; p. 1.

BIBLIOGRAPHY

Alangaram, A., S.J. *Christ of the Asian Peoples*. Bangalore: Asian Trading Corporation, 1999.

Aliño Leyson, Ildebrando Jesus. *Pedro Calungsod: Prospects of a Teenage Filipino*. Cebu, Philippines: Claretian Publications, n.d.

Arévalo, Catalino G., SJ. *Pedro Calungsod: Young Visayan Proto-Martyr*. Second edition. Quezon City, Philippines: Paulines Publishing House, 2000.

Attwater, Donald. *Saints Of The East*. London, England: The Catholic Book Club, 1962.

Bibliotheca Sanctorum. Rome: Istituto Giovanni XXIII Della Pontificia Universita Lateranense, 1968. Volumes I – XII, and Two Appendices. Roma, Italia: Instituto Giovanni XXIII Nella Pontificia Universita Lateranense, 1961.

Blessed Damien of Molokai, Servant of God, Servant of Humanity. Honolulu, HI: Knights of Columbus Kamiano Council #11743, 1997.

Bl. Mariam Thresia. Mannuthy, Kerala, India: Holy Family Generalate, 2000.

Blessed Mother Mariam Thresia Beatification Souvenir. Mannuthy, Thrissur, Kerala, India: The Congregation of the Holy Family, 2000.

Borzaga, Mario. "To Be a Happy Man," Ed. Lucia Borzaga. Rome, Italy: Oblate General Postulation, 1992.

Boxer, C.R. *The Christian Century in Japan 1549-1650*. Berkeley, CA: University of California Press, 1967.

Bunson, Matthew, Margaret, and Stephen. *Encyclopedia Of Saints*. Huntington, IN: Our Sunday Visitor, 1998.

Butler's Lives of the Saints. Herbert Thurston and Donald Attwater. Eds. Four volumes. Westminster, Maryland: Christian Classics, 1990.

Cappella Papale Presieduta Dal Santo Padre Giovanni Paolo II per la Canizzazione Dei Beati Agostino Zhao Rong E 119 Compagni. Vatican City:Tipografia Vaticana, October 2000.

Chacko, Chevalier K.C. *Sister Alphonsa*. Bharananganam, India: The Vice Postulator Cause of Blessed Alphonsa, 1990.

_______. *The Vigilant Shepherd: Bishop Mar Thomas Kurialacherry*. Alwaye, Kerala, India: The Cenacle, 1986.

Chavara, Kuriackose Elias. *Complete Works of Blessed Chavara, Vol. II.* Tr. by Sr. Mary Leo, C.M.C., and others. Mannanam, India: The Committee for the Cause of Blessed Chavara, 1989.

Cheers, Gordon. Gen. ed., and others. *Geographica. The complete Illustrated Atlas of the World.* New York, NY: Barnes & Noble, 2001.

Ciszek, Walter, S.J., with Flaherty, Daniel L., S.J., *With God in Russia.* New York: The America Press, 1964.

Clark, S.J., Francis X. *Asian Saints.* Quezon City, Philippines: Claretian Publications, 2000.

Congregatio de Causis Sanctorum. Index ac Status Causarum. Città del Vaticano, 1999.

Costelloe, Martin Joseph, S.J. Tr. *The Letters and Instructions of Francis Xavier.* St. Louis, MO: The Institute of Jesuit Sources, 1992.

Cumming, John. Ed. *Letters from Saints to Sinners.* New York, NY: The Crossroad Publishing Company, 1996.

Da Silva Rego, A. "Patronato Real. Padroado of Portugal." *New Catholic Encyclopedia.* Vol.10, pp. 1113-1115.

Davitt, Thomas, C.M. "The Cause for the Canonization of John Gabriel Perboyre, C.M." *Vincentian Heritage*. Vol. XVI. No. 2. 1995. pp. 209-211.

De Santo Domingo, Juan, O.P. Tr. by The Congregation of Dominican Sisters of St. Catherine of Siena. *The Beatorio De Santa Catalina. The Cradle Years Of The Dominican Sisters In The Philippines.* Second edition. Quezon City, Philippines: GPV Printing Ventures, Co., 2000.

De Maleissye, Marie-Therese, F.M.M. *A Short Life of Mary of the Passion.* Mumbai, Maharashtra, India: St. Paul Press Training School, 2002.

Dung Lac Tan Cao Tuong, Duong Song cac Thanh Tu Dao Viet Nam; www.Vietcatholic.net; no pagination.

Ephrem, J., C.R., Cleopatra, Sr., C.M.C. Ed. *The Praying Mother: Servant of God Mother Euphrasia.* Tr. by C. A. Regina. Kerala, India: Holy Trinity Convent, 1999.

Episcopal Commission for Canonization of Saints and Martyrs of China. *The Newly Canonized Martyr-Saints of China.* Taiwan: CRBC, 2000.

Fanego, Justina, F.M.M. *In Order to Give Life: A Community That Delivered Itself Up To Death.* Tr. by Sheila Patenaude, F.M.M.. France: Nouvelle Imprimerie Laballery, 2000.

Fitzpatrick, James M., O.M.I. *Priest and Martyr: Blessed Nicholas Bunkerd Kitbamrung, 1895-1944.* Bangkok, Thailand: Assumption Printing Press, 2003.

Fox, Thomas C. *Pentecost in Asia: A New Way of Being Church.* Maryknoll, NY: Orbis Books, 2002.

Francy, Sr., C.H.F.; Annie Grace, Sr., C.H.F.; and Varghese, Sr. Ruby, C.H.F. *Blessed Mariam Thresia: A Biography.* Kerala, India: Holy Family Publications, 2000.

Froehle, Bryan T. and Gautier, Mary L. Eds.. *Global Catholicism: Portrait of a World Church.* Maryknoll, NY: Orbis Books, 2003.

Gelinas, Andre. "Vietnam." *New Catholic Encyclopedia.* 1967 edition. Vol. 14. pp. 661-63.

Gheddo, Piero. *Il Santo Col Martello: Felice Tantardini: 70 anni di Birmania.* Bologna, Italia: Editrice Missionaria Italiana, 2000.

Gomes, Herma, SS.CC. *Damien, Servant of God, Servant of Humanity.* Honolulu, HI: Hawaii Province of the Congregation of the Sacred Hearts of Jesus and Mary, 2002.

Guennou, Jean. *Missions Étrangères de Paris.* Paris: Missions Étrangères de Paris, 1984.

Habig, Marion A. *Saints Of The Americas.* Huntington, IN: Our Sunday Visitor, 1974.

Hanley, Mary Laurence, O.F.M. *Representative Writings of the Servant of God Mother Marianne of Molokai..* "Letter to Paul Cope." Syracuse, NY: Sisters of the Third Franciscan Order, n.d., p. 17.

Jalabert, Henri, S.J. "Damascus, Martyrs of," *New Catholic Encyclopedia.* Vol. 4. Pg. 624.

Jenkins, Philip. *The Next Christendom: The Coming of Global Christianity.* New York: Oxford University Press, 2002.

Jeyakumar, D. Arthur. *History Of Christianity In India: Selected Themes.* Delhi, India: ISPCK, 2002.

John Paul II, Pope. *Ecclesia In Asia. Apostolic Exhortation of the Holy FatherJohn Paul II on Jesus Christ the Savior and His Mission of Love and Service in Asia.* Pasay City, Philippines: Paulines Publishing House, 2000.

Jourdain, Vital. *The Heart of Father Damien.* Tr. by Francis Larkin and Charles Davenport. Milwaukee, WI: The Bruce Publishing Company, 1955.

Kim Chang-seok Thaddeus. *Lives Of 103 Martyr Saints Of Korea.* Seoul, Korea: Catholic Publishing House, 1984.

Launay, Adrien. *Histoire Générale De La Société des Missions-Étrangéres.* Paris: Téqui, 1894.

_______. *Les Trente-Cinq Vénérables Serviteurs De Dieu: Francais, Anamies, Chinois Mis A Mort Pour La Foi En Extreme Orient, De 1815 A 1862.* Paris, France: P. Lethielleux, Libraire-Editeur, troisieme edition, 1907.

Launay, Marcel. *Helene de Chappotin and the Missionaries of Mary.* Paris, France: Editions du Cerf, 2001.

The Liturgy of the Hours. Vol. I-IV. New York: Catholic Book Publishing Co., 1976.

The Liturgy of the Hours. Proper of the Congregation of the Mission. New York: Catholic Book Publishing Co.; 1978.

Loup, Robert. *Martyr In Tibet:The Heroic Life and Death of Father Maurice Tornay, St. Bernard Missionary to Tibet,* Tr. by Charles Davenport. New York: David McKay Company, Inc., 1956.

MacMahon, Hugh. Gen. Ed. and Trans. *The Korean Martyr Saints: Founders Of A Church.* Seoul, South Korea: St. Hwang Sok Tu Luke Publishing House, 1995.

Marin, Rosanna, F.M.M.. *That They May Have Life: The Martyrs of Taiyuan-fu and the FMM.* Tr. by General Secretariat F.M.M. Roma, Ialia: Franciscan Missionaries of Mary Generalate, 2000.

Mathias, Teresa, F.D.C.C. *Fernanda:Fragrance of Humble Love.* Mumbai, India: Canossian Daughters of Charity, 1996.

Mathothu, Kurian. *Blessed Father Kuriakose Elias Chavara.* Tr. by T. V. Thomas. Palai, Kerala, India: Pastoral Service Centre, 1988.

_______. *Kunjachan: The Missionary Among The Harijans in India.* Palai, India: Resmi Printers, 1995.

_______ and Joseph, Baby. Eds. *The Little Liberator: Servant of God, 'Kunjachan,' Fr. Augustine Thevarparampil.* Kerala, India: The Vice-Postulator St. Augustine's Forane Church, n.d.

Mattam, Joseph and Marak, Krickwin C. Eds. *Blossoms From The East: Contribution of the Indian Church to World Mission.* Mumbai: St Pauls, 1999.

Mode, Daniel L. *The Grunt Padre.* Oak Lawn, IL: CMJ Marian Publishers, 2000.

Moffett, Samuel Hugh. *A History of Christianity in Asia, Volume 1: Beginnings to 1500.* San Francisco: HarperSanFrancisco, 1992.

Molinari, Paolo, S.J., "Takayama Ukon," *Bibliotheca Sanctorum, Prima Appendice*, col. 1350-1354.

Moolayil, Thomas and Joseph, Matthew. Eds. "The Passion Flower: Commemorative of the 25th Death Anniversary of Servant of God Sister Alphonsa, Vol. XV, No. 5" Palai, Kerala, India: St. Thomas Press, 1971.

Moozhoor, Zacharias M., C.M.I.. *Blessed Chavara: The Star of the East.* Tr. by Sheila Kannath, C.M.C. Kottayam, Kerala, India: D.C. Offset Printers, 1993.

Mundadan, Mathias, C.M.I. Ed. *Writings of Mother Mariam Thresia.* Mannuthy, Trichur, India: Holy Family Generalate, 1991.

Murphy, Edmund, S.J. *The Walter Ciszek Story.* Scranton, PA: The Association of Jesuit University Presses, n.d.

Nedungatt, George, S.J. *Crucified With Christ For All: A Biography of Bl. Mariam Thresia.* Kerala, India: Holy Family Publications, 2002.

Neger, Doris C. "The Little Arab: Blessed Mariam Bouardy." *Sophia.* Vol. 31. No. 1. Jan.-Feb. 2002. Reprinted in http://www.melkitge.org/sa33.htm; pp. 1-4.

The New American Bible. Nashville, TN: Thomas Nelson Publishers, 1971.

The Newly Canonized Martyr-Saints of China. Taiwan, Roc: CRBC, 2000.

Noronha, Agnelo, S.F.X., *Venerable Father Agnelo de Souza — A Saint For India.* Pilar, Goa, India: Cause of Fr. Agnelo, 1988.

Novena to Our Lady of Vailankanni. Pamphlet.

Park, Hee-bohng, ed. *Chol-Du San Martyrs' Shrine: Twenty Year Anniversary Album.* Catholic Press, 1987.

Pastor, Sister, C.M.C. *Thirsting For God: The Spirituality of Venerable Mother Euphrasia.* Tr. by Sister Bianca, C.M.C. Kerala, India: C.M.C Publications, 2002.

Peregrin, Sister., C.M.C. *Servant of God: Mother Euphrasia*. Tr. by Sister Leo, C.M.C.. Kerala, India: Holy Trinity Convent, 1998.

Phan, Peter C. *Christianity with an Asian Face: Asian American Theology in the Making*. Maryknoll, NY: Orbis Books, 2003.

_______. Ed. *The Asian Synod: Texts and Commentaries*. Maryknoll, NY: Orbis Books, 2002.

Phúc, Hồng, C.Ss.R. *Đức Mẹ La Vang và Giáo Hội Công Giáo Việt Nam*.

Picken, Stuart, D. B. *Christianity and Japan:Meeting, Conflict, Hope*. New York: Harper & Row, Publishers, Inc., 1983.

Plathottam, Valerian, C.M.I. *The First Indian Saint: Blessed Fr. Kuriakose Elias Chavara*. Mannanam, India: Sanjos Book Stall, n.d.

Porras, Willaim M. "Patronato Real. Patronato of Spain." *New Catholic Encyclopedia*. Vol. 10. Pp. 1115-1116.

Puthenkalam, Joseph, S.D.B., and Mampra, Anthony, S.D.B. *Sanctity In India*. Chennai, Tamil Nadu: Salesian Institute of Graphic Arts, 2000.

Quitugua, David Cruz. *The Vicar Apostolic in the 1983 Code of Canon Law*. Romae: Pontificiam Universitatem S. Thomae In Urbe, 1995.

Raj, Felix, S.J. "St. John de Brittó, 1647-1693." Published in *Himmat* weekly on February 11, 1977. www.goethals.org/life.htm.

Rao, Belona Vittal. *History of Asia: From early times to A.D. 2000*. New Delhi: Sterling Publishers Pvt. Ltd., 2001.

Rouleau, Francis Albert. "Ricci, Matteo." *New Catholic Encyclopedia*. Vol. 12. pp. 470-722.

Saint Lawrence, Ignatius. *Francis Xavier*. Bangalore, Karnataka, India: Claretian Publications, 1998.

Santiago, Luciano P.R. *Stars of Peace: The Talangpaz Sisters*. Manila, Philippines: Congregation of the Augustinian Recollect Sisters, 2001.

Schwartz, Aloysius. *Killing Me Softly: The Inspiring Story of a Champion of the Poor*. New York: Alba House, 1993.

Segalla, Giuseppe. *Martyr Of Charity — Sister Rani Maria*. Schor Series #9. Tellicherry, Kerala, India: Institute for Research in Social Sciences and Humanities, 2003.

Sendlein, Thomas, C.M.. "The 120 Martyr Saints of China" in *China Sparks: Vincentian Reflections On The Church In China*. Vol. V. No.1. 2000.

Sfeir, Paul. *Blessed Nimattullah Kassab Al-Hardini: His Life, Words and Spiritualities.* Tr. by Kozhaya S. Akiki. Kaslik, Lebanon: Holy Spirit University, 2001.

_______. *Saint Rafqa The Lebanese Nun: Her Life and Spirituality.* Tr. by Kozhaya S. Akiki:Holy Spirit University, Kaslik, Lebanon, 2001.

_______. *Saint Sharbel: The Hermit of Lebanon.* Tr. by Kozhaya S. Akiki: Holy Spirit University, Kaslik, Lebanon, 2001.

Stella Maris, Sister. *Servant of God: Bishop Thomas Kurialacherry. A Short Biography.* Palai, India: Adoration Congregation, 1986.

Stockwell, Foster. *Religion in China Today.* Second ed.. Beijing: New World Press, 1996.

Sylvestre, Andre, C.M. *Jean Gabriel Perboyre, Pretre De La Congregation De La Mission Saint-Lazare, Martrise En Chine Le 11 Septembre 1840.* Peuch-Montgesty, Catus: Association Jean Gabriel Perboyre, n.d.

Thiên Hùng Su: 117 Hiên Thánh Tú Đạo Việt Nam. San Jose, CA, Hoa Kỳ: Cộng Đồng Công Giáo Việt Nam, 1990.

Thorpe, Osmund, C.P. *Mary MacKillop.* Second edition. Rydalmere, Australia: The Petty Publishing Company Limited, 1980.

Tylenda, Joseph N., S.J. "A Greater Love, Damien de Veuster, SS. CC. (1840-89)" in *Portraits in American Sanctity.* Chicago, IL: Franciscan Herald Press, 1982.

_______. *Jesuit Saints & Martyrs: Short Biographies of the Saints, Blesseds, Venerables, and Servants of God of the Society of Jesus.* Second edition. Chicago, IL: Loyola Press, 1998.

United States Conference of Catholic Bishops. *Asian and Pacific Presence: Harmony In Faith.* Washington, DC: USCCB, Inc.; 2002.

United States Commission on International Religious Freedom. *USCIRF Annual Report*, released April 26, 2006. http://www.uscirf.gov;

Vannini, Fulgentius, O.F.M. Cap., *Bishop Hartmann.* Allahabad, India: St. Paul's Press Training School, 1966.

Villarroel, Fidel, O.P. *Lorenzo de Manila: The Protomartyr of the Philippines and His Companions.* Manila, Philippines: UST Press, 1988.

Wahl, Joseph Anthony, C.Or. "Vaz, Joseph." *New Catholic Encyclopedia.* Vol. 14. p. 580.

www.achievers-odds.com.au/topac.mmackillopfull.htm

www.Bisitaguam.com/Episodes/14/body.html

www.sspxasia.com/Seven Blessed Martyrs of Thailand

www.vidasejemplares.org/BeatoSalvador.pdf
www.xavier.sa.au/subjects/religed /mackillop/mackillop2.htm
Zambon, Mariagrazia. *Crimson Seeds: Eighteen P.I.M.E. Martyrs*. Detroit, MI: P.I.M.E. World Press, 1997.

INDEX OF SAINTS AND FEAST DAYS

Kunjachan Thevarparampil, October 16
Kuriakose Elias Chavara, C.M.I., January 3
Lawrence Imbert, M.E.P., September 20
Lorenzo Ruiz and Companions, September 28
Lucy Pak Hŭi-Sun, May 24
Lucy Wang Cheng and Companions, June 24
Magdalene of Nagasaki, October 20
Mariam Thresia Chiaramel Mankidiyan, C.H.F., June 8
Marianne Cope, O.S.F., August 9
Marie Baouardy, O.C.M., August 25
Marie Hermine, F.M.M., and Companions, July 9
Mario Borzaga, O.M.I., and Thoj Xyooj Paolo, April 22
Martyrs of China (1648-1930), July 9
Martyrs of Japan (1597-1650), February 6
Martyrs of Korea (1838-1867), September 20
Martyrs of Viet Nam (1745-1862), November 24
Mary MacKillop, R.M., Aug. 8
Mary of the Passion, F.M.M., November 15
Mary Zhu Wu and Companions, July 20
Matthew Kavukatt, October 5
Matteo Ricci, S.J., May 10
Matthew Kadalikkattil, May 23
Maurice Tornay, M.E.P., August 12
Melchior Marion de Brésillac, S.M.A., June 25
Michael Hồ Đình Hy, May 22
Nicholas Bunkerd Kitbamrung, January 12
Nimattullah Youssef Kassab al-Hardini, December 14
Our Lady of La Vang, November 22
Our Lady of Vailankanni, September 8
Paul Chŏng Ha-sang, September 22
Paul Lê-Báo Tịnh, April 6
Paul Miki, S.J., and Companions, February 6
Pedro Calungsod, April 2
Peter Chanel, S.M., April 28
Peter Kibe Kasui, S.J., July 4
Peter ToRot, July 7
Peter Yu Tae-ch'ŏl, October 31
Philip Siphong Onphithah and Companions, December 16
Rafqa de Himlaya, March 23
Rani Maria Kunju Vattalil, F.C.C., February 25
Rudolph Aquaviva, S.J., and Companions, July 27

INDEX OF COUNTRIES WHERE THESE SAINTS MINISTERED

Japan

Bartolomeo Gutierrez Rodriguez, O.S.A.; Francis Pacheco, S.J.; Francis Xavier, S.J.; Gonzalo Garcia, O.F.M.; Lorenzo Ruiz and Companions; Magdalene of Nagasaki; Martyrs of Japan; Matteo Ricci, S.J.; Paul Miki, S.J.; Peter Kibe Kasui, S.J.; Takayama Ukon

Laos

Mario Borzaga, O.M.I.; Thoj Xyooj Paolo

Lebanon

Nimattullah Youssef Kassab al-Hardini, Rafqa de Himlaya, Sharbel Makhloof

Myanmar

Clemente Vismara, P.I.M.E.; Felice Tantardini, P.I.M.E.

Oceania

Peter Chanel, S.M.

Palestine/Israel

Marie Baouardy, O.C.M.

Papua New Guinea

John Baptist Mazzucconi, P.I.M.E.; Peter ToRot

Philippines

Aloysius Schwartz, Bartolomeo Gutierrez Rodriguez, O.S.A.; Francisca Del Espiritu Santo, O.P.; Lorenzo Ruiz and Companions; Pedro Calungsod, the Talangpaz Sisters: Dionicia, A.R., and Cecilia Rosa, A.R.

Russian Federation

Walter Ciszek, S.J.

South Korea

Aloysius Schwartz, Andrew Kim Tae-gŏn and Companions; Paul Chŏng Ha-sang, Lawrence Imbert de la Motte, M.E.P.; Lucy Pak Hŭi-Sun, Martyrs of Korea, Agatha Yi, Peter Yu Tae-ch'ŏl

Sri Lanka

Joseph Vaz, C.Or.

Syria

Emmanuel Ruiz, O.F.M., and Companions

Taiwan

Vincent Robert Capodanno, M.M.

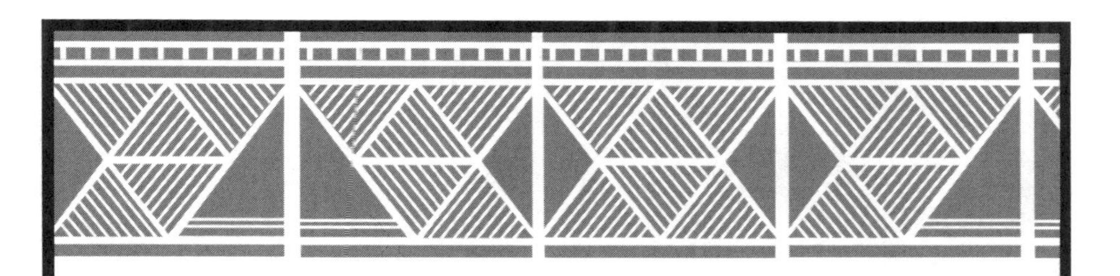

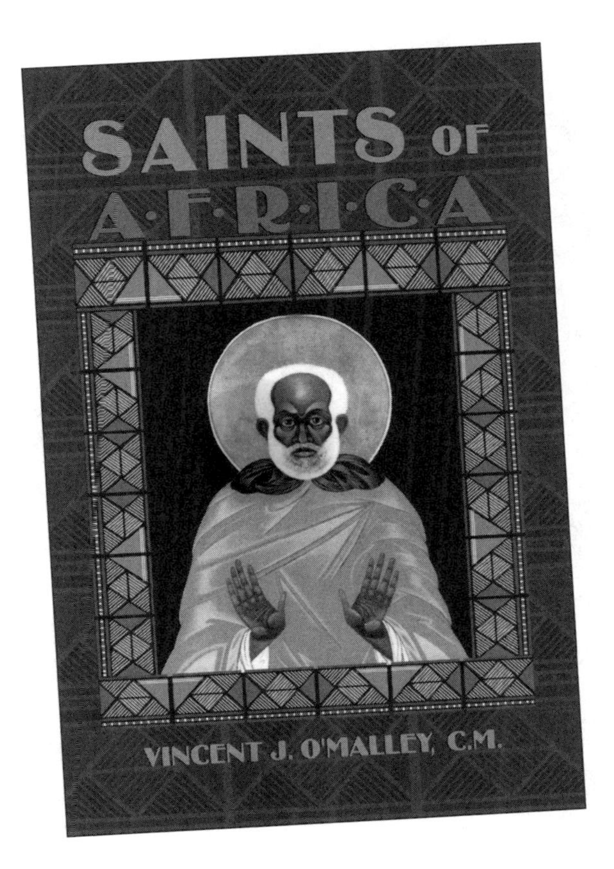
SAINTS OF
A·F·R·I·C·A
VINCENT J. O'MALLEY, C.M.

Saints of
NORTH AMERICA
Vincent J. O'Malley, C.M.